JUSTICE IN THE ROUND

ROUND

THE TRIAL OF ANGELA DAVIS

JUSTICE IN THE ROUND

THE TRIAL OF ANGELA DAVIS

Reginald Major

THE THIRD PRESS
Joseph Okpaku Publishing Co., Inc.
444 Central Park West,
New York, N.Y. 10025

Library of Congress Catalogue Card Number: LC 72–84108
SBN 89388–052–3

First printing, March 1973

Designed by Bennie Arrington

ACKNOWLEDGMENTS

There is more to a lawsuit than what goes on in court and I was helped to an understanding of that fact by almost everyone connected with the Angela Davis trial.

There were the newspeople, the Davis family, bailiffs and many trial watchers with whom I talked and from whom I learned. I received substantial help from the defense team, Leo Branton, Jr., Margaret Burnham, Howard Moore, Jr. and Doris Walker; from Prosecutor Albert Harris, Jr., Judge Richard E. Arnason, Jury fore-person, Mary M. Timothy.

NUCSAD, particularly their man-of-all-work, Rob Baker, detailed the intricacies and problems of mounting a national political campaign around a trial, and Bettina Aptheker Kurzweil gave me some insight as to the creation of a legal defense committee.

Angela Davis and Howard Moore, Jr. contributed considerable time to giving me their over-view of the entire trial proceedings.

My wife, Helen, helped me put it all together. All of the conclusions and opinions not otherwise identified are mine. More over, much of what might at first appear to be bias on my part is derived from the presummation of innocence one is supposed to accord an accused.

R.M.

1 : Political Prologue

A political trial is a sham, a show, a carefully staged bit of theatrical legerdemain in which the state, uttering newspeak guarantees of non-existing constitutional rights, hides its inevitable reflex to repress behind a cloak of procedural flim flam that is inherently unfair to the defendant.

In theory, there are no political trials, although constitutional purists can occasionally be cajoled into admitting that there have been courthouse decisions that were affected by political considerations. Under the constitution a person can only be tried for an act, not a belief.

To be sure, there is the possibility of confusion between those trials that are politically motivated, those which have political considerations and those which are purely political. The libel trial of Adam Clayton Powell, which resulted in his being unceremoniously dumped from Congress, is a prime example of the politically motivated trial. Adam was of the system that sought to limit his growing power. His fellow congressmen opposed him, not his beliefs or political orientation.

The Scottsboro boys, who were convicted in the nineteen-thirties of rape, is an example of a trial with an outcome determined by political considerations. It was obvious to many that the four blacks were being railroaded. But the courts, local, state and federal, did not see fit to stop the persecution or modify the sentences which resulted.

To save the Scottsboro boys would unduly antagonize the south, which in the midst of depression-caused unrest was hardly ready to be deprived of the entertaining social balm that is the spectacle of bringing black rapists of white women before a large and attentive red-neck audience. The Scottsboro boys were not political, they were simply the victims of a political reality.

Concerned blacks who pointed to the basic unfairness of the trial were offered a sop to their concerns; the four defendants were not lynched. This fact was announced as though it represented the triumph of liberalism over mob rule. And, when the death sentences were commuted, again a political consideration, blacks were told that the commutation was living proof that the system, although flawed, was on the way to perfection.

Angelo Herndon, a black, was convicted in 1933 of insurrection. He was arrested for passing out leaflets and sentenced clearly because of his membership in the Communist Party. Stokely Carmichael was convicted under the same state law 30 years later. The law was declared unconstitutional by the United States Supreme Court in 1967. Howard Moore, Jr., Angela Davis' chief counsel, was the attorney who handled Carmichael's case.

Henry Winston, along with 12 other members of the Communist Party, was convicted in the 1950's of advocating the overthrow of the United States government through force and violence. That he would be found guilty could be easily predicted. Winston's blackness was not the cause of the conviction, any more than Herndon's was. They were communists, pure and simple, and as such were guilty before the law. Following these convictions, the four black communists were sent to maximum security federal prisons, while their white comrades were housed in lighter security institutions. Winston lost his eyesight in prison, a fact which led him to remark, "I lost my sight not my vision." Prison authorities refused to release him for an operation which could not be performed in the prison with the medical facilities available.

There have been other political trials involving blacks, but they were largely petty harassments, occurring mainly in connection with civil rights activities. Thus, Martin Luther King was sentenced innumerable times for misdemeanors such as parading without a permit, illegal assembly and disturbing the peace. Stokely Carmichael, James Foreman, H. Rap Brown and other civil rights activists found themselves repeatedly charged with a variety of offenses ranging from dubious traffic violations to misdemeanor charges connected with civil rights activities.

None of these cases involved the death penalty, and in most instances the possible outcome of the trial was no more threatening to the defendant than a few days or weeks in jail or a fine. Furthermore, because of the blatantly prejudiced position of the courts which sentenced them, civil rights activists could pretty much guarantee that somewhere along the appeals road the original conviction would be reversed. A major contribution to these reversals has been the movement that has been built up around particular defendants. Law issuing from both legislatures and courts has always been sensitive to public pressure. A mass movement, even when it receives no official notice, has proved to have an effect on both courts and legislatures.

Again, these dismissals were hailed as proof that the American system of justice worked. Unnoticed in the hullabaloo was the fact that the original convictions served their purpose. A leader was taken out of circulation right at the point that he was successfully mobilizing a mass of people. A group of demonstrators were illegally detained just at the moment that their efforts were beginning to create difficulty for those demonstrated against. But these were petty political prosecutions doomed when the thrust of black politics shifted to specifically seeking effective political power. When the shift began to show results the political repression machine had to be cranked up and put into motion.

The main determinant of the political trial is the defendant. If the defendant is a political person whose views are sharply at variance with what is considered political orthodoxy, if all or part of the case against him involves evidence drawn from observing his political activities, then in all probability you are dealing with a political trial.

The crime with which the defendant is charged is only incidental to the purpose of the political trial. The object is to discredit the individual and his politics, and to convince the public that unorthodox political activity and criminal behavior is inextricably linked. Ultimately, the basic purpose of political trials is the reconfirmation of the primacy of the state.

In these trials the individual, while protesting his innocence, restricts his assertion of the government's motives in bringing him to trial only to matters dealing with the charge, thus making possible a verdict of not guilty.

In countries where the move toward armed revolution had become irreversible, the plea of "innocent" put forth by Fidel Castro, Regis Debray, the Algerian rebels and Nelson Mandela were not anticipatory of a possible verdict of innocence, and involved a belief that the government was illegitimate.

Nelson Mandela, a leader of the African National Congress, was tried in 1964 for sedition and sabotage. "I am prepared to die," said Mandela, robbing the South African trial court of any control over the terror that often accompanies the realization that one is on trial for one's life.

". . . I do not . . . deny that I planned sabotage. I did not plan it in a spirit of recklessness, nor because I have any love of violence. I planned it as a result of a calm and sober assessment of the political situation that had arisen after many years of tyranny, exploitation and oppression of my people by the Whites . . . we felt that without violence there would be no way open to the African people to succeed in their struggle against the principle of White supremacy. All lawful modes of expressing opposition to this principle had been closed by legislation, and we were placed in a position in which we had either to accept a permanent state of inferiority, or to defy the government. We chose to defy the law. We first broke the law in a way which avoided any recourse to violence; when this form was legislated against, and then the government resorted to a show of force to crush opposition to its policies, only then did we decide to answer violence with violence." [1]

Conceptually, the trials of Angela Davis and Ruchell Magee linked the two.

The rallying cry "free all political prisoners" is lofted in support of many individuals who have heretofore not been associated with political thought, political principles or political activities. Ruchell Magee is one of those who are now considered political prisoners, although they were convicted and jailed for crimes that had no political overtones whatsoever. Magee was a political prisoner, a victim of the larger politics of racist repression, and he came to recognize that fact long before he had to defend himself in the killing of a judge.

[1] From ANC pamphlet issued 1964.

The courts do not dispense justice as even-handedly as public school civics classes would have us believe. Defendants who are represented by lawyers are convicted of crimes less frequently than those who are unrepresented. Defendants who depend on the services of public defenders are convicted more often than those who can provide their own attorneys. The poor are convicted more often than the rich. Proportionately more members of minority groups, particularly blacks, are sentenced to prison than are whites.

Violent crimes, more often associated with class status, are punished more severely than non-violent crimes, without regard to the social harm done by the criminal. Thus, a youth who takes a few dollars at gun point from a grocery store can expect to receive a sentence of several years in jail if convicted, and an embezzler, whose activities might have ruined the financial lives of a number of people, can count on a relatively short term.

The consistently harsher sentences given to the black and the poor represent a politics of repression. The disenfranchised are expected to conform to a rigid set of expectations promulgated and enforced by officials who do not want to face the implications of their racist behavior. Criminality is often an inchoate political expression in which an individual seeks power over his own destiny through recognition that "them thats got can afford to get took."

Under this formula an outsized proportion of prison inmates can be considered political prisoners. But, one more step is necessary before they can logically be defined as such. It is self realization, awareness of the political nature of their travail, and a determination to do something about it. Ruchell Magee became a political prisoner after he gained an understanding that his jailed condition was due to the operation of the system, rather than his poor luck in facing tribunals.

A prime example of the politics of racial repression in jails occurred in the California prison system several years ago. The object was the Black Muslims, an organization which owes much of its numerical strength to recruiting practices in prisons. In 1961 there was a race riot at Folsom Prison, started by a white inmate who threw a potentially lethal metal tray at the head of a black prisoner. The reason was that the black had violated the unofficial custom of apartheid at Folsom by sitting at a table normally occupied by whites.

Blacks immediately retaliated, and for a while there was nothing but hostility on both sides. Prison officials resorted to their usual method of handling disturbances, by identifying and isolating the assumed troublemakers. Who did they pick on? Black Muslims.

Logic would dictate that Muslims would be the last people to look at when searching for someone who would want to fight for integration. But the logic was beyond prison officials. Essentially, prison officials do not want any group organized for any reason, at any time, unless of course that organization meets with their approval. The Muslims were organized and that was enough.

It took several court actions before California prison officials were forced to recognize the Muslims as a religious group, and to cease and desist from singling out Muslims for disciplinary action. It was later determined that Muslims were seldom involved in racial struggles within the prison. But, that discovery was made after Muslims were successful in establishing through court procedures some recognition of their status as a bona fide religious organization. The attempt of prison officials to block this recognition was political, not religious. The victory of the Muslims over prison officials also reflected a political reality, as the Muslims had succeeded in building a movement around their demands for religious freedom within prison walls.

Courts are not totally oppressive and many of their decisions have been against the state. But ultimately the court is responsive to the interests of the state.

An individual cannot oppress or take advantage of the state. Their positions are much too unequal. The best that one can do in any prosecution is to hold his own, and that is a hell of a problem. Despite all procedural safeguards, the truth is that the state has the upper hand. This occurs because the state makes the first move. It decides when and whom to prosecute. It decides the grounds. The state decides who will hear the case, who will prosecute and how much energy it will put into obtaining a conviction. The defense does little but respond to the aggressive stance of the state.

When the state brings charges against a political person, it is often the state that is on the defensive. To be sure, its stance, except in a narrow tactical sense, is aggressive. But, the state's position is one of defense, for in a political trial the state must make the crime fit the punishment. Essentially, it must manufacture a crime with which to charge a political defendant or else magnify an assumed crime way out of proportion. In a political trial, the state is defending itself from accusations made out of court.

The political trial is inherently unfair, simply because the state uses the cloak of its legitimacy to punish political acts which are constitutionally guaranteed. The state, it is averred, has a right, yea a duty, to protect itself against subversion, violent overthrow or illegitimate seizure of power. But, that is untrue; it is a sophistry that can only be entertained by those who like the idea of power. It is very clear, for instance, that the majority of American people are against the war in Southeast Asia, and have been for some time. So what!

The nation's politicians respond to this fact with all kinds of fantasies, none, of course, dealing with the facts of the matter, particularly that fact which is the concept of majority rule. Anti-war sentiment is projected as the product of subversion. The American people are protected from being duped. President Nixon behaves like a dove, who reluctantly has to temporarily assume the mantle of a hawk. And so much for democracy.

To be anti-war is to be subversive on some level, and therefore, the American people are coerced into supporting a military effort for which they have no real liking.

The same can be said for a host of national priorities. The current administration is critical of the poor, particularly those on welfare, implying somehow that they are draining our national resources. But, primarily because America is a country which is exceptionally nice to big business, subsidies, which are nothing more than welfare for the rich, are deemed to be a good national policy.

Tax expert Joseph Pechman, of the Brookings Institution, estimated that if all "unnecessary," as opposed to all, subsidies were eliminated, including those exemptions which allow millionaires to pay little or no taxes, the result would be enough money—at least $25 billion annually—to totally eliminate poverty. This procedure would not eliminate rich people; it would only raise the level of the 26 million poverty stricken Americans to something that resembled living.

These are the considerations which prompt the formation of political opponents to the status quo. Historically, America has been fanatical in its opposition to anything resembling socialism. The idea of sharing the wealth has been handled as though it is the most horrendous of heresies and a violent attack on American principles.

When it comes to accepting the challenge to create true political, social and economic equality for all, regardless of racial, national or ethnic background, this country is regressive. The problem is not just that it is racist. It is that the nation as a whole bitterly resents examining its racist attitudes, even though those attiudes are clearly bringing chaos to the land.

There is a revolution going on. Buildings have been bombed and policemen ambushed. Official records are being destroyed, as in the case of the draft boards, or stolen for the sole purpose of embarrassing government bureaus such as the FBI in Media, Pennsylvania. There was recently the occupation of the Bureau of Indian Affairs in Washington, D.C., in which Native Americans raided the files and exposed some of the inner workings of the Bureau. The flag is being debased, the army is being avoided, deserted and subverted, colleges are being turned into centers of resistance and the ability to raise a clenched fist is coming a little easier to many whites and most blacks.

It is within the context of revolution that political trials must be witnessed. The political trial is the method by which the Establishment maintains the political status quo. Before the present racially oriented upheavals the government was very successful in its political persecutions. The reason, perhaps, is that its targets had no real revolutionary zeal. Sacco and Vanzetti, Tom Mooney, the Rosenbergs, Owen Lattimore, Benjamin Spock, Howard Levy, and to some extent the Fathers Berrigan, were easy to convict.

None of them could develop a rhetoric of resistance, which when uttered, remained within constitutional limits, but which had implications for action that could transcend the constitution and develop ambitions to replace it with something else. Only the Berrigans had a program of action which consisted in deliberately becoming involved in illegal acts that are deemed to be moral, and therefore reasonable to perform. The other political prisoners only talked, or advocated, or said good things about mainland China, or bad things about our involvement in Vietnam.

The victims of political persecution who have come to our attention, have been, with few exceptions, white, middle class members of the system. They took positions within the system widely at variance with official dicta.

Routine racist political repression directed primarily toward members of racial minorities, was not so widely publicized. This has left the impression that comparatively few blacks have been subject to coercive political control. There have always been black movements. Every one which attracted a mass of people has experienced the arrest of its most visible members.

The current spate of political trials involves revolutionaries. All of them are guilty of the political crimes of which they are suspected.

Political repression in America is not new, but never before have so many people been brought into court whose politics aim at basically changing the system. They are subversive. They do seek the overthrow of the government. They are not opposed to criminality, that is to say, that illegal activity which disrupts the orderly processes of the state. They seek and promote dissension. They do not rule out revolutionary violence as a means of correcting what they see as evil. And, moreover, they are proud of it.

But, a revolution cannot be put on trial and its proponents can only be displayed in court. They are never placed on trial for advocating a revolution. To do that would subject the state to entertain in a court of law, serious questions about its own validity. A revolutionary is placed on trial because of his politics, and charged with performing acts which grow out of his political convictions and can be interpreted or transformed into crimes. It follows, therefore, that a revolutionary cannot get a fair trial simply because he is not made to answer to the actual reasons for which the state indicted him. The state, in attempting to sharply prune the revolutionary tree, can never admit that its fruit has a right to ripen and be appreciated.

A revolutionary does not come to court seeking, expecting or even thinking in terms of a fair trial. If he had any belief that a fair trial in these institutions was available to him he would not be a revolutionary.

The revolutionary comes to court to attack the system, to expose its contradictions, to educate the people to the imperfections of the institutions which govern their lives. The revolutionary comes to court to do symbolic battle. He is convinced that not too long after his beliefs are placed on trial the courts will be considered irrelevant by the people. The revolutionary gives a court two choices. The first is to simply shoot him, or jail him, or do whatever the prosecution wishes. The other choice is exposure. The revolutionary, in submitting to trial, seeks the widest possible audience. He is convinced that if the people can be exposed to the details of political persecution in the courts they will tend to support his position.

No country can stand the spectacle of too many political trials. For a time, the state can make political persecution with the charge that they are dealing with criminality. But sooner or later, primarily because of the stance of the defense, the state is forced to admit to the political nature of some of its prosecutions.

The state has a method of dealing with this problem. It holds secret trials. It attempts to insure secrecy in two ways. First, is the nature of the accusation. The state seeks to force a defendant in a political trial to answer only to the crime charged and not to place their defense within a political context. That is secrecy through indirection.

Secondly, the state can count on the mass media. Although it might report on the political statements made by the defendants, the mass media directs its attention to the charge itself, and reports on the defendants' reactions to those charges to the almost total exclusion of all else. The media is more responsive to the authority that licenses it and gives it generous subsidies in the form of low mail rates and free use of publicly owned airwaves, than it is to the moral and political indignation of revolutionaries. And, when the media slips up and begins to assume postures that tend to expose the government as less than legitimate, there is always the FBI and FCC and ultimately an Agnew to bring it back into line.

The modern political trial is a substitute for, and a precursor of, politically motivated violence that would control and repress those who would change the system.

2 : The Revolutionary Set

"We say that the evidence will confirm that four human beings lost their lives in the vicinity of the Marin County Courthouse . . . Judge Harold Haley was killed. Jonathan Jackson was killed, as were James McClain and Willie—William Christmas, two prisoners from San Quentin.

"There were three human beings wounded on that day. Gary Thomas, an Assistant District Attorney from Marin County was wounded, as was a juror, Mrs. Maria Graham, and Ruchell Magee from San Quentin.

"We do not dispute these facts that lives were lost and people were wounded on that day, facts as the evidence will show you, has now become a matter of public knowledge. But we remind you again . . . There are two separate issues involved here. There is the issue of whether deaths occurred and how those deaths occurred. Then there is the issue of whether I had anything to do with the occurrence of those deaths . . . There are basically three things which must be proved in order to establish my guilt. First of all, the Prosecutor must prove beyond a reasonable doubt that there was a plan which predated the events of August 7.

"Secondly, he must prove beyond a reasonable doubt that I had foreknowledge of a plan which predated the events of August 7.

"Third, he must prove beyond a reasonable doubt that I took steps to deliberately promote the execution of that plan."

These were Angela Davis' opening remarks on March 29, 1972 at her trial.

The Marin County Civic Center is probably one of the most elegant, costly and architecturally prestigious civic centers in America. It was Frank Lloyd Wright's 770th commission, his first for a government agency and the last of his life. He died in 1959 at age 88, a year before the construction began. His original plans cov-

12

ered a span of 30 years of intermittent construction which would, in addition to housing all county governmental functions from the library to the jail, also have a 3,000 seat amphitheatre, a 12 acre lagoon, an Olympic size pool and a small scale "Disneyland" county fairgrounds.

Two wings, totaling 1,500 feet in length and joined together by a dome-shaped rotunda to form a wide angled V, are suspended between three four-story-high hills that dominate the rolling terrain north of San Rafael, the county seat. Entrance to the building is gained through one of the three giant arches that support the building, each with a roadway running beneath. The upper floors, which fade into the hills to allow direct access to the outside, have balconies running the full length of the building, set off by a series of smaller arches repeating the main motif. Inside, the wide gallery-like corridors are pierced with long lightwells that transmit light from the rounded, transparent plexiglass roof to the lush indoor gardens four stories below.

Wright did not attempt to design a fortress. The structure was modeled after an ancient server of peoples needs, the Roman aqueduct, which utilized massive arches to span a series of hills. But, an aborted escape attempt which resulted in the death of four people, followed two months later by a courtroom bombing, resulted in the establishment of stringent security measures.

On the second floor of the north wing are nine wood-paneled courtrooms, set out in groups of three. Two circular corridors flank the middle group. Each has an immense planter box, a set of stairs and a bank of two elevators. All of the courtrooms face a glass wall, on the other side of which is a balcony running the length of the corridor. It looks out over a large parking lot, past a freeway, and toward Mount Tamalpais in the background, ten miles away.

Aaron Green, the West coast representative of the Frank Lloyd Wright Foundation, supervised the actual construction. When the second wing—the hall of justice—was completed he said of the courtrooms: "The circular courtrooms are theatre really. They are designed to make people more related visually and audibly to each other." [1] And they did.

[1] *San Francisco Chronicle,* 1966.

The jury box, with three rows of comfortable, royal blue arm-chairs, forms part of the circle on one side, and a 16-foot curved table serving both prosecution and defense continues the circle on the other side. The walls complete the circle, and a curved railing separates the audience from the trial.

It was there, in the round, that two avowed revolutionaries asserted that they could not be fairly judged by a jury composed of white, middle class people reared to accept racist institutions and to believe that those institutions express and promote democratic ideals.

Courtroom 2 is where it all began. On August 7, 1970, a tall, thin, 17 year old, whose sharp-featured, coffee brown face was framed in a large afro, entered the courtroom wearing a trenchcoat and carrying a small satchel.

Jonathan Jackson had probably been in the building before—there were two prosecution witnesses who said he had been. One of them, Mrs. Lois M. Leidig, a thin woman of about 60, dressed in a powder-blue iridescent suit, testified that she saw Jonathan Jackson on the afternoon of August 6, 1970, in Judge Haley's courtroom. Mrs. Leidig lives in Portland, Oregon, and had been spending a vacation with a Marin County resident, Barney Joseph. The two, who apparently attend trials as though they were updated versions of the Christian versus Lion games once popular in Rome, arrived in courtroom 2 fifteen minutes to a half hour before court recessed for the day, and listened while the defendant, James Mc-Clain, an inmate at San Quentin, defending himself against a charge of stabbing a prison guard, was questioning a witness.

"I expected to hear a better defense," Mrs. Leidig volunteered. She said she saw Jonathan Jackson come in. "A young Negro male . . . I heard the rattling of paper behind me and I turned around. He had a sack, a brown paper sack like a grocery sack. He was in the act of putting it down with both hands . . . After he sat down he rested his elbows on his thighs and his hands were over his knees . . . shirt open at the neck, jacket or sweater around his waist. Mr. McClain stared at the gallery. He stared so long that I looked in his direction."

Mrs. Leidig insisted that McClain became distracted after Jonathan came in, and that she detected a glance, several glances, in fact stares, pass between them.

Defense Attorney Leo Branton, Jr. cross-examined her closely. "I'm not interested in what you have to say, but why you feel you have to say it," Branton began.

"Any biases? No. Haven't you once held the position that a conviction in this case would be welcome? No. Don't you believe she is an anarchist? I don't believe everything I read.

"Look at this letter dated January 11, 1971—Is it your handwriting? Oh it's my handwriting. And you did write that letter? I wrote it. What you said there was the truth? I admit I was a little angry when I wrote that."

Branton then read part of the letter. He ignored the beginning: "Dear Barney: It was so nice to hear your voice on the telephone tonight, and I will comply with your request to recall about our visit to Judge Haley's courtroom the day before he was killed . . . It makes me sick to think what happened the next day when we arrived at the courthouse just after the shooting. Although a death penalty will not bring back Judge Haley, or Mr. Thomas' health . . ." Branton read aloud, "I am hoping for this verdict for all those anarchists involved. Our national courts need a verdict like this. Our former Governor Hatfield, who was too much of a dove had capital punishment done away with in this state."

Mrs. Leidig seemed shocked to hear her words of almost 17 months before read to her. Her already pale complexion visibly lightened.

"You would have to be talking about Angela Davis," Branton persisted.

She admitted that was true.

"Now isn't it the truth that you don't remember having seen anything in that courtroom on August 6?"

"It is not the truth. I am under oath and don't you call me a liar."

"What color was his hair?"

"Black."

"It wasn't blond?"

"It's not important what color his hair is."

"You might be surprised . . . He didn't have a long trench-coat?"

"No."

Branton asked if Jonathan was carrying a brief case or an attaché case.

"No," she replied. "He had a paper sack."

"You didn't see any books on top?"

"No."

"As a matter of fact you thought he brought his laundry, didn't you?"

Lean, personable, with a voice that would thrust out accusingly one minute and purr in the next instant, Branton said softly:

"Describe Jonathan. What kind of a complexion did he have?"

"Sort of a warm Indian tan, a very fresh complexion . . . Like someone who has a good suntan."

"Why was it so important for you to remember what happened in that courtroom that you can never forget?"

"McClain . . . he kept staring . . . I turned to see what he was staring at and every time I looked Jonathan Jackson was in my view."

"The picture was burned in your memory to the extent that you could pick out his picture two years later."

"I told you I have very good visual recall . . ."

"Including the black hair?"

Jonathan's hair was reddish blond, combed in an afro that heightened his 6 foot 2 inch, well-muscled frame. Everyone else who testified to seeing him described him as wearing a tan trench-coat. James H. Layne, a Marin County bailiff who once worked in Judge Haley's court, said that he had seen Jonathan after court had recessed August 6, and described him as wearing a trenchcoat and carrying a black attaché case.

What Layne had to say partially contradicted Mrs. Leidig. He said that Jonathan came up to him and asked if the McClain trial was in session. According to Mrs. Leidig, Jonathan was in the courtroom when Judge Haley recessed the trial until 10:00 the following morning.

Layne said he also saw Jonathan the next day, August 7. The bailiff testified that something bothered him about Jonathan when he walked into the courtroom and took a seat. He remembered that McClain was questioning a witness. The bailiff said that he decided to ask Jonathan a few questions, stood up to walk towards him, only to see Jonathan stand up and take a small automatic from his coat pocket, and say, "All right gentlemen, I'll take over now."

It was then about 10:45 a.m. James McClain had been in the building about an hour. He, Ruchell Magee, William Christmas, Willie Reddicks and Marc Cisneros, all prisoners at San Quentin, had been handcuffed, placed in ankle restraints which require an individual to hobble across a floor, placed in cars and driven to the Civic Center.

The other four inmates were to testify that McClain could not possibly have stabbed a prison guard on March 2, 1970.

At the time Jonathan stood up, Ruchell Magee was on the stand. McClain, standing near the edge of the curved table was questioning Magee. Outside in the corridor, sitting on one of the cushioned benches that curved around pillars, his back to the view, was a shackled William Christmas, with two San Quentin guards.

Cisneros and Reddicks were in a holding cell, outside of which were still more guards. Courtroom 2 did not have a holding cell of its own, and these two were in the cell adjacent to courtroom 1. Christmas was waiting to testify, Reddicks had already been on the stand. Some of the guards outside the cell were seated on the steps which led up to a security corridor through which prisoners are brought from the county jail to the courts.

Just before the trial session had begun McClain held two meetings with his witnesses in that holding cell. After the second meeting he changed the order of the witnesses so that Christmas, rather than Reddicks, would be the person waiting in the hall.

Jonathan ordered everyone to lie down, except one of the guards who was told to remove the restraints from both Magee and McClain, before joining the others face down on the floor. At least one of the bailiffs slipped out, turned right, ran past the holding cell into the sheriff's department, and told them what was happening in courtroom 2.

After whipping a carbine out from under his coat, and snapping out the collapsible stock, Jonathan opened a zippered, rectangular black bag. From the bag came a sawed off shotgun. One witness said that McClain asked Jonathan, "Where's the tape?," and that Jonathan produced a roll of adhesive tape.

McClain taped the shotgun to Judge Haley's neck, and ordered him to call Louis Mountanos, the sheriff of Marin County. Haley did. He told the sheriff what was happening in the courtroom, and said that he did not want anyone hurt.

Meanwhile, hostages were being selected. Gary Thomas, the prosecutor who was married to Judge Haley's niece, the judge, and three women jurors, Maria Graham, Doris Wittmer and Joyce Ridoni were chosen.

More people came into the courtroom. A couple with a baby, who were surprised to find a gun pointing at them, Willie Christmas, who was brought in by Magee, and Inspector Earl Cummesky, who was walking by when Magee invited him in at gunpoint, decided he and Cummesky were about the same size, and had Cummesky give him his brand new, green plaid sports coat.

McClain explained to the jurors that he was innocent of all charges. He also told the ladies in the jury not to be scared, explaining that his own mother had been afraid when she came in to court. The four hostages, wired together at the arms, began to move out of the courtroom and turned left down the corridor, past courtroom 3, to the elevators.

McClain and Judge Haley went right, to the room where the holding cell was located. It was closed, having been locked by Sgt. John Mitchell, the guard in charge of the detail which had brought the prisoners to court. Mitchell had heard running; he stepped out to see what was happening, and saw Judge Haley coming towards him with McClain, his hand on the shotgun, right along side.

Mitchell and the other guards retreated up the stairs as Haley opened the door with his own key. The judge did not have a key to the cell and was demanding that the door be opened at the same time that McClain was shouting for Reddicks and Cisneros to join the group. Mitchell, a trained guardian of men, responded with a prison guard's first priority, that prisoners will not escape, and threw the keys on the other side of the locked door that opened onto the jail passageway. He preferred locking himself in, rather than letting a prisoner out. The two decided not to join the others so the judge and McClain went back to the group.

The corridor was dotted with policemen and sheriff's deputies with their hands up. Some had been disarmed. Sheriff Mountanos, who had earlier given orders to protect the hostages, was among the group, as was Dan Terzich, the police chief of Mill Valley, another Marin County town.

James Kean, a photographer for *The Independent Journal,* a Marin County newspaper, arrived on the floor just before McClain and Haley caught up with the group. They allowed Kean to take a number of photographs which documented the events in Civic Center that day. There were shots of Jonathan disarming policemen, Magee with a gun in each hand, one showing Christmas with a gun at the head of one of the hostages, and a shot of Judge Haley and McClain. Kean estimated that he took between 24 and 30 pictures of the events in the corridor.

The news of the escape attempt had been put on the air. Police units streaked toward the Civic Center. A broadcaster from one of the local stations showed up and began an on the spot report. San Quentin guards scrapped earlier plans to barricade a portion of the highway where they expected the escapees to pass, and drove five miles to the Center.

Meanwhile, Jonathan's party went down an elevator and exited from the building under one of the large arches.

Directly across from them was a garage-like structure called the sheriff's sally port, into which the prisoners had been driven less than two hours before. They discovered another photographer, Roger Bockrath, hiding behind a car parked in the port, and waved him out at gunpoint. The men also disarmed two deputies who had been hiding in two immense concrete planter boxes that flanked the glassed-in rotunda from which the group had exited. The prisoners and their hostages walked across the parking lot towards a yellow rental van at the very time that San Quentin guards were setting up a roadblock 100 yards away.

The balconies above were lined with people, a 300 pound inspector drove his "undercover unit" into the lot to get a better look at the group. Jonathan, walking backwards, bringing up the rear, swung his carbine toward the car which sped away. The group reached the van, removed the wire from the hostages' arms, and climbed in through the double doors at the back.

The road block had been completed with the arrival of a gunnery instructor, John W. Matthews, who parked his San Quentin vehicle nose to nose with another guard's car, across the wide driveway. He then issued rifles and handguns to some of the guards, selected a 30-30 rifle for himself, and took position behind a car parked at the curb immediately in front of the hastily improvised barricade.

Jonathan was driving, with McClain crouched beside him. There was only a driver's seat. The seven people in the body of the van shifted about as they sat on the floor. Gary Thomas perched on a projecting shelf formed by the wheelwell.

Thomas was behind McClain, his back to the wall; Maria Graham was on the floor in front of him and Joyce Ridoni was behind the driver. Judge Haley was to the left of Thomas, with Magee behind him. Christmas, facing forward as was the judge, was in the center of the van next to Haley, and Wittmer was behind and to the left of him. The back was crowded, and the positions relative, as everyone was moving around trying to get adjusted.

The van came forward toward Matthews' position, as he checked his weapon, placing a shell in the chamber and crouching a little lower. The entire parking lot was silent. Those standing on the balconies leaned forward. Guards and deputies nervously fingered their weapons, waiting for an order, or for some event that would tell them what to do. Suddenly gunfire. Matthews ducked, and came up immediately shooting.

He testified that he fired at the driver who, "flew down, away from the sitting position." Then at the passenger, who "flew down too. His body went violently away from the direction of the line of fire . . . then a man exposed himself from the rear of the van facing me with a pistol in his hand, and I fired at him . . . He went down . . . he either was pushed up or bounced back up, and I fired again . . . he went down and stayed down . . . The next thing that happened was, a gentleman in a gray suit, I think it was gray, pushed himself up and said 'stop firing. I am hit.' "

The gunfire ceased and the officers went to the van. There were four dead men. Jonathan, who was still moving when officers entered the van, James McClain, whose body was found under the dashboard, William Christmas who was sprawled over the judge, and Judge Harold Haley, who had only half a face left. Maria Graham had been shot through the right arm, Ruchell Magee in the chest, and Gary Thomas in the spine. The others were unhurt, provided one does not count the emotional shock of participating in such an event.

Bodies and guns were passed from the van. Theodore V. Hughes, a deputy with 25 years experience, recognized one of the guns being passed from the van as the one he had bought 15 years before, and which had been taken from him in the courtroom corridor. He retrieved it and put it in his holster, and did not notice until the next morning that the gun was empty. Ballistics tests indicated that a bullet from this gun had gone into Judge Haley's chest.

A total of 12 guns were removed from the van, three of which Jonathan had brought into the courtroom, a fourth which had been left in the van, two shotguns and six handguns, all taken from police officers. All except Hughes' gun were tagged for evidence. Other evidence found at the scene included a number of shell casings (12 were found in the van), an attaché case full of ammunition, two coils of wire, a spool of adhesive tape, the van and the rental agreement showing it had been rented in San Francisco the day before, three flares taped together to resemble dynamite which had been brandished in the courtroom, a blue satchel, some revolutionary pamphlets—including the *Mini-Manual of the Urban Guerrillas* by Carlos Marighella, who was killed in Brazil, November 4, 1969—and six books. Three of the books were in French and three in English. All were concerned with some aspect of revolutionary activity. Two of them, *The Politics of Violence* and *Violence and Social Change,* had "Angela Y. Davis, 1969" inscribed in them. There was also a telephone number, 588-9073, which was found on a slip of paper in Jonathan Jackson's wallet.

Some of the evidence, primarily fragments of bullets, were recovered by John H. Manwaring, who conducted autopsies on the four dead men. Ballistics tests were conducted, but the weapons fired by San Quentin guards did not figure in the investigation. The guards reportedly returned their weapons to the prison armory where they were stored along with similar weapons and could not, therefore, be properly identified.

The expert who conducted the ballistics tests, Fred Wynbrandt, Supervising Criminalist for the CII (Bureau of Criminal Information and Identification) is by coincidence an expert in the use of blood and bloodstains in criminal identification. He has written a number of papers on the subject and makes it his business to keep up with the latest developments in this field. Despite his expertise, he was unable to come up with useful information regarding the origin of the blood which was found on some of the weapons.

The fingerprint evidence collected at the site was limited to a print of Jonathan Jackson on a rear view mirror. The guns, tape, wire, rental van and even the clothing Jonathan wore (a trench-coat in 80 degree weather) clearly indicated that he had some kind of plan. Jackson went to the Civic Center prepared for action. But, what was the plan?

One newspaper suggested that Jackson's action was part of an overall revolutionary scheme hatched by the Panthers. Huey Newton had been released from prison on August 5, two days before Jonathan went to the courthouse. That week the Panther paper had featured a drawing showing black men being released from prison with the legend under it: "The time is now for prison walls all across decadent Babylon to crumble, for prison gates to be blown to pieces, and for prison hallways to vibrate with the sounds of gunfire, hand grenades, and shouts of liberation!!!" [2]

Someone said that they had heard members of the group demanding the release of the Soledad Brothers, and surmised that the escape attempt was related to them, that it was geared to effect their release by exchanging their freedom for the safety of the hostages. That, in fact, was the theory that finally helped to shape the prosecution case.

The telephone number found in Jonathan's wallet was the same as the number in a phone booth near the American Airlines ticket counter at the San Francisco airport. The four guns brought in by Jonathan had been purchased by Angela Davis, who, it developed, had taken a flight to Los Angeles at 2 p.m., just three hours after the shooting at the Civic Center had ended. A statewide intelligence

[2] *The Black Panther*, Saturday, August 8, 1970, page 15.

network determined in short order that Angela Davis and Jonathan Jackson had frequently been seen together, twice when she was purchasing guns.

Those who identified themselves as revolutionaries responded to the August 7 incident. Huey Newton stated, on the day he was released from prison, that the Soledad Brothers were innocent of murdering a prison guard. He told news reporters that the guard had indeed been killed by revolutionary elements within the prison, but that the Soledad Brothers were not those revolutionaries. George Jackson had been identified with the Panthers because of the support they gave his case, and also because he had been contributing articles to the Black Panther newspaper. When news of August 7 flashed around the world, Huey P. Newton announced that the Black Panther Party would hold its first revolutionary funeral.

The funeral was held August 15 at St. Augustine's church in Oakland. An estimated 3,000 people turned out, filling the pavement from one side of the street to the other. The roof of the large supermarket across the street from the church had lines of spectators on it. Roofs further removed were covered with law enforcement agents, observing the goings on through binoculars and telescopes. The church was packed, and Huey Newton delivered a eulogy.

"We have gathered today not only to give respect to Comrades Jonathan Jackson and William Christmas, but also to pledge our lives to the accomplishment of the goals exemplified in the actions of brothers Jonathan Jackson and William Christmas.

"There are no laws that the oppressor makes that the oppressed are bound to respect. Laws should be made to serve people. People should not be made to serve laws. When laws no longer serve the people, it is the people's right and the people's duty to free themselves from the yoke of such laws. . . .

"Our comrades Jonathan Jackson and William A. Christmas have taught us a revolutionary lesson. They have intensified the struggle and placed it on a higher level."

Revolutionary greetings were sent from all over the country, many of them from men in prison who identified with Jonathan Jackson's action.

Warden Louis Nelson of San Quentin said that long before August 7 he sensed growing ugliness among the self-help groups in prison, which he at one time thought were constructive, but now felt had come under the influence of revolutionaries. Prison authorities in California place those they label as revolutionaries in adjustment centers, prisons within prisons, and in isolation cells away from the general prison population.

"Now most of the people we have in here are pretty violent to begin with," Nelson said in a newspaper interview. "Standing up and shouting about revolution is not the right way to deal with them . . . (such behavior) may result in the form of added time coming to all men confined within our walls. For if the prisons of California become known as 'schools for violent revolution' the Adult Authority would be remiss in their duty not to keep the inmates longer." [3]

Nelson's remarks confirm the charge that there are political prisoners in California prisons, namely revolutionaries, or at least those labeled as such by prison officials. But, the label 'revolutionary' is avoided when discussing individuals. What is described is not their political beliefs, including those that have to do with overturning the government, but their character. Nelson, in the wake of August 7, said that he suspected that George Jackson was the prison contact for the escape plot, but he did not identify Jackson as a revolutionary. On an individual level inmates are troublemakers, but are not political.

San Quentin's Associate Warden, James Park, refused to subscribe to the theory that the escaping convicts had been revolutionaries. "Not everybody who says they are revolutionaries are, some are just plain hoodlums. I think these guys fall in that category. From their temperaments and past experience these men wouldn't hesitate to kill." [4]

Men who have served time with them describe the three—Christmas, Magee and McClain—as revolutionaries, men who had been active behind the walls preaching black liberation, teaching some version of Marxist-Leninist revolutionary analysis and reaching for an opportunity to strike a blow at the prison system. An

[3] *San Francisco Chronicle*, August, 1970.
[4] *San Francisco Examiner*, August 10, 1970.

indication that they were not the hoodlums described by Park came out in some of the trial testimony.

Mrs. Norene Morris, one of the jurors at the McClain trial who testified at the Angela Davis trial, recalled McClain's admonishment to his companions not to harass the jurors in any way: "Leave the jury alone, we don't want to hear that . . . cut that out . . . I think you would have had enough of that . . . we're not animals, we're not going to act like that." It was McClain, said Mrs. Norris, who picked up Joyce Ridoni's purse and handed it to her.

There was no question about Jonathan Jackson's politics. He had made it clear to his brother, to his family, to his companions, and ultimately to the world. "Manchild, black manchild with submachine gun in hand, he was free for a while. I guess that's more than most of us can expect," [5] wrote George Jackson of his younger brother, Jonathan, two days after his death.

George, in another letter speaking of Jonathan said: "I guess now that he is dead, and the guilty are safe from the muscle of his mind and arm, it is safe to reveal some of his thoughts and functions within the matrix of the party and movement. He felt as I did that the military and political branches, though married in purpose and direction, in these opening stages should function separately from each other for very obvious reasons . . . The situation allows for such activity as the August 7th movement, because it can be accomplished without giving the enemy—state forces—the pretext they need to move in and destroy the political apparatus—under the very convenient and much used Anglo-Saxon conspiracy laws . . . So Jonathan's raid on the military and judiciary that Friday was at once an expression of his own aggressive consciousness and that of the party. It is easy to infer all of this in retrospect that Jonathan was head of a clandestine army which saw the Black Panther Party as its political leader. Operating on his own, he was able to at least attempt to support some of the minimum demands of the people. . . ." [6]

Their mother, Georgia Jackson, denied that Angela Davis gave Jonathan the weapons. "It's ridiculous to think Angela Davis would

[5] Jackson, George, *Soledad Brother*, Coward-McCann, NY, 1970.
[6] Jackson, George, *Blood In My Eye*, Random House Inc., NY, 1972.

give a 17 year old a gun. Anytime something comes up, the Panthers or Angela Davis are blamed . . . I think he did what every black man—or white man—would do. If you can't get justice one way, you take it another." [7]

Jonathan's sister, Penny Jackson, summed it up for herself, and for those who sympathized with Jonathan: "We won't forget he died in the streets trying to free the brothers, trying to free the people." [8]

[7] *Los Angeles Times,* August 12, 1970.
[8] *Los Angeles Times,* August 20, 1970.

3 : The Leading Lady

Marcia Lynn Brewer, who sells tickets for Pacific Southwest Airlines, saw Angela Davis at 2 p.m. on August 7. She could not remember whether Miss Davis had luggage. She did recall however that Angela was in a hurry, thinking that she might miss the plane. The flight, scheduled to leave for Los Angeles at 2 p.m. took off 13 minutes later.

On August 12, authorities began to look for her. What began as a request for Angela to come in and answer a few questions, quickly intensified into a full scale hunt. They went to her 35th Street apartment. Nobody was home.

Angela's old Rambler sedan was found parked in front of Franklin Alexander's house. He too was wanted for questioning in regard to the 9 mm Browning automatic used that afternoon by Jonathan Jackson to interrupt the court proceedings at the Marin County Civic Center. Although the gun was registered in Angela's name, Los Angeles police department records indicated that in 1968 it was in Franklin Alexander's possession. No one was home there either.

During the days and weeks that followed rumors of Angela's whereabouts led police to conduct raids and investigations throughout the United States, as well as in Canada and Europe. Fania Davis Jordan, Angela's tall, fair skinned, Afro-coiffed younger sister was taken into custody when San Francisco police, acting without a warrant and under the direction of Assistant Attorney General Albert Harris, Jr., broke into the Soledad Brothers Defense Committee Headquarters. It was 3 a.m. the following day before two attorneys forced Harris and two investigators from the Attorney General's office to stop questioning her and admit that he and the San Francisco Police Department could not hold Mrs.

Jordan since she was not charged with any crime and was not under arrest.

Members of the Che-Lumumba Club in Los Angeles were rounded up and questioned. They refused to make any statement by invoking the Fifth Amendment.

FBI men broke into Angela's apartment on August 15, "with the express intention to arrest Miss Davis." The leader of the expedition, James William McCord, was later to be one of the prosecution witnesses. After kicking in the back door, McCord and four other FBI agents opened doors, drawers and cupboards, and looked in closets, under the bed, and in every conceivable place that a person might hide. None of the FBI men had an arrest or search warrant with him. McCord explained that the FBI normally does not carry warrants. He said that he had been notified by teletype that Angela was wanted by Marin County authorities and that on August 14 a Federal warrant charging unlawful flight across state lines to avoid prosecution had been issued. McCord did not answer when asked by what authority he could arrest Angela Davis in Los Angeles for crossing state lines to avoid prosecution.

Angela later said that her disappearance was motivated by her fear of police authority, and the construction that might be made regarding her ownership of guns involved in the Marin County affair. The raid on her apartment justified those fears.

If she had returned to her home so that she could be surrounded by the familiarities of her books, pictures and papers, and immerse herself in the music of Bach while reflecting on what was happening in her life and how she would respond to the demand that she appear in Marin County and be questioned, one night her back door would have been kicked in, and five men would have seized her. If she resisted, or if they thought for some reason she was armed, she would have been shot, possibly killed, by FBI men acting as bounty hunters, enforcing a warrant which they had never seen, and which spelt out a crime that could not be proved by her presence in Los Angeles.

Police swarmed all over Birmingham, Alabama, Angela's home town, and questioned and harassed her friends and relatives. A police source reported that they had received information that Angela had met with a group of Black Panthers in Birmingham who had congratulated her on doing a fine job in California. Reportedly, Angela left with a $1,200 check given her by a wealthy white sympathizer. In fact, she was never in Birmingham.

The father of a friend who had known Angela in Birmingham, said he doubted that Angela had been within a thousand miles of his home in Toronto, Canada.

J. Edgar Hoover, head of the FBI until his death, placed Angela Davis on the ten most wanted list, which meant that she could be shot on sight, despite the fact that she was not charged with killing anyone, or, for that matter, of committing any crime at all.

In Frankfurt, German police, alerted by American authorities, descended on friends she had known there in 1965, while a student at the Johann Wolfgang Goethe University.

Connie Matthews, who is associated with Eldridge Cleaver's group in Algiers, was living in Paris when Angela disappeared. One night she had a phone call informing her that her school teacher friend was coming to Paris from Montreal, and would be staying at a particular address. When she arrived at the apartment she found that several large, menacing men had preceded her looking for Angela Davis. When she left the apartment, she was followed. Connie Matthews left France and went to Geneva.

Angela did go to Chicago, Detroit and Florida. She stayed in an apartment complex in Miami for about a month. Rumors that she was trying to get to Algiers or to Cuba cropped up. A charter boat captain claimed that two men and a woman tried to force him at gunpoint to take them to Cuba. He identified Angela from photographs. It turned out that he was lying. A pilot claimed that Angela had tried to hire him to fly her to Cuba. This story also was false.

The FBI traced Angela to a midtown Manhattan motel, following some leads provided by Robert Loman of Chicago, who had been a friend of David Poindexter, the man arrested with Angela. The FBI had also learned that Poindexter owned a blue Toyota. Lawrence J. Monroe, the FBI man in charge of the Angela Davis fugitive investigation in New York, assigned his agents to 12 parking lots attached to midtown motor hotels. They spotted the car in the Howard Johnson Motel, staked out the rooms adjoining Angela's, and waited for her to show up. Angela Davis and David Poindexter, the man she had been traveling with, were arrested.

Angela was held on a $250,000 bail and Poindexter was jailed pending the posting of $100,000, an unusually high bail.

John H. Doyle III, an Assistant United States Attorney, told the US Commissioner before whom Angela and Poindexter were brought, that "there was tangible and material evidence of her involvement" in the Marin County killings.

He said of the 36-year-old Poindexter that, "his life is a complete mystery as far as this court is concerned," and warned that "there is a very high risk of flight." Doyle did not get an opportunity to resolve the contradiction of assessing a "high risk of flight" in a situation where a person was a complete mystery to him. The following day, Mrs. June Hunzinger, Poindexter's mother, came from Florida, posted $100,000 cash, and left with her son. Howard Moore, Jr. subsequently sent a book to the manager of the bonding agency that provided the cash for Poindexter, inscribed, "to the one who freed Poindexter for a price."

Doyle prosecuted Poindexter in Federal court for aiding and abetting a fugitive. He produced FBI agents, motel clerks, employees of the Miami apartment complex where the two stayed and three of Poindexter's friends—44 prosecution witnesses in all. The issue was whether Poindexter knew that Angela Davis was wanted by federal authorities. Doyle insisted that Poindexter could not have missed the saturation of news about her being wanted in California and the issuance of a federal fugitive warrant for her arrest.

Poindexter's defense was that he didn't watch TV, didn't read newspapers and had no idea that the FBI were looking for Angela. He was acquitted in April 1971.

During her trial Angela never explicitly stated why she "made herself unavailable." She was familiar with a parallel in history—the flight of Frederick Douglass in 1864, following John Brown's attack on Harpers Ferry with a group of men that included Sheilds Green, a fugitive slave whom Douglass had introduced to John Brown just days before the raid.

"It may be asked," said Douglass, "why I should have objected to being sent to Virginia to be tried for the offense charged. The explanation is not difficult. I knew that if my enemies could not prove me guilty of the offense of being with John Brown, they could prove that I was Frederick Douglass—they could prove that I was in correspondence and conspiracy with Brown against slavery —they could prove that I brought Sheilds Green, one of the bravest of his soldiers, all the way from Rochester to him at Chambersburg—they could prove that I brought money to aid him, and in what was then the state of the public mind I could not hope to make a jury of Virginia believe I did not go the whole length he went, or that I was not one of his supporters; and I knew that all Virginia, were I once in her clutches, would say 'Let him be hanged.' " [1]

Many of these elements were exactly the same for Angela Davis. There was no problem in proving who Angela Davis was and in so doing cast inferences on what she might do. Angela became known in California in 1969, immediately after she accepted a position as a temporary Acting Assistant Professor in the Philosophy Department at the University of California in Los Angeles.

At the time she was offered the appointment she was enrolled as a Ph.D. candidate in Philosophy at the University of California in San Diego. In Los Angeles she continued the involvement with black political concerns that had been part of her life in San Diego. Angela worked with the Black Panthers in Los Angeles, and although she was not a member of the organization, had been associated with them by the Los Angeles police department's "red squad." And, Angela was a communist, a member of the Che-Lumumba Club, an all black collective of the Communist Party USA.

Angela was a socialist and a revolutionary before she joined the Communist Party USA. She believed in the theory popularized by the Panthers that black people, because of their position at the bottom of the social scale and political heap, and because of the all embracing oppression visited upon them through racist practices, were, by virtue of that position, a potential revolutionary force.

She viewed the black community as the vanguard in a socialist revolution, a Panther position before Huey Newton decided to opt in favor of black capitalism. Angela's entrance into the CPUSA

---

[1] *Life and Times of Frederick Douglass,* Bonanza Books, New York.

was preceded by months of conversation with her sister Fania, and her close friends Franklin and Kendra Alexander, who were members of the Che-Lumumba Club, and who also shared her views about the political position of blacks in this country.

Angela did not join the Panthers because she had no particular attraction for the internecine squabbling that was beginning to emerge in the national Panther organization. At that point the Panthers were attempting to resolve seemingly opposing strategies within the organization. One position saw the Panthers as a vanguard organization which would bring about mass participation in its activities by setting revolutionary examples for other blacks to follow, and by tailoring their programs to meet the basic needs of the community. Central to this were the defense movements built around Huey Newton, Bobby Seale, Erica Huggins and a host of lesser known Panthers. The other position dismissed even token attention to the masses, insisted that black revolutionaries not relate to the court system, and that the Panthers, through urban guerilla warfare, should take their case directly into the streets. The assumption was that protracted guerilla warfare would eventually attract mass support.

The positions were not irreconcilable. All revolutionaries base their political analysis and tactics on the supposition that a point will be reached in the struggle when the masses of people will support armed revolution. The problem was how that support would be generated, what tactics would raise revolutionary consciousness while maintaining, within the organization, a pure revolutionary position which sought to dissolve all institutions founded on racist capitalism.

But Angela did not feel that she wanted to be a part of that resolution, particularly as she felt that the Black Panther Party was beginning to move away from the revolutionary principles on which it was founded. She was critical of Panther relationships with white revolutionary groups such as the Weathermen, because of her belief that it was not possible to develop revolutionary nonracist politics within an all-white group. The Weathermen, as young white people, took the position that, through their revolutionary acts, they were going to spur the development of revolutionary consciousness among other young white people. They would then find some way to relate to black and brown and Third World people, but they were going to be separate. Perhaps as a result of that notion of what struggle is all about, all kinds of subtle racist influences seeped into their position.

"I think that the party's position (CPUSA) is really the best position of the relationship that should exist between black and white workers, and that is that black formations within the struggle are necessary, in order to develop the revolutionary potential of black workers, in order to develop the kind of national consciousness and identity which is a necessary element of black liberation. On the other hand, all-white formations are reactionary, all-white formations are going to do nothing but promote racism, including the politics of Weathermen." [2]

The Communist Party became Angela's choice. With, and through the Che-Lumumba Club, she could actively pursue the political goal of black liberation, coupled with a socialist revolution the vanguard of which would be black workers. She did not begin to believe that the Communist Party was the absolute revolutionary answer to the problems that exist in America.

Angela believes that the times require the creation of a revolutionary structure, which would give leadership and meaning to the movements that have been created around particular issues or individuals. The problem, she explained, is to reach the masses by successfully bringing to their attention the issues and principles upon which a revolutionary movement could be built.

She chose the Communist Party, partly because of her background in Marxist theory. The final impetus was blackness, the existence within the Communist Party of the Che-Lumumba Club, an all-black collective. She maintains that a genuine revolutionary movement cannot exist until progressive whites recognize the need to eradicate racism, and in doing so accept black leadership.

The Che-Lumumba Club was working on two fronts. They operated in the black community in Los Angeles around particular issues. Among themselves they agreed on the need for armed self defense as well as on the practical approach to self defense involving securing weapons and learning how to use them. They also

[2] Angela Davis, in interview with author.

operated within the CPUSA, seeking to transform it into a genuine revolutionary organization that could and would accept black leadership in the struggle against both capitalist exploitation and racist cant.

A few months after Angela joined the Communist Party, the Chairman of the Philosophy Department at UCLA recommended her appointment as an Assistant Professor. She was a Phi Beta Kappa who had graduated from Brandeis in 1965 with a Bachelor of Arts degree in French literature, having spent her junior year at the Sorbonne. She spent 1965–67 doing graduate work at the University of Frankfurt. In September 1968 she received an M.A. in Philosophy from the University of California at San Diego studying under Herbert Marcuse who was later to supervise her doctoral work also at San Diego.

Although Angela was not looking for a job, she accepted the UCLA offer.

Negotiations were begun in March and completed in April. On June 3, 1969, a letter of appointment was sent to her and on July 1 the UCLA newspaper printed a story saying that the Philosophy Department had hired a communist. A week later an "exposé" appeared in *The San Francisco Examiner* written by Ed Montgomery, probably the leading radical rightist of all newspapermen on the nation's big dailies. His news career has been dedicated to attacking anyone to the left of the late Senator Joseph McCarthy, or anyone more racially moderate than Governor George Wallace.

Montgomery's world is political, and his is the politics of repression. He has consistently "exposed" communists, attacked all facets of the civil rights movement, excoriated students seeking meaningful changes in the institutions which control their education, and acted as the unofficial mouthpiece for the inquisitorial tribunals of Congress which seek out subversion and label citizens as un-American. He identified the communist at UCLA as Angela Davis. To emphasize her alleged capacity for subversion Montgomery described her as "a known Maoist," and characterized her as being active in the Students for a Democratic Society and the Panthers, thus giving Angela political breadth on the left that has never before been experienced. In addition, Montgomery charged her with being a "gun runner" for the Panthers.

The University of California is governed by a single board of 24 Regents. Four of these are elected state officials—the Governor, the Lieutenant Governor, the Speaker of the Assembly, and the Superintendent of Public Instruction—and four others serve ex-officio; the remainder are appointed by the Governor for 16-year terms. The position of Regent of the University of California has long been regarded as one of great prestige in the state and among a Governor's most important appointments.

The Regents are spiritually, financially and politically the heirs of men who believed that the greatest disaster to befall mankind was the 1917 Bolshevik revolution. Most are capitalists who deal in millions of dollars annually, and who collectively are in touch with much of California's corporate wealth through memberships on interlocking boards of directors, ownership of factories, large farms and transportation industries, and manipulation of oil fields.

In 1949 the Regents banned the hiring of communists. In 1962 their General Counsel advised them that he thought this order had been rendered illegal by subsequent Supreme Court decisions. He also pointed out that the Regents themselves had passed a Standing Order 102.1 saying, "No political test shall ever be considered in the appointment and promotion of any faculty member or employee." The Regents' position was that to eliminate Communist Party members from teaching at the University did not constitute applying a political test. They then directed UCLA President, Charles J. Hitch, to ask Miss Davis if it were true, what the papers were saying about her.

President Hitch wrote a letter to Angela, which she did not receive for almost two months; she was in Cuba for the summer. On her return she answered "yes" to Dr. Hitch's question. "While I think this membership requires no justification here, I want you to know that as a black woman I feel an urgent need to find radical solutions to the problems of racial and national minorities in white capitalist United States . . ."

On September 19, the Regents directed President Hitch to terminate Miss Davis' appointment "in accordance with regular procedures as prescribed in Standing Orders of the Regents." This meant that Angela would still be on the payroll until after the procedures (which included a hearing) were completed.

She requested that she be allowed to teach Philosophy 99 in the Fall quarter, which was already scheduled and pre-enrolled but lacked an instructor. Angela took the position that by teaching she could demonstrate her general competence, while assuring those concerned that she did not consider the classroom a place for convincing students to be communists. The Department agreed.

When the Regents learned of this arrangement they called a special meeting and instructed UCLA not to assign Angela teaching duties. The college directed the Registrar not to accept enrollments for credit in courses Angela might teach.

The struggle was resolved in the courts in the latter part of October, when Superior Court Judge Jerry Pacht ruled that the Regents' anti-communist hiring policy was unconstitutional. He was ruling in a suit filed by three of Angela's fellow professors and joined in by Angela. Due to the notoriety of the Regents' anti-communist ruling, Angela Davis' first lecture had to be held in a hall large enough to accommodate the over 1,500 students and faculty members who attended it and gave her a standing ovation.

The course, "Recurring Philosophical Themes in Black Literature," revolved around the notion of freedom as one of those recurring themes. She talked about slavery within the context of Frederick Douglass' Autobiography.

"Already we can begin to concretize the notion of freedom as it appeared to the slave. The first condition of freedom is the open act of resistance—physical resistance, violent resistance. In that act of resistance, the rudiments of freedom are already present. And the violent retaliation signifies much more than the physical act; it is refusal not only to submit to the flogging, but refusal to accept the definitions of the slave master; it is implicitly a rejection of the institution of slavery, its standards, its morality, a microcosmic effort towards liberation." [3]

According to Angela, the slave, when he understands the fact of his slavery, begins to comprehend freedom in a manner that is unavailable to his master. "He knows that it means the destruction of the master-slave relationship. And in this sense, his knowledge of freedom is more profound than that of the master. For the

[3] Lecture: "Recurring Philosophical Themes in Black Literature," UCLA, Fall 1969.

master feels himself free and he feels himself free precisely because he is able to control the lives of others. He is free at the expense of the freedom of another. The slave experiences the freedom of the master in its true light. He understands that the master's freedom is abstract freedom to suppress other human beings. The slave understands that this is a pseudo concept of freedom and at this point is more enlightened than his master for he realizes that the master is a slave of his own misconceptions, his own misdeeds, his own brutality, his own effort to oppress." [4]

The lectures were a success. They were properly academic, philosophically intact and compellingly relevant. She was convinced that any appraisal of black thought in America had to proceed from the recognition of black subjugation through slavery, and include in its final analysis the fact that today's relationship between blacks and American institutions are to a large extent an extension of relationships begun when it was legal to own people.

During the 1969 Fall semester UCLA and its Regents investigated Angela in depth. A secret committee was formed to monitor her classes, and also to determine whether her off campus speeches constituted unprofessional conduct. They were not capable of finding her either incompetent to teach, or guilty of unprofessional conduct in her off campus activities. They found that the charge of utilizing her position in the classroom to indoctrinate students was not substantiated, that the claim that her extra-university commitments interfered with her duties as a faculty member were without foundation, and "that evidence supporting the charge 'that her public statements demonstrate her commitment to a concept of academic freedom which . . . would ultimately be destructive of that essential freedom itself' does not warrant special disciplinary action by the University against her."

The committee's observations about Angela's speeches included the observation that, "she has frequently sacrificed accuracy and fairness for the sake of rhetorical effect. We deem particularly offensive such utterances as her statement that the Regents 'killed . . . brutalized . . . (and) murdered' the 'people's park' demonstrators, and her repeated characterization of the police as 'pigs.'

[4] Idem.

Regrettably, the use of lurid imagery and the excessive resort to hyperbole have become the hallmark of extremist rhetoric. Its use is by no means confined to the militant left. Compared with some of the writings of Classics Professor Revilo P. Oliver of the University of Illinois in the John Birch publication, *American Opinion,* for example, most of what Miss Davis has said in public seems rather bland." [5]

The Regents seized on this mild criticism as a basis for denying her further employment. She had originally been hired for one year, with the understanding that there would be an automatic renewal for another year if she proved satisfactory as a teacher. All of the appropriate faculty committees evaluating her performance recommended that the second year teaching appointment be offered to her. Chancellor Charles E. Young, therefore, recommended to the Regents that she be rehired. The Regents' reaction to the Chancellor's recommendation was a resolution:

"The Regents hereby relieve the President of the University, the Chancellor of the Los Angeles campus and all other administrative officers of any further authority or responsibility in connection with the reappointment or non-reappointment of Acting Assistant Professor Angela Davis, and direct that the Board of Regents, acting as a Committee of the Whole, review the record relating to this matter and recommend appropriate action to the Board at its next regular meeting." [6]

Six of the Regents, including President Hitch, opposed the action. The rest, led by Governor Ronald Reagan and the then Superintendent of Public Instruction, Max Rafferty, asserted their loyalty to anti-communist politics, and voted to ignore their reversal of the 20-year-old ban on hiring communists. Governor Reagan told the press that he cast his first Regent vote to remove her from the faculty because she was "a member of the Communist Party."

"The Communist Party is considered to be not a political party *per se,* but a subversive organization . . . It is listed as a subversive organization by the Attorney General's office since its members have prior allegiance to another country."

The fact that the Supreme Court has declared that such lists

[5] AAUP Bulletin, September, 1971.
[6] Idem.

cannot be used to bar employment from any except a few "sensitive" positions, in no way affected Governor Reagan's actions.

Rafferty, an outright right-wing racist could be expected to come down hard on Angela. He later called her "a fugitive gun moll" he would not even hire as a custodian.

Rafferty rode himself into office on a campaign which opposed effective measures to integrate California public schools and an educational philosophy that would see political conservatism enshrined as a permanent part of all educational curriculum beginning with child care centers and ending as the organizing principle behind those committees that award doctorate degrees.

He was defeated for re-election in 1970, as Wilson Riles, a black career educator who was projected as opposed to Rafferty at every point, scored a surprise victory. Rafferty left California, taking a job in Alabama where he settled down comfortably as a supporter of Governor Wallace.

Two of the Regents, both attorneys, filed written dissents.

"The action of the Governor and a majority of the Board firing Miss Davis is unlawful and unconstitutional, for it violates the Federal Constitution, including the First Amendment, Equal Protection Clause, Due Process Provision, and *Ex Post Facto* Prohibition, Federal Civil Rights Statutes, the California Constitution, state law, and the Board of Regents' own long standing rules and procedures," wrote Regent Frederick Dutton.[7]

"In essence," Dutton continued, "Governor Reagan and his Regents have again unleashed vigilantism on our state. They have carried out a public lynching of this 26-year-old black girl for their own exploitive purposes."[8]

Regent William K. Coblentz, in his dissent, touched coincidentally on a case which had particular relevance to Angela Davis. He quoted the United States Supreme Court decision in the case of Julian Bond versus the Georgia legislature noting that: "Miss Davis' posture and obligations as a teacher are comparable to those of Julian Bond's as a legislator." Bond had been refused a seat after having been elected to the Georgia legislature because of

[7] Fred Dutton, "Dissenting Statement to Report of the Regents' Committee of the Whole," June 19, 1970.
[8] Idem.

his various statements opposing the war in Vietnam, urging Negroes as "second class" citizens to seek alternatives to the draft, and expressing admiration for those who burned their draft cards.

Julian Bond's case had been argued before the Supreme Court by Howard Moore, Jr., a veteran of southern civil rights battles, and an attorney who has more than 15 US Supreme Court decisions in his favor. Moore was later to become Angela's chief counsel in her murder and conspiracy trial.

Coblentz' reference to the Julian Bond case provides another insight into the reasons for which Angela faded from view immediately following the August 7 incident—fear of the abuse of state power. She had grown up in Birmingham and had experienced those legalistic extremes supportive of white rule, which effectively disenfranchised the one-fourth of the state's population that was black.

She received her B.A. the same month that Julian Bond was elected to the Georgia State legislature, and was in Germany when the legislature refused to seat him despite the fact that he was overwhelmingly elected (82%) by the voters in his district.[9] Angela was thoroughly aware that the United States House of Representatives summarily dismissed the late Adam Clayton Powell from their midst, and when he was subsequently re-elected to his seat, dismissed him again. Furthermore, when the courts finally determined that Powell was entitled to his seat, his fellow Congressmen stripped him of his seniority, therefore reducing the most powerful black politician in the country to the status of a freshman Congressman, after 20 years of continuous membership in the House of Representatives.

It took two years of litigation before higher courts found that the Regents had dismissed Angela without cause. By that time she was in jail awaiting trial for murder, kidnapping and conspiracy. Sanctimonious sounding editorials in local newspapers hailed the reversal of the Regents' decision as indicative of the fact that the system worked, and snidely suggested that Angela, if she were in Russia, would not have been afforded the constitutional guarantees

---

[9] An interesting sidelight is that after the NAACP Legal Defense Fund refused to participate in either the Julian Bond or the Angela Davis case, Howard Moore, Jr. successfully took on the defense.

which she enjoyed at the hands of the system she was dedicated to destroy. But no mention was made of the destruction and erosion of all constitutional rights that comes from officials acting according to their sense of politics rather than their knowledge of law. No sanctions were applied to the Regents. There was no fine or jail term for depriving Angela Davis of her rights. And, if Angela had not taken her case to court, there would have been no automatic review of the Regents' actions.

Governor Reagan and Lieutenant Governor Ed Reineke, after the reversal of their decision as Regents, and after Angela was acquitted, still declared her ineligible to teach at the University of California. Their reasons? Angela's use of the classroom as a forum for her communist beliefs, and her radical remarks made outside the classroom. Governor Reagan seems to have abandoned his law and order position when called upon to obey laws he cannot live with. The law says that an individual cannot be denied employment solely because of membership in the Communist Party. "It won't happen in my state," is Reagan's attitude, and it is an absolute certainty that if Angela attempts to regain her position at UCLA the Governor will attempt once more to find some stratagem to deny her employment.

So-called moderates, who utilize a rhetoric that eschews extremism of the right and the left, conveniently ignore the fact that both liberals and moderates have always made a political accommodation for right wing extremists. Ironically, Max Rafferty, the right-wing supporter of racist orientations toward education was replaced by Wilson Riles, who was no more "moderate" about Angela Davis than Rafferty was. Riles, a black man and professional educator, was the choice of liberals and moderates to replace Rafferty. In August 1970, Riles was campaigning for the position. At that time, faculty members at UCLA were not only clamoring for Angela's rehiring but had started a fund to pay her salary.

Riles described faculty members who wanted Angela rehired as "myopic visionaries who've lost their glasses." He described the professors who were collecting money to pay her salary as "jumping with lead shoes on the very tender toes of academic freedom." Angela became a campaign issue for Riles. In a paid radio spot

Riles said that Angela would not have been hired at UCLA had he been in the post that Rafferty held. He had two debates with Rafferty and told him, "Angela Davis is your baby."

Angela was shocked to find that Wilson Riles had attacked her in a bid for votes. Riles' most intensive campaigning coincided with the time that Angela was being sought. His election took place just three weeks after she had been arrested in New York. She noted that she had been on a panel with Riles at a Negro Leadership Conference held in January 1970, after Riles had let it be known that he would be a candidate for public office. At the conference, Riles, though obviously less left-oriented than Angela, gave no hint that he disapproved of her membership, as a communist, on the UCLA faculty.

H. L. Richardson, a state senator from Arcadia, who had once been a John Birch staff member, circulated a memo to all state legislators on June 16, 1970, which anticipated the prosecution theory that Angela was purchasing firearms and making them available to militants. Richardson's memo outlined her purchase of a Browning automatic and a Plainfield carbine, both of which were used on August 7. He said he was trying to make his colleagues "aware of the revolutionary nature of this woman" and that she was "not just a quiet teacher but a revolutionary in every sense of the word." The memo was circulated just three days before the Regents made their final decision to fire Angela.

One of the Regents voting against her was Jesse Unruh, who was a Regent by virtue of his position as Speaker of the Assembly. Unruh, a liberal, whose name is on the state's basic anti-discrimination law, was unequivocal in his opinion of Angela Davis. He said that she never should have been hired, and that she should be fired.

Much of Angela Davis' liberal support at UCLA began to fade away in April 1970, after she became active in the Soledad Brothers Defense Committee. The professors who supported her right to have and to hold dissident or unpopular political opinions resented the fact that Angela, during the time they were supporting her, had the bad form to exercise those rights.

Montgomery Furth, head of UCLA's Philosophy Department, in August 1970, noted in an interview published August 16, that there were indications that faculty support for Angela had been damaged critically because of the charges that had been brought against her. Arnold Kaufman, a Philosophy professor and president of the UCLA chapter of the American Federation of Teachers, put it on the line. "We are not jumping to any conclusions," he said, "but it's absolutely indispensable that we have a public explanation of the circumstances concerning allegations that the guns were hers. Until a full and truthful account is forthcoming, our effort to protect her rights will be severely hampered."

In theory, all of Angela Davis' rights were protected by the presumption of innocence prior to a guilty verdict. In practice, a person accused of a crime is responsible only to the court trying the case to factually contradict those items which· unexplained might indicate guilt. In truth, the presumption of innocence is a legalistic formalism that has never been able to supplant the folk legend "where there's smoke there's fire" with the more accurate observation that where there's smoke, there's smoke, and if fire exists that fact will soon be obvious.

Angela's philosophic concentration with the idea that black life represented a bourgeois democratic extension of slave relationships netted her additional enemies after she became active in defense of the Soledad Brothers.

"Historically the prison system has been an integral part of our lives," she wrote in an article. "Black people emerged from slavery only to encounter the prison labor system as one element of the new apparatus of exploitation. . . . The mere fact that almost half of the 28,000 convicted felons in California's prison system are non-whites—Blacks and Chicanos—is enough to reveal the intrinsic racism of the courts, Youth Authorities and Parole Boards to which George Jackson, John Cluchette and Fleeta Drumgo fell victim at a very early age. . . . The mindless, sadistic guards whose carbines at any moment could let loose bullets aimed at their brains, could not deter the Soledad Brothers from reaching out to every other inmate whose ears were receptive to their teachings on liberation." [10]

Even while her fight to retain her position at UCLA was going on, and during the time that she had to prepare lectures, correct

[10] "The Soledad Brothers," in *The Black Scholar*, April–May 1971.

papers and otherwise satisfy the requirements of being a temporary Assistant Professor, Angela moved around the state mobilizing support for the Soledad Brothers.

She became an outspoken foe of the prison system, stressing Frederick Engels' observation, "that along with the army and the police, prisons are the most essential instruments of state power. The prospect of long prison terms is meant to preserve order, it is supposed to serve as a threat to anyone who dares disturb existing social relations, whether by failing to observe the sacred rules of property or by consciously challenging the right of an unjust system of racism and domination to function smoothly." [11]

She attacked the California indeterminate sentencing which allows the prison system extreme flexibility in determining who is eligible to be released from prison. She spoke of the psychological torture practiced in California prisons by medical personnel who used aversion therapy such as that depicted in "A Clockwork Orange" to condition the minds of some inmates, and condemned the move of the Department of Corrections to destroy the minds of those they could not condition through brain surgery. In the process of campaigning for the Soledad Brothers, and against the Adult Authority and the Department of Corrections, Angela met and became intimate with the Jackson family, and fell in love with George Jackson.

"I was not seeking love when I walked into a Salinas courtroom on Friday, May 8, 1970," she wrote in a letter to George Jackson dated June 2, which was submitted by the prosecution as evidence of Angela's motivation in her alleged participation in aiding and abetting Jonathan Jackson's foray. ". . . But one thing remains to be said—my feelings dictate neither illusionary hopes nor intolerable despair. My love—your love—reinforces my fighting instincts, it tells me to go to war."

The letter was apparently a response to two letters written by George Jackson on the 28th and 29th of May. ". . . I promised not to be brash with you," he wrote on the 28th. "It's crazy, all women, even the very phenomenal, want at least a promise of brighter days, bright tomorrows. I have no tomorrows at all." [12]

[11] Quoted in "Soledad Brothers," op. cit.
[12] In George Jackson: *Soledad Brother,* Bantam Books, 1970.

On the 29th he wrote, "I love you like a man, like a brother, and like a father. Every time I've opened my mouth, assumed my battle stance, I was trying in effect to say I love you, African —African woman. My protest has been a small one, something much more effective is hidden in my mind—believe in me, Angela. This is one nigger who's got some sense and is not afraid to use it. If my enemies, your enemies, prove stronger, at least I want them to know that they made one righteous African man extremely angry. And that they've strained the patience of a righteous and loving people to the utmost." [13]

The letters that Angela and George wrote to each other should be published as a book. The mutual devotion to each other within the context of revolutionary struggle and the phenomenon of two revolutionary minds bridging the gap between the non-freedom of prison and the un-freedom of black existence in that minimum security prison that is the second class citizen status assigned to all non-whites; the magnificent premise on which their correspondence was based—that the liberation of mankind from all forms of oppression, while violent in execution, is based in a tender regard for the potential of human beings to love themselves and their fellow human beings, deserves the adulation of posterity and demands the attention of those who presently find their lives restricted by the so-called democratic institutions that obscure the meaning, the promise and the vibrancy of a society truly dedicated to the development of the best potential of all its citizens.

George Jackson had written of his younger brother in an earlier letter: "He is at that dangerous age where confusion sets in and sends brothers either to the undertaker or to prison."

In June, Angela sent a letter in which she mentioned Jonathan: his promise to work on an essay, their meeting in San Jose with a statewide Soledad Brothers Committee, his request that she stop smoking.

"I stopped," she wrote. "First day in 11 years I have spent eleven hours without a cigarette."

Jonathan had added a postscript: "Brother, I heard some of the tapes that Gregory did with you. I wish that you would not even mention my age at all. It is very hard for me to command authority

[13] Idem.

from anyone if he knows that I am 17. You should understand. Jon."

California prison authorities censor the most intimate of exchanges between inmates and their families and friends. They determine who can visit and who can correspond. In Angela's case, prison authorities denied her the right to correspond with George Jackson. The two found other ways to write to each other. A letter dated June 22, 1970, which was mailed in an envelope bearing the address of Jackson's attorney, John Thorne (in theory, correspondence between inmates and their attorneys is only subject to inspection for contraband) was confiscated by Soledad Prison officials, and subsequently was used as evidence against Angela.

Raymond W. Kelsey, a prison guard, testified that he had found the letter from Angela to George Jackson and had taken it to his superior, Captain Charles Moody.

"Did you have a policy not to read letters from attorneys?," asked defense attorney Leo Branton, Jr.

"Yes."

"Did you read that letter?"

"I did not read the complete letter; I just determined who it was from and took it to the captain."

"Why did you look? What was your purpose?"

"To look for contraband, like a money order."

Prosecutor Harris, in questioning Kelsey, determined that the envelope included a petition to be signed by prisoners and, in addition to the letter an article by Mao Tse-tung, entitled "Combat Liberalism." The letter, which certainly did not sound like something a lawyer would send, was handwritten and covered both sides of a sheet of yellow paper and began, "Dear George, what activities am I supposed to take time off from? Since that day described to you, my life, all my life's efforts have gone in one direction. Free George Jackson and the Soledad Brothers."

Branton had asked: "Did you make a determination that the letter did not involve a legal matter?"

"Yes and no," Kelsey replied. "I knew it wasn't from Attorney Thorne, and I didn't believe it was legal."

Jackson got the Mao pamphlet, but Angela's letter was withheld and not seen until it turned up as evidence.

Usual prison practice is to return all unauthorized correspondence to the sender. In this case the letter was kept. The apparent reason for this confiscation was that prison authorities were building a file on Angela Davis, for George Jackson could not reasonably be charged with being responsible for the actions Angela Davis took in violation of arbitrarily applied rules promulgated by the Department of Corrections.

Angela, by this time, had completed her UCLA stint, and was working full time on behalf of the Soledad Brothers. A change of venue was ordered, and the case was transferred to San Francisco at a time when Angela Davis, through George Jackson's attorney, was officially attempting to become an investigator on the case.

San Francisco Superior Court Judge Robert J. Drewes did not want Angela associated with his trial, and would not allow her to act as an investigator. The decision was obviously political. Most investigators have fewer qualifications than Angela, and defense attorneys usually can select an investigator and be certain of court approval. The practical effect of the denial of investigator status was that it prevented Angela from visiting George Jackson in either San Quentin or in the holding cell in San Francisco where the Soledad Brothers trial was taking place. One of the items of information which contributed to her being denied investigator status was the fact that Soledad Prison officials had denied Angela the right to visit or correspond with Jackson in May. Judge Drewes was aware of this.

Angela, in working for George Jackson's acquittal, came into the San Francisco Bay Area frequently. She was part of the committee which secured Soledad House, a headquarters for the Soledad Brothers Defense Committee. She could not be at the opening of the house on Sunday, August 2, but did show up in the Bay Area the following day. Her prime interest at that time was persuading blacks to join the Soledad Brothers Defense Committee in greater numbers. Support for the Soledad Brothers in Los Angeles was solidly based in the black community while the northern California committees were predominately white.

Jonathan Jackson was also in the Bay Area at that time, having become a familiar figure to members of the defense committee. Angela and Jonathan were together several times during the week of August 2, 1970, including Wednesday, August 5, when she purchased a shotgun in a downtown San Francisco pawnshop.

Angela left San Francisco Friday, August 7, and returned to Los Angeles where she remained in hiding for a week, leaving that city on August 14 on a trip that ended in her arrest in midtown Manhattan, New York.

A warrant had been issued in San Francisco on August 14, by Federal District Judge Gerald S. Levin. Jerrold Ladar, the Assistant US Attorney who applied for the warrant, argued before the judge that Angela bought a gun in San Francisco two days before the August 7 shooting, and that the purchase placed her in the area at the approximate time of the shooting, which was enough of a link to obtain a Federal warrant.

"We also pointed out," Ladar said later in an interview, "that she had been at Soledad House, a center for defense activities for three accused killers of a Soledad prison guard."

Ladar told the court that Angela had obtained a US passport. He failed to inform the judge that Angela had had a US passport for a number of years. He also insisted that there were "reasonable grounds" to believe that she had fled across state lines to avoid prosecution. Ladar notified Judge Levin of his reliable and confidential information that Miss Davis had been in Birmingham the previous Saturday. He pointed out that Angela was born in Birmingham and that her parents lived there. Moreover, he referred to a newspaper, *The Birmingham Post Herald,* which received a telephone call from a man who said he had seen Miss Davis at a local shopping center. A Federal warrant, with a minimum $100,000 bail requirement, was issued following these arguments.

The night of her arrest, John Abt, General Counsel for the Communist Party, Margaret Burnham of the NAACP Legal Defense Fund, and Haywood Burns of the National Conference of Black Lawyers, went to the basement of the Federal Building in New York, to represent Angela. Federal authorities were only prepared for John Abt, and so Margaret Burnham and Haywood Burns were about to be forcibly ejected from the building when Angela was brought into the basement and she recognized Margaret Burnham, whom she had known in Atlanta.

The three spent the next two months and ten days fighting in the courts to prevent Angela's extradition to California. John Abt said he went from precinct to precinct in search of Angela after the Federal charges were dropped, and Angela had been turned over to New York authorities.

New York policemen, who are past masters at transferring people in custoday from one precinct to another to avoid attorneys with writs, had gone into their act. When Abt finally caught up with her at a night court arraignment the day after she was arrested, he found the courtroom guarded by approximately 200 policemen.

After the arraignment, Angela was placed in the Women's House of Detention in Greenwich Village, and placed in the cell block reserved for psychiatric cases. After her attorneys protested Angela was transferred to a regular cellblock, and 24 hours later was placed in solitary confinement.

The New York Times interviewed "a spokesman for the Correction Department" who contended that there was no such thing as solitary confinement at the Women's House of Detention. He said that Angela had been transferred to a large room which previously was part of the jail's clinic, and had been provided with books, furniture, library privileges, and the constant companionship of a corrections official, even during recreation periods.

Three days later the same spokesman confirmed that Angela was on a hunger strike. After protests and ineffeetual appeals to city and state courts, Angela's attorneys had a hearing before Federal Judge Walter Mansfield, who extracted from Leonard Bernkow, the Assistant Corporation Counsel of New York, the admission that Angela was in solitary, "because she could possibly have a serious and destructive influence on the rest of the population."

"It is also for her own safety," the attorney threw in as an after thought—an argument which did not impress Judge Mansfield. After a two week hunger strike and vigorous argument by her attorneys, another Federal Judge, Morris E. Lasker, ordered that Angela should be "transferred to quarters shared with the general inmate population and accorded all privileges enjoyed by them."

Released from solitary, Angela issued a statement charging that she was framed, and that there was no evidence against her. She criticized the "bourgeois press" for focusing the bulk of its articles on her personality and background, and thereby camouflaging the political issues involved.

At this juncture the Federal charge was still being maintained even though Angela had been released from Federal custody. By her being held without bail, supporters of Angela Davis who might have come up with the original quarter of a million dollars were blocked. She spent from October 14 to October 21 in a procedural limbo. She was being held by New York officials pending a complaint which had not been filed prior to her arrest. In the end she was arrested on a warrant issued in response to rumor and conjecture.

On October 19, Bruce Bales, the Marin County District Attorney, swore to a complaint charging that Angela Davis had aided and abetted the murder of Judge Haley. She was not accused of actually killing him, and the alleged murderer was not named. The affidavit stated that Angela owned the guns which Jonathan Jackson carried into the courtroom, but it did not even make the claim that she provided Jonathan with them. The Marin County Grand Jury had met on September 4, and had indicted Ruchell Magee for the murder of Judge Haley. The Grand Jury had not been asked to consider charges against Angela at that time. Governor Reagan immediately signed the request for extradition, which was supported by Bales, and Governor Rockefeller of New York signed the extradition order without holding hearings or in any way looking into the legal issues involved.

Angela's attorneys filed a petition with the New York state courts on November 5, which pointed out the deficiencies in Bruce Bales' affidavit. But Bales was busy straightening things out. He convened the Grand Jury on November 10, and had them indict Angela and Ruchell as co-defendants, charging both with kidnap, murder and conspiracy. Ruchell was charged in addition with assault under California Penal Code 4500, which mandates an automatic death penalty and applies only to inmates serving an indeterminate sentence.

Bales had corrected his faulty affidavit by securing a Grand Jury indictment. But then he faced another legal hurdle. California law requires that an accused be given a transcript of the Grand Jury proceedings within ten days after the indictment. Once the accused has the transcript he can attempt to have the indictment quashed by convincing a judge that insufficient evidence was given the Grand Jury.

Marin County Superior Court Judge Joseph Wilson took care of that problem procedurally. He issued an order denying Angela a copy of the transcript as long as she was out of the state—a decision which deprived her attorneys of the opportunity to attack the indictment. Although it is rare, requests for extradition have been denied.

In an effort to block extradition, John Abt said he went on "the fastest Cook's tour of the appellate courts that I have been given in 45 years of practice. On the average it takes well over a year to exhaust the appellate process in a New York extradition proceeding—and this where the defendant's points are insubstantial to the point of the frivolous. In Angela's case, our constitutional arguments received a brush-off by five courts in as many days." [14] The matter was settled on December 21, when US Supreme Court Justice Harlan denied a stay of the extradition order.

Margaret Burnham and Haywood Burns were also busy in the courts. It was Burns who argued in Federal Court that Angela should be removed from solitary confinement. The two lawyers were also instrumental in convincing Angela to have a black-directed legal defense.

While in the Women's House of Detention, Angela spoke with several attorneys and decided on Howard Moore, Jr., who is also a member of the National Conference of Black Lawyers, and who subsequently won their 1972 Lawyer of the Year award. Margaret Burnham was also a member of the National Conference of Black Lawyers, as well as a part of Angela's legal team. The National Conference of Black Lawyers finally became an important part of the legal defense.

Burns organized a National Panel of Black Law Professors, headed by Paul Miller, Dean of Howard University Law School, to provide legal support services. In addition to doing legal research and working on some of the many briefs that were filed in the case,

[14] John Abt in Angela Davis *et al.: If They Come in the Morning,* Third Press, New York, 1971, p. 209.

the panel involved itself in fund raising for Angela's legal defense.

Angela was taken from her cell at 3 a.m. on December 22, on the pretext that her lawyer wanted to talk to her about extradition. She was taken to a room which she found filled with plain clothesmen and matrons, but could see no lawyer. There, she was notified that a skin search, preparatory to being taken back to California, would be performed. Angela refused to submit. She maintained that she had a right to consult with her attorney, and also that a skin search under those circumstances constituted an extreme violation of privacy.

The latter objection was handled first. Two male law enforcement agents simply grabbed her, and supervised the search. And then, she was hauled off. She was wearing a cotton dress and sneakers, and managed to convince a matron to get a pair of jeans (which she hurriedly put on under the dress) and a coat which was thrown over her shoulders.

She was turned over to California authorities, placed in a car that was located in the middle of an automobile convoy and driven to McGuire Air Force Base in New Jersey. Security precautions were so elaborate that the Holland Tunnel (between Manhattan and New Jersey) was closed to other traffic during the time the convoy was in it.

She was placed aboard a four-engine C-97 cargo plane belonging to the California Air National Guard, which Will R. Wilson, Assistant US Attorney General, said had been arranged for at the request of the California Attorney General's office. Angela was in Marin Superior Court the following day.

John Abt and Margaret Burnham had made a hurried trip from New York in order to represent her. Marin Superior Court Judge E. Warren McGuire gave her a copy of the Grand Jury transcript and immediately sealed the transcript so that the defense would not give out details of the testimony. In addition, McGuire issued a gag order:

"This Court is of the firm conviction that the impossible task of attempting to choose between the constitutional guarantees of a free press and fair trial need not be made, but that they are compatible with some reasonable restrictions imposed upon pre-trial publicity." McGuire's 'reasonableness' forbade everyone connected with the case from saying anything or revealing any information other than what had been previously released.

But nothing had been released. The Grand Jury transcript was sealed. The assumed even-handedness in gagging both defense and prosecution did not take into account the fact that most of the printed information linking Angela Davis to August 7 came from prosecution sources, and was not calculated to make Angela appear innocent. Judge McGuire made several exceptions to the gag rule which essentially allowed the press to report anything that happened in open court, and to receive such bare-bone facts as names, circumstances of arrest, and the nature of the charge. The judge also allowed the release of "Any information as to any person not in custody who is sought as a possible suspect or witness . . . any statement aimed at warning the public of any possible danger as to such person not in custody."

Only the prosecution could benefit from the modification as it was nothing more than a license to release whatever information they wanted to about anyone else who might be named as a suspect. There were no other suspects, but Judge McGuire's order remained in force throughout the trial. It became the first of a number of decisions which would lead Angela to emphasize that the only fair trial would have been no trial at all.

4 : Dress Rehearsal

Pre-trial publicity had begun four and a half months before Judge McGuire's gag order, and with a vengeance.

Bruce Bales, the District Attorney of Marin County, noted for the newspapers immediately after August 7 that Angela and Jonathan were "observed crossing the border from Tijuana, Mexico, into California on July 31, 1970, in an automobile registered to Angela Davis." Bales also revealed that Jonathan Jackson accompanied Angela when she purchased a carbine on July 25, and a shotgun on August 5.

These were items of evidence which corresponded to Judge McGuire's proscription against "any out-of-court statement for public dissemination as to the weight, value, source, or effect of any purported evidence alleged to have been accumulated as a result of the investigation of this matter," which it can be assumed had the effect of preventing any person directly related to the trial (including law enforcement personnel in the jurisdiction) from making "any statement for public dissemination as to the content, nature, substance, or effect of any testimony which may be given in any proceeding related to this matter."

Attorney General Albert Harris, who prosecuted, also released information to the newspapers that Angela had been seen in the company of Jonathan Jackson before the shooting.

There were also items which fell outside the gag rule in practice, but could not be refuted by the defense by means which were clearly not in violation of Judge McGuire's orders.

The San Francisco Examiner said that it had learned that David Poindexter, Angela Davis' companion while she was in hiding in Florida, was active in the organization of such militant groups as JOMO (Junta of Militant Organizations) in the St. Petersburg and Gaiesville areas of Florida.

Guy Wright wrote in *The San Francisco Examiner* less than a month after the shooting: ". . . Miss Davis' faculty defenders shouldn't have been all that surprised when she traded her mortarboard for a place on the FBI's most wanted list. Her performance is just a repeat on a grander scale of what Eldridge Cleaver did to them a few years ago."

The gag rule guaranteed that Angela or her attorneys could do nothing at all to combat the image of her that had been created by a press exposed only to alleged factual material produced by prosecution sources.

August 4, 1971, over seven months after the gag order, radio station KNX, a CBS affiliate in Los Angeles, let loose the first of two scathing editorials:

"Months ago, we predicted that the left-wing would turn the Angela Davis trial into a propaganda showcase. The question of her involvement in the killing of a Marin County judge would be ignored.

"Now the propaganda campaign has begun with the inevitable full page ad in *The New York Times* that has become mandatory today. In it, a group of ultra-liberal professors claim Angela is being persecuted because she is black; a communist; a woman; and, a teacher.

"They ignore her purchase of the fatal guns. They ignore the admission by Black Panther attorneys that it is possible for black militants to get a fair trial in America. They ignore other cases that make their position about Angela crumble before the truth."

"They cry out," the second editorial concluded, "that Angela Davis cannot get justice in America. We ask what kind of justice she would get *for doing the same thing* (emphasis added) in Albania, Cuba, Algeria, Russia, Red China or the Sudan?

"KNX believes these members of the left-wing Angela Davis propaganda machine are either hypocrites or fools. Maybe they are both."

KNX was supported in its position by Warren Dohrn, a Los Angeles County Supervisor, who suggested that instead of a change of venue to Los Angeles, Angela, "should be sent back to Russia, the country she loves." Los Angeles Mayor Sam Yorty suggested Algeria.

There was an attempt to counter much of this pre-trial publicity by the National United Committee to Free Angela Davis

(NUCFAD), which as a defense committee was not bound by the gag rule. However, any direct reference to the Grand Jury testimony might be interpreted as information which came from the attorneys, and therefore a violation of the gag.

The gag order suited the prosecutor. He could piously proclaim his scrupulous observation of the rule, while allowing a free press to print anything it wanted. The prosecution had made its press statements prior to McGuire's pronouncement. After the imposition of the gag, all the prosecution had to do was to monitor any seeming violations of Judge McGuire's order.

Prosecutor Harris found it necessary to complain about the defense violating the order. There was first the publication of *If They Come in The Morning,* an anthology published in 1971, which described and defined many of the issues, legal and political, faced in Angela's case, placing it in the perspective of other political trials. The only piece in the book that could possibly fall afoul of McGuire's edict was written by Howard Moore, Jr. who discussed the state's entire case against Angela and still remained within the letter of the order. He did defy the spirit, however, for the purpose of the gag was to shut the lawyers up. Then came the telecast, *Vibrations For a New People.*

In February 1972, three weeks before the trial actually began, the Westinghouse network televised a conversation between Angela and the Reverend Cecil Williams of Glide Memorial Church in San Francisco. Now Harris could not get ready for Cecil Williams, who is the prototype of a hip preacher Harris usually does not encounter in church or in court.

The Reverend Cecil Williams is first and foremost an activist. He is active from sun-up to sun-up with a brand of new politics. A fully bearded, bespectacled, slightly paunchy, peace-symbol-wearing, hugging preacher, he has transformed the morning services at Glide with rock bands, light shows, poetry and folk singing, justice seeking, good feeling, sometimes rocking love feasts, into something called "celebrations." To visit Glide Memorial Church[1]

---

[1] In the pre-Cecil days, up until 1967, it was a staid Methodist church located near downtown, that had a dwindling, mainly elderly, white, middle-class congregation, a substantial endowment dedicated to social purposes, and a need for a preacher who would head the foundation.

is to enter a bazaar of causes. The reception hall of the church, where sedate coffee hours and bake sales were once held, is now a forum for every radical and revolutionary cause in the San Francisco Bay Area. Gay liberation, prison reform, bail funds, defense committees, peace demonstrations, sickle cell anemia testing, school integration committees, support for popular labor strikes, all flow from Glide.

Williams began visiting Angela when she was first brought back from New York. Even though the gag rule was in effect, newspeople and others had access to interviews with her. She gave details of her background, discussed political ideas with reporters, but stayed well within the guidelines of the gag order.

The telecast was filmed at the Santa Clara County Jail in Palo Alto, California, on January 20, 1972. Angela and Cecil never discussed anything to do with the trial. They started by exchanging a few views about revolution and then launched into a discussion of the Soledad Brothers' case and how Angela came to be associated with it. They discussed George Jackson's death, the need to work for revolutionary change of the system, and discussed the system of justice.

"What is justice? I mean, what does justice mean?" asked Angela. "Does justice simply mean that a person who has been charged with this crime is going to be acquitted? And that's what happened, of course, to Ericka and Bobby and Huey and the New York 21 and partially in the case of the Los Angeles Panthers who were just recently on trial. They were acquitted, or the charges dismissed against them, but that appears to me to be a purely formalistic view of what justice is—it's empty, it has no content.

"If you can show, or pick out someone, single a black person, a black revolutionary out, charge him with an unbailable offense, put him or her in jail for two years or two and a half years as in the case of the New York 21, I think, and then afterwards, get up with the case that you have that doesn't have any water at all and have the jury acquit them, is that what justice is all about? They've lost years of their lives. See, what has happened in those cases is that the black revolutionary leaders have been effectively silenced. They have been separated from their people, isolated from the community, for one year, two years, three years."

Angela had expressed one of the central concerns of her defense committee in relation to black political figures who had been similarly charged, and she did not feel the necessity to refer specifically to her own case.

She answered several letters during the telecast, including one from an inmate in the Ohio State Reformatory. "I've endorsed your actions," he wrote, "but, I've spoken at churches and one main question which they ask is 'Why is Angela Davis communist?' This is a very hard question to answer, mainly because I don't think I've been taught the true meaning of communism. This is one of my reasons for writing you at the time."

Angela replied, "Because I have a very strong love for oppressed people, for my people. I want to see them free and I want to see all oppressed people throughout the world free. And I realize that the only way that we can do this is by moving towards a revolutionary society where the needs and the interests and the wishes of all people can be respected."

She went on to one of her main concerns: ". . . I don't see myself as any different, any more important, than all of my captive sisters and brothers . . . What about all of the other thousands and thousands who are in America's prisons today. People should begin to realize that they have a responsibility to see to it that America does not head in the direction of fascism and it begins right at the level of the prisons. That's why the prison struggle is so important, because I see it as being a signal as to what the entire society will be about in the future and that's why I think it's in the interest of all people, many of whom may not know anyone personally in prison, but most black people, of course, have had some contact with the prisons, people should really begin to express themselves aggressively and boldly and demand that something be done about the prisons in their society today."

Albert Harris had seen a preview on Friday, February 4, and had sent a protest to William Osterhaus, the manager of Channel 5. "The broadcasting of this discussion makes clear the patent falsehood of the charge that there is, or has been, any effort to prevent Miss Davis from expressing her views," he said, and continued: "On the other hand, it is for you to decide whether the nature of the discussion, the identity of the interviewer and the timing and circumstances of the broadcast, result in a form of 'special pleading' for Miss Davis that is consistent with the right of both the defendant and the people to a fair trial. This decision rests with the news media."

Angela was able to conduct interviews because of an order handed down by Judge Richard Arnason granting her access to the press under certain conditions, most of them to be determined by the Sheriff. Santa Clara County Sheriff James Geary had been very cooperative; he not only made Angela available to the press, he made himself available. He referred to Angela as a model prisoner, spoke in favor of her being released on bail and generally let it be known that he, as Sheriff, had a high regard for his well-publicized prisoner.

Geary also spoke freely of the security arrangements that were being prepared for Angela. He would not venture an opinion as to whether the trial would be held in Palo Alto or San Jose, but he would be prepared to handle the trial in either location. On that point Geary need not have commented. Stanford University is in Palo Alto, and the University administration feared that a trial in Palo Alto would set off protests and confrontations similar to those experienced at Yale in May 1970, when Bobby Seale was being tried in the University town of New Haven. Stanford Vice Provost, Robert Rosenzweig, said that the university administrators, "did our best to do what we could to see the trial was held in San Jose."

Stanford President, Richard Lyman, said he met with Santa Clara County Executive, Howard Campen, because "some people did not know about the New Haven situation and we just wanted them to consider that piece of history." Sheriff Geary said that in his opinion the university was "overconcerned." Stanford had political clout, however, and the trial was moved to San Jose.

There had been no condemnation of Geary's genial attitude toward the news media until the telecast was announced. *The San Francisco Examiner* reported that the wife of either Judge James Scott, the supervising criminal judge in Santa Clara County, or the wife of Judge Bruce Allan, saw an advertisement announcing the television showing of *Vibrations For a New People* scheduled for a 9 p.m. showing Monday, February 7. This concerned woman called her husband, who in turn conferred with Judge Arnason by

phone over the weekend. On Monday morning, the day of the telecast, Judge Arnason announced that he had rescinded his June,
1971 order allowing press interviews.

At the same time, Judge Scott, who had no connection with the
case before or after, issued an order: "Good cause appearing, it
is hereby ordered that the Sheriff of Santa Clara County, James
Geary, shall henceforth make no statements for public dissemination of his opinions regarding the above defendant, matters relating
to the trial or the cause of security provisions pertaining to the trial
or any other security provisions relating to the Criminal Division
Trial Departments of this court."

Geary was shut up, and just in time. It so happened that at that
moment a group of 35 inmates in the Santa Clara jail, mainly
Mexican-Americans, went on a five-day hunger strike. They were
specifically protesting the harsh sentences handed down by Judges
James Scott and Bruce Allan. There were also comments about
the conditions at the jail, but before they could be spelled out
Judge Scott's order took effect. These judges were making damn
sure that Angela's invitation to the public to investigate conditions
in jails and prisons would not be taken too literally by the mass of
press people who hung around the County Civic Center day after
day.

Leo Branton, Jr. one of the defense counsel, was outraged. He
accused Judge Arnason of not being man enough to run his own
court, and charged the county counsel with complicity in the silenc-
ing of Angela Davis. Arnason's withdrawal of press privileges to
Angela effectively kept the press away from her, by placing, in the
hands of the Sheriff and his superiors, including Judge Scott, the
discretion as to whether she would see newspeople or not.

Howard Moore, Jr. insisted that the new orders were designed
to handicap his client. "All this activity is aimed at continuing the
prosecution made image of Miss Davis as a nappy haired, big
mouth firebrand." He accused the prosecution of attempting to
prevent the American public from seeing Angela as the person she
really is—a serious, thoughtful individual who has reasoned out
her politics and acts accordingly.

Attorney General Evelle Younger, Harris' boss, got into the act.

"I can't help but wonder," he mused after seeing the show, "how Miss Davis and her supporters would react if a special on the late Judge Haley, with his family and dreams and aspirations were shown this close to the time of the trial."

Doris Walker, another defense attorney, attacked this statement.

"Yesterday Evil Younger made remarks regarding Miss Angela Davis," Miss Walker began, and proceeded to refer to the Attorney General as "Evil" Younger throughout her entire speech. The Attorney General is the state's lawyer, she pointed out. He could not be in the least confused, or afford not to understand what he was doing. His remarks constitute an attack on the defendant, she explained, because they assume a connection between Angela and Judge Haley.

Calling the Attorney General's remarks, "a most improper insertion" in the case, Miss Walker demanded that Arnason reprimand the Attorney General, and order the prosecutor, Albert Harris, to hand-deliver an order to both Younger and Governor Reagan, informing them that statements they make about the trial could lead to contempt of court citations.

Harris rose to his feet, his normally ruddy face having turned an incredible shade of red. He was mad, insulted, outraged that the defense would have the nerve to suggest to the judge that he play Western Union and personally deliver a warning to his boss, the Attorney General, and the superboss, the Governor, telling them to stop making their remarks about Angela or be cited for contempt—and all because of a television show which he found in poor taste.

Almost sputtering, Harris pointed out that the defendant appeared on TV at "prime time, preempting Lucy and Doris Day." He described Cecil Williams as, "a man who is her supporter, a member of her defense committee who uses his church to support Angela . . ." He called Williams a cheerleader, and again complained about the use of prime time to put on what he called a "maudlin performance."

He reminded Miss Walker that the Attorney General's name was "Evelle," not "Evil," and suggested that the accusation that Younger was in contempt for making "fair comment," was ridiculous. "It may be that the totalitarian mind is using free speech as a one way street. As sickening as I find that performance, it is a free country. I have not commented in court."

He promised at some point to place both the book, *If They Come in the Morning,* and the film in the record to use as evidence of violation of a pre-trial publicity gag rule.

Doris Walker retaliated. "I think Mr. Harris is carried away. All I ask is for him to effect personal service . . . What has happened to the presumption of innocence held by the prosecutor? . . . If there is a totalitarian atmosphere about this case, it can be laid to those two, Evil Younger and Ronald Reagan."

The atmosphere in the courtroom was seething. The defense was demanding that Arnason reinstate his order granting press interviews. Arnason, practically running out of the door, noted, "We recognize the great strength of this country is that we do have rights and liberties and sometimes they may be attacked. But we have confidence that with perseverance, what should be done, will be done." No one heard his, "court is adjourned."

After the court session Doris Walker explained that "Younger is the top lawyer of the State of California. He is not ignorant of the total impropriety of his statement attacking the defendant. The trial is not yet under way, yet on the face of his statement some guilt connecting Miss Davis with the death of Judge Haley is most improper."

As for Reagan, she noted his "capacity for ignoring the most basic precepts of due process . . . the importance of court orders and the importance of obeying court orders" and characterized him as "an extremely stupid man." But the gag orders held, and that was one of the last candid statements made by any of the attorneys for the defense to the press during the entire length of the trial.

The proliferation of gag rules, combined with security problems, created difficulties for the press which were never completely surmounted. This was more than a political trial, it was an international political event with over 400 people accredited to the press corps, among them representatives of 31 foreign news media agencies, wire services and magazines, representing ten countries

(Australia, Denmark, East Germany, Great Britain, France, Italy, Luxembourg, Sweden, USSR and West Germany). There were 133 American news gathering agencies, including the Voice of America.

The courtroom was hardly large enough to contain the press that wanted to attend the trial. Of the total of 75 courtroom seats, 30 were assigned to the press. Seven of these seats were assigned on a rotating basis; the balance went to the big dailies, wire services, national news magazines and selected members of the local press. In an adjacent building an auxiliary courtroom, equipped with a closed circuit TV, was provided exclusively for the overflow press corps.

There were no correspondents from black nations, a fact which undoubtedly reflects the economic realities faced by countries whose political independence has not yet secured for them the wealth which would allow them to engage in such international news gathering events. From Nigeria, the ninth most populous country in the world, with a population of 66 million, only letters and telegrams of support for Angela were sent.

The 25 million blacks in the United States were hardly in better shape. There were two black reporters with permanent seats at the trial, Earl Caldwell representing *The New York Times,* and the author, covering for *The Sun Reporter,* a San Francisco based black weekly. *The Sun Reporter* was the only black newspaper in regular attendance. The only other news coverage directed to a black audience was provided by reporters covering for three black-oriented radio stations.

There were other black newspeople present, but their job was to report the trial to a predominately white audience. Their coverage could not deal directly with those aspects of the trial that were of particular interest to black people.

A black revolutionary was on trial, a woman who said that her politics, including membership in the Communist Party USA, was an expression of her experience as a black person in America. She was accused of conspiring with a 17-year-old black youth in a scheme purportedly designed to free his brother and two other men from prison. The alleged conspiracy resulted in four deaths, three of whom were black people. A wounded survivor of the incident, who for a time was Angela Davis' co-defendant, was also black.

Three of the four defense attorneys were black, Leo Branton, Jr. from Los Angeles, Howard Moore, Jr. from Atlanta, and Margaret Burnham from New York, via Birmingham—all cities with large black populations. Four of the six members of the legal defense committee, those who did most of the work and made most of the decisions about the conduct of the political campaign surrounding the trial, were black.

The general media is neither equipped nor prepared to deal with the implications of police political activity directed solely against blacks. When Martin Luther King's forces were being brutally assaulted by southern racists ignorant of the first amendment the daily press referred to the incidents as "violent demonstrations." The events of August 7, 1970, were referred to by most of the press as a "bloody shootout." Bloody it was, but was it a shootout? All the evidence gathered indicated that no more than two of the shots fired came from the van containing Jonathan Jackson, his three compatriots and the five hostages. The 19-second barrage of bullets that must have made the Marin County Civic Center resemble a free fire zone in Vietnam, could therefore hardly be called a two-sided affair.

The press was interested in even-handedness, in presenting both sides of a guilty or innocent equation in an "objective" fashion. It had no interest in the why of the indictment, or what its significance was or, more important, whether any of the political statements being made by Angela and her defense team were worthy of objective news treatment. As a result, the press was guilty of excesses, some subtle and others glaring, either of commissions or omissions, which gave a one-sided, nay, a no-sided picture of the event that was the Angela Davis trial.

Rumor-ridden news stories, or distorted versions of events were common enough, but this fault was secondary to the abject acceptance by the press of a series of gag rules that effectively hampered their gathering of complete information about the trial and truthfully informing the public.

Leo Branton, Jr. tried to explain racist differential treatment at a dinner gathering of reporters. He said the press was not reporting many of the injustices which they experienced or participated in. He led them through their restrictions at the trial, the fact that by court order they were restrained in performing their function, even to the point of getting background information from defense counsel in what was a very complex case. Branton then pointed out that many of the press people in the room had covered the Charles Manson case which was tried at the same time that he was defending the Panther 13—a group of Panthers charged with assault, conspiracy and possession of illegal weapons, in the aftermath of a five-hour exchange of gunfire following a 300-man police attack on Panther headquarters in which police dynamited the roof of the building holding the Panthers.

"We would come into court," said Branton, "my clients in chains, shackled around the arms and around the legs. And coming down the corridor, strutting like debutantes, smiling for the television cameras, joking for the press, were four women who along with Manson were accused of murdering people. My clients were not accused of murder. There were no allegations that they caused bodily harm. But they were in chains, and you ladies and gentlemen of the press, did not see fit to report that blacks accused of assault must be chained, while whites accused of murder can walk freely in the halls of justice."

The press was incapable of reporting the injustice inherent in the trial because they were insensitive to the repression they accepted. If the press cannot complain under conditions where they cannot do their jobs, they are hardly in a position to be sympathetic to the complaints of an accused who cannot live her life.

"I think the press was derelict," Howard Moore, Jr. remarked in an interview immediately after the verdict, "in not challenging the security measures which had been established here. I felt that those security measures did pose a substantial threat to first amendment freedoms, that is the freedom of the press to come in and report on a public event. . . . You were told when you could come into the courtroom, when you could leave, the circumstances under which you could leave—in other words you were told when you could reach the public and how you had to conduct yourself in order to reach the public. I think that those measures had the potential of having an adverse impact on the freedom of the press. And I think that the press was obligated to speak out against them. Its failure to do that I think was a dereliction on the part of the press."

The press was so lost in the pageantry of the prosecution, so captured by the assumptions of those who wield power, that it transmitted the sum of the Angela Davis trial without dealing with the substance. That substance was politics, the way America is run, and the difficulty in making appropriate changes.

Whether or not August 7, 1970, was a "bizarre" event as reported, there was an important aspect of it which was a serious exercise of predetermined political alternatives. That aspect is revolution—world revolution—and its object is violence. Here, the question is not violent versus non-violent change, but rather who controls the violence which brings about change.

The story of the Angela Davis trial lay not in Angela's guilt or innocence, but in her complicity in a political world that makes Jonathan Jackson an inevitability. The challenge was not whether Angela could get a fair trial, but whether the American public could get a fair look at the system of justice which tried her.

Between the restrictions placed by the judge, the paucity of black reporters to observe the trial and the general inflexibility of whites to adopt new modes of thinking about racial matters, a number of defense positions or arguments were lost to the press. The press could not accept the fact that they were set up in a way calculated to block their understanding. They found Angela easier to understand than Ruchell, partly because she cooperated with the four attorneys who were defending her.

Howard Moore, Jr. had set the tone for the defense, calling the indictment, "pure speculation, guessing and conjecture . . . Angela Davis is the target of a vicious political frameup . . . No responsible and fair-minded prosecutor would ever bring three capital charges against a person on the basis of this kind of circumstantial evidence."

Two hundred pages of briefs attacked the Grand Jury—both its composition and the way it came to indictments. "These same judges, including the deceased judge, selected from among their friends and associates the very grand jury who weighed the evidence and voted the indictment."

Defense attorneys asked for the "suppression of the testimony of all spies, provocateurs, informers and undercover police agents who obtained their evidence by deceit, trickery or artifice." They pointed out that the testimony before the grand jury "provided no evidence of criminal intent," stressing the fact that, "close association with even the obviously guilty is insufficient to uphold an indictment."

All attacks on the grand jury failed.

Moore argued that bail should be granted:

"Judge, I have to say first of all that I am really overwhelmed . . . I am concerned about the fact that Miss Davis has been here since December 22 and she has been locked up here on the third floor. There is no sunlight up there. Her life is restricted to moving from one 7 by 7 or 8 by 8 cell to one cell that is 10 by 10. No contact with other people on a social, sisterly basis. Her whole contact is with the matrons who follow her every step, or with her lawyers, witnesses or investigators. That goes on day after day after day after day for 24 hours and there doesn't seem to be any end in sight.

"This four-legged monster that Mr. Harris has brought into court—neither has a head nor a tail, nor a body for that matter, it just jumps around. It is a sort of Disneyland North. It is sufficient just to keep a person in jail like that for maybe a year, two years, three years, regardless of what the outcome is. The client is just plain punished."

Bail was denied.

The prosecutor played his role to the hilt. He insisted that Angela was not being persecuted, but had been charged for very serious crimes because the evidence warranted it. He emphasized the fact that a judge was killed, and challenged any of the six men, who at one point or the other sat as judges in the trial, to act leniently with the accused who had conspired to kill one of their colleagues.

The first battle was for a larger courtroom, a motion which Judge Wilson denied. Then came the move to quash the indictment, which Mike Tigar argued. He said that the indictment of Miss Davis was a sham. While he was speaking, Harris signalled from his seat at the counsel table to an aide standing near the door leading back to the judge's chambers. The aide proceeded to push a shopping cart with guns in it across the courtroom floor.

"Miss Davis is an articulate and concerned advocate for social change," said Tigar, as Harris was transferring the guns from the cart to the table before him.

"The institution of a prosecution against this brave woman is an outrage. The case simply should not be."

Then it was Harris' turn.

"The test of the validity of the indictment is a strong suspicion," began Harris. He absolutely refused to be moved by arguments with which he did not agree.

"The only question before the court (an aide was unpacking the guns) is whether there is enough evidence to raise a strong suspicion in the minds of reasonable men." The guns were out. He picked up the carbine.

"The August 7 incident took place 50 feet from where I stand. Judge Haley was seated pretty much where you are judge . . . ," and he was interrupted by Attorneys Bell and Carrow, representing Magee. They pointed out that Harris was violating a previous order sealing the grand jury testimony, and that the guns were a part of that testimony insofar as they had been submitted to the grand jury as evidence to back up the testimony.

Harris asked that the seal be vacated, saying that he had no way to reply to Tigar's attack on the indictment unless he could produce some of the evidence which made the indictment valid. Judge McMurray kept the seal on the weapons, and Harris had to put his toys away.

Throughout the trial Harris projected himself as a victim, an employee of the Attorney General's office, who had a job to do in the face of overwhelming odds. He constantly made reference to the phalanx of attorneys surrounding Angela, pointing out that only he and Clifford Thompson, his assistant, represented the state. In truth, the Attorney General's office has a couple of hundred attorneys, investigators and criminologists who are involved solely in criminal prosecutions.

Harris is head of the criminal division, an Assistant Attorney General. He has instant cooperation from any police jurisdiction in the country and has the money of the State of California behind him. His witnesses, some of whom had appeared at the grand jury hearings, came from Florida, New York, Missouri, Oregon and various parts of California. While investigating a case, the Attorney General's office is in command of the full police powers of the state —an amount of power that is generally not in the hands of an underdog.

He nevertheless did not have absolute control of the trial. California's discovery laws tie the defense into the prosecution preparations insofar as the prosecution is required to turn over to the defense all of the potential evidence available to it. It is not an automatic gift. The defense has to make a demand that is couched in language that will produce the evidence looked for. And even at that there are untoward occurrences.

Part of the prosecution's case involved eyewitnesses who would say that they saw Angela Davis at San Quentin prison in the company of Jonathan Jackson on the days preceding August 7. The prosecution was to claim that Angela Davis used the alias Diane Robinson in order to gain entrance into the prison. Handwriting experts had determined that the name Diane Robinson, which appeared under Jonathan Jackson's signature, had been written by Jonathan.

The defense contacted everyone who visited San Quentin between August 4 and August 6. They attempted to find someone who saw Jonathan and his companion, and would be able to describe her in sufficient detail to convince a jury that the lady in question was not Angela. They did not succeed in finding anyone who remembered seeing Jonathan Jackson or a lady who was, or was not, Angela Davis. But they did contact one lady, Madeline Lucas, who would not make a statement for the defense, but ended up, apparently as a result of the defense contact, testifying for the prosecution.

It is the prosecution which makes the decision about who to charge and what to charge them with. Criminal charges seem straightforward. Someone is suspected of committing a crime, evidence is gathered that seems sufficient to charge him, and then an indictment is secured, either through information, a hearing conducted before a judge (where the accused has the right to be represented by an attorney who can cross-examine witnesses) or a grand jury—a procedure which is the prosecutor's show and which does not afford any challenge to the accuser.

A basic inequity exists here, as an accused person has more chances of being indicted before a grand jury insofar as he has no opportunity to face his accusers and demonstrate whatever contradictions might exist in the testimony. One of the arguments raised in the Angela Davis and Ruchell Magee trials was that indictment by a grand jury, as opposed to a hearing, violated the equal protection clause of the 14th amendment, insofar as an individual can be indicted by a grand jury on evidence that would not succeed in getting past the information hearing.

Then there is the problem of indictment itself. Who gets indicted for what, and what penalties do they face upon conviction?

One of the seemingly obvious facts about August 7, was that three people, James McClain, William Christmas and Ruchell Magee, were taking leave of Marin County, without the blessings of prison authorities. That is escape. And yet, escape was never charged.

San Quentin is a state facility, and had escape been charged the State of California would automatically assume all costs of the trial. At first there was a loud complaint from county officials, but a Marin County Assemblyman subsequently maneuvered a bill through the legislature which required the state to pay a major part of the expenses for any trial in any county where the cost of the trial, including security, exceeded a stated amount.

A count of the dead and wounded leads to the possibility of charging four murders and possibly two assaults. California's felony murder rule allows the court to hold a person convicted of a felony guilty of any homicides that occur as a direct result of that felonious activity. There have been murder convictions in California of individuals because their crime partner had been killed by police, or by the intended victim, in the course of an attempted robbery. But, this rule, according to a California Supreme Court decision, does not apply to escapees. The court determined that the act of escape, though a felony, is not inherently dangerous to life as other felonies apparently are. The felony murder rule, therefore, does not apply when escape is being charged.

The effect of the framing of the indictment was that only one homicide, the death of Judge Haley was charged, meaning that it was Judge Haley's death, rather than the others, which had been emphasized and for which the state sought retribution.

"Well, I don't think it's really intended that way," was Albert Harris' response to the observation that Judge Haley's death was stressed above all else. "You may get that impression. The indictment, of course, focuses on the death of the judge. That's the murder, that's the kidnapping, that's not exclusive of the kidnapping but that is the murder charge."

"And I think we probably could have charged, on one theory or another, the deaths of the other persons, Jonathan and McClain and Christmas. But the law is very, very complicated on that. You have these cases where two or three guys go to rob a store or something, and one of the robbers gets killed. There are circumstances under which you can charge the surviving robber with the death of his accomplice. But it's very complex . . . We had enough legal issues without adding that whole element and so we didn't charge. That doesn't mean that their deaths are not as important as Judge Haley's, but it would have complicated the case enormously."

It undoubtedly would have complicated the case—both the presentation and framework within which it would have to be tried. The indictment was framed for Angela Davis. She was to be held just as responsible for the death of Harold Haley as the person who pulled the trigger. It would not have worked as well to have a jury consider that three others had also died. There could be no confusion in a jury's mind between those who deserved, and those who did not deserve, to die on August 7.

Despite the prosecutor's disclaimer, there absolutely could not be an implication that the deaths of the other three men were as important as the death of Judge Haley. Throughout the trial Harris stressed that Haley died, not that four people died. It was a kind of subliminal appeal to the jury's consideration of human worth.

Further, by not charging four murders, the prosecution might have limited the possibilities of the defense. One line of defense available if four murders were charged was that the situation did not warrant the firepower used by police forces. To an extent the defense did make this assertion in the cross-examination of a prison guard, which brought before the court some details of the policy of the Department of Correction which mandates that escapes be prevented at all cost—even if hostages were sacrificed in the process.

But the fact that prison guards were trained to shoot anyone, including hostages, to prevent an escape, was reduced to something extracted from cross-examination, rather than an item which could possibly explain the carnage of August 7. It was in the prosecution's interest to avoid an area where, as a part of the defense, serious questions about the implications of a deadly policy of the Department of Corrections could be challenged, and the failure to charge escape meshed with this interest.

A clue to the political nature of the indictment lies in the discovery that the evidence submitted to the grand jury—with the sole exception of the alleged statements made on August 7 demanding the freedom of the Soledad Brothers by 12:00—could link Angela with the Soledad Brothers only by inference. That inference rested on an assumption about Angela's state of mind. If the evidence submitted had any meaning other than that Angela might have been implicated in the attempt to free Christmas, McClain and Magee, that meaning rested solely on her politics and associations.

The indictment charged Angela and Magee with five counts of kidnapping, one count of murder—namely that of Judge Harold Haley—and a third count of conspiracy, that: "defendant Angela Y. Davis and Jonathan P. Jackson, now deceased, did, after February 16, 1970 and continuing until on or about August 7, 1970 . . . willfully, unlawfully, feloniously and knowingly conspire, combine, confederate and agree together with the other persons whose names are unknown to the Grand Jury, to willfully and knowingly and feloniously commit felonies."

Four felonies were listed: the kidnapping of Judge Haley, his murder, the escape of "state prisoner James B. McClain and other state prisoners," and the criminal rescue of the Soledad Brothers.

A fourth count charging Ruchell Magee with assaulting Judge Haley completed the indictment.

The evidence which resulted in the indictment included guns which Angela had purchased, testimony that she had filed an application to correspond with George Jackson which contained the false statement that she was his cousin, statements from people saying that they had seen Angela Davis in the company of Jonathan Jackson, and a description by the FBI man who arrested Angela in New York, of how her appearance had been altered by the wearing of a wig.

The prosecution knew of letters written to George Jackson, and writings and speeches by Angela. These were not presented to the grand jury. A picture of Jonathan carrying a sign reading "End Political Repression in the Prisons" was introduced. Also, there was a photograph of a demonstration which included Angela and Jonathan, where signs were displayed saying "Free John Cluchette, Free Fleeta Drumgo, Free George Jackson, Free the Soledad Three and All Political Prisoners."

The link which the prosecution was trying to make between the events of August 7, and the possible subsequent rescue of the Soledad Brothers could not, in fact, be supported by the evidence presented to the grand jury.

There was more evidence available to them to support the idea that Angela may have conspired with Jonathan in an effort in which only Ruchell Magee had survived. Angela had made public statements equating prisons with slavery. If prisoners are slaves, and if slaves should seek freedom, and if a prosecutor has to rely on statements supposedly protected by the first amendment in order to put an indictment together, that statement, coupled with the thinking which resulted in the indictment, might be twisted to show that Angela had a state of mind that could lead her to conspire in an escape attempt. The logic then would be to charge her with conspiring to free the three prisoners, who were in fact freed, even if only for a short period of time.

Harris' claim that he did not want to complicate the trial with a complex indictment does not hold up. To charge Angela with being part of a conspiracy to free three inmates would have avoided the complicated issue of the impending rescue of the Soledad Brothers, for which Harris did not have one piece of documentation. But that was not his purpose.

He had Angela's correspondence with George Jackson, he had a history of her political activities prior to August 7, he had documentation of her weapon purchases and her association with Jonathan Jackson, and he had a grand jury who were responsive to the social and political perjudices which his presentation, unhampered by defense objections, could activate. All that was necessary was for Harris to introduce into evidence the criminal records of George Jackson, Fleeta Drumgo and John Cluchette. Harris knew that a grand jury would return an indictment, and that with a little bit of luck he might convince an all-white jury somewhere else to convict.

He had middle American sensibility on his side. Angela Davis is black, but she is also middleclass and a college professor. A stereotype belief of many whites is that middleclass blacks are somehow betraying America when they become involved in radical politics. Middleclass blacks are not considered to be victims of racism.

Angela's treatment in jail and in the courts is a reflection of her being recognized as a member of the middle class. There have been a number of trials of blacks—Bobby Seale's for instance—in which legal and financial resources for the defendant were comparable, and the arguments for self representation no less persuasive. The others were not eligible for favored status in jail because they were militants, dissidents, people from a lower level whose activities were galling to authority. But Angela was cut from better cloth. Yes, she should be convicted, but until convicted, she had to be afforded all of the protection and some of the privileges available to that small portion of the "responsible" middle class whose conflicts with society result in court action. The extent to which people accused of crimes can expect a fair trial is directly related to the degree to which their life styles or activities deviate from a middle class ideal.

Central to the effectiveness of the court system is the assumption that serious social inequities do not exist. The system is therefore geared to condemn a disproportionate percentage of minority and poor people to prison by holding on to that egalitarian fantasy, while not affording the defendant an opportunity to make certain that the procedures by which he is to be condemned afford him all of the rights and privileges due a defendant.

But those of the middle class, particularly those blacks who become middle class by sufferance, who are recognized as deserving of all of the procedural rights that accompany their prosecution, are subject to the imponderables of a prosecution that is partially impelled by the belief that the accused middle class member has betrayed his position. That's part of the indictment. Angela was charged with the enormity of attempting the criminal rescue of the Soledad Brothers because she could be charged with abdicating the responsibility of a middle class citizen to stick to middle class business, a charge which reduces the idea of freeing the Soledad Brothers to nothing more than a logical extension of helping to get three less well-known inmates out of prison. Her indictment was just as much a warning to others of her class who might think of defecting, as it was a charge that she actually involved herself in criminal activity.

Angela directly faced the charges against her for the first time on January 5, 1971. "I now declare publicly before this court and before the people of this country," she said in her own defense, "that I am innocent of all charges which have been leveled against me by the State of California."

"I am innocent, therefore I maintain that my presence in this courtroom today is unrelated to any criminal act. I stand before the court as the target of a political frame-up, which, far from pointing to my culpability, implicates the State of California as an agent of political repression. Indeed, the state reveals its own role by introducing as evidence against me, my participation in the struggles of my people—black people—against the obvious injustices of this society, specifically my involvement in the Soledad Brothers Defense Committee."

The prosecution did not bring an indictment against George Jackson. In order for its case to seem reasonable it was necessary that George Jackson be the courier who transmitted messages between Jonathan and James McClain. George Jackson's active involvement in the conspiracy is essential to the prosecution's case simply because they averred that the conspiracy existed prior to

August 7, while implying that Jonathan, in visiting his brother on August 4th, 5th and 6th, was providing him with information meant for McClain.

But, to indict George Jackson would not strengthen the case against Angela Davis. It would instead leave the Department of Corrections open for another attack in court. George Jackson, as a defendant in this political trial, would have to have included in his defense a description of the workings of the Department of Corrections, including the categories of prisoners considered to have greater criminal potential because of their politically oriented statements and actions.

Albert Harris as Assistant Attorney General, is the state's lawyer. He represents each and all state agencies, including the Department of Corrections. Because of this attorney-client relationship, Harris had to avoid putting together a case which in any way threatened his client. That is why all of Angela's alleged co-conspirators who were not dead, with the exception of Ruchell Magee, were not indicted. The framing of the charges had to be done in a way that avoided the possibility that the Assistant Attorney General would find himself prosecuting Angela Davis and at the same time defending the Department of Corrections from allegations made as a part of the defense.

The prosecution had made Angela and Ruchell co-defendants, but their status was not to be equal. And everything that was done to bring them to justice was calculated to convict Angela. The prosecution wanted them both. But Ruchell was to be convicted because he was a brute, and Angela because she was a traitor to the opportunity she had been given.

5 : Ruchell's Walk On

For a while it was Ruchell Magee rather than Angela Davis who occupied center-stage of the trial. His conduct in the case so tied up the trial that Angela's plea of not guilty was not entered until June 4, 1971, five months after their initial appearance in court. Magee, who had been projected by reporters as the "other" defendant in the trial, refused to have his defense subordinated to Angela's.

Angela and Ruchell were linked by more than the fact that they are both black and were associated, by indictment, with the same alleged crimes. They both viewed the American prison as an institution of slavery. They were both advocates of revolution and they both believed that as defendants they had the right and the duty to participate in their defense. Despite these points of agreement, the link between the two defendants was severed July 19, 1971, on a motion by Angela Davis.

In some respects the separation of the co-defendants, with the scheduling of two different trials dealing with the same event, is a measure of the current inability of America's revolutionary movement to organize itself. Differences between Angela and Ruchell were to a large extent tactical. He wanted to force the trial out of the state courts, while Angela and her attorneys were maneuvering to get the best possible combination of trial site, judge and jury within the Superior Court system. But, that tactical difference was based on differing views of the law, which in turn arose from totally dissimilar backgrounds and experiences.

Ruchell Magee is from Franklin, Louisiana, a town located in the midst of active Ku Klux Klan sentiments. On February 6, 1956, 39 days before his 17th birthday, he was convicted of attempted aggravated rape. Aggravated rape is apparently Louisiana's way of charging that a black man tried to take advantage of a sexual invitation coming from a white woman and was caught. Records indicate that the supposed victim identified Magee on the street days after she failed to recognize him in a lineup. Supposedly Magee had accosted her at her home, and was interrupted in his move to take the young woman to bed only by the screams of her young child.

The court appointed an attorney to represent Magee, and when the trial was over he was sentenced to Angola State Penitentiary. He emerged from Angola, a place where many full grown men have not survived their sentences, after serving six years and eight months of the original 12-year sentence. Parole was based on his promise to leave Louisiana, which he did immediately and went to Los Angeles to live with an aunt and uncle. In Los Angeles he worked as a part-time house painter and as an attendant at a car wash.

Magee is not a big man. He is about 5 feet 7 inches tall, and weighs no more than 150 pounds. His voice is soft and his speech patterns reflect his southern upbringing. When angry or agitated Magee's voice grows hard, and he spits out his syllables with precision, in an ever flowing barrage of invective, logic, reason and inflexibility.

He carries himself loosely, walking with an easy bounce and a built-in alertness that allows him to move quickly in any direction at the slightest hint of trouble. He is obviously strong. Gary Thomas, when testifying about the events of August 7, said that Magee, upon leaving the courtroom, picked up with one hand a bailiff who had been lying face down on the floor, and moved him by the belt out of the way without apparent effort. That physical strength parallels the strength of purpose that has sustained him since he moved to Los Angeles in October 1962.

Ruchell Magee was arrested on March 23, 1963, just six months after arriving in California. He has been behind bars ever since. The incident which caused his arrest arose from an argument which he had with Ben Howard Brown, a black musician who brought charges against him. Brown claimed that Magee asked for a ride to a bus stop on a rainy night, and after getting in his car produced a gun and held him up. Brown testified that Leroy Stewart, Magee's first cousin, who had arrived in Los Angeles from Louisiana just two weeks before, was Magee's accomplice in the holdup.

Magee insists that the incident grew out of an argument over a young lady in whom Brown was interested. He said that there was a gun, but that it belonged to Brown. Magee says that he took the gun at a point when he felt that Brown was looking for it. The gun in question, according to Magee, was under the seat in Brown's car.

Whatever the facts of the incident, the truth is that Magee was sentenced to prison for life for committing, at its worst, a holdup involving $10 and no bodily harm. One of the most striking things about the case is that there was a witness in the car at the time of the incident, the girl who Magee said was the cause of the friction between himself and Brown. Brown, in filing his complaint, never mentioned the presence of this potential witness, and in fact made no reference to her during the trial until pressed by the defense attorney. At that point he could not remember her name.

Magee was convicted, had the conviction reversed, and was convicted again. The public record indicates that Magee was poorly represented, that the presiding judge acted in a prejudicial manner, and that a number of moves of doubtful legality on the part of both the judge and Magee's attorneys contributed to his imprisonment.

Attorney Leonard Mayer received $650 for defending Magee after submitting a bill which reflected no more than five hours in preparation for a case which had the possibility of a death sentence, and which actually resulted in a life sentence:

4–30–63   Read transcript—one hour
5–7–63   Visit with defendant at county jail—one hour
5–20–63   Visit with defendant at county jail—one hour
5–21–63   Reread transcript—one hour
5–22–63   Conference with co-defendant's counsel—½ hour maximum
5–22–63   Conference with witnesses and co-counsel—½ hour

This approach to defense represented the beginning of Magee's vocal opposition to being represented by attorneys who did not seem to be taking care of his business.

The conviction began a process which has continued unabated for ten years. Magee began filing writs, appeals, letters, observations, and accusations, with every court that would receive them. His filings were more than voluminous, they represented a line of legal defense that was totally separated from any defense produced by any of the attorneys who subsequently represented him. Magee's experience with Mayer convinced him that the best defense was self-defense.

"Defendant contends that during the trial court proceedings he was unjustly restrained, refused and denied the right to a fair and just trial in a direct violation of the rights guaranteed by the 14th Amendment of the Constitution. . . . It is a denial of due process and equal protection of law and also a violation of the constitution of the US to deprive a person of his property because of his indigence . . . There can be no equal justice where the kind of trial or treatment a man gets depends on the amount of money he has." [1]

Magee pointed out in subsequent affidavits upon which he based his appeal, that a tape recording of an alleged confession of Stewart had been illegally introduced as evidence. None of his letters or affidavits were acknowledged or answered.

Ernest Graves, one of the attorneys appointed to represent Magee on the August 7 murder charge, filed an extensive brief dealing with the 1963 conviction, and the subsequent reconviction in 1965. In it the attorney summarized what he believed to be the development of Magee's thinking:

"(1) Ruchell became convinced that he had been framed by the trial procedures. (2) He concluded that the reason for the frame was to cover up his police-administered beating and subsequent hospitalization. (3) He believed that the prosecutor, the attorney for Stewart and the Judge were all parties to the trial 'framing'. [Stewart's attorney in the 1963 trial, J. Stanley Brill, a Public Defender, openly attempted to have the trial court place all the blame on Magee, basing his argument on the contention that Stewart had cooperated with police in making a tape recording and pointing to Magee's uncooperative attitude in court]. (4)

[1] Ruchell Magee Affidavit, June 3, 1965.

He opined that thereafter the record was fraudulently and incompletely prepared. (5) He believed that the reporter and the appointed lawyer on appeal wouldn't 'correct' the record and (6) he believed that the appellate court had joined the 'frame' by not 'correcting' the record, ignoring his motion to dismiss the appeal, and reversing the judgment on the incomplete record, which reversal, instead of releasing him, brought him back to the trial courts for a retrial of the case."

Magee's reputation for disrupting a trial began with his conduct in 1963. Actually, he interrupted the trial at three critical points. The first was his attempt to dismiss his attorney after becoming convinced that Mayer had handled his defense ineptly. The dialogue which followed his walking out when the judge refused to dismiss Mayer indicated that there was some conflict, insofar as Mayer, who was supposedly working to achieve an acquittal, was at the same time attempting to work out a deal whereby Magee would plead guilty to a lesser offense. Whatever the value of plea bargaining, it is usually done prior to the formal beginning of a trial.

Magee interrupted to contradict a statement by a police officer that no physical force had been used when he was arrested, and he spoke again during the prosecution's closing arguments to complain that he was being framed. The judge shut him up. He finally attempted to fire his attorney after the verdict was delivered but before the sentence. At the time, Mayer was attempting to have the charges reduced, and also was announcing his intention to appeal for a new trial on the grounds that the trials of Magee and Stewart had been improperly joined. Magee objected forcefully, stating that he did want a new trial, but not on the grounds presented by his court-appointed attorney.

The document submitted to the Appeals Court did not include the grounds that Magee wanted explored. Moreover, it did not go into the fact of Judge Walker's attitude toward Magee, which according to the record seems decidedly prejudicial. The judgment was reversed.

When Magee received the news he concluded that a reversal of a guilty verdict amounted to not guilty. Imagine his shock when he walked into court in June 1965, to find Judge Herbert V.

Walker, whose improper joinder of two cases had become the basis for the reversal, sitting on the bench.

The acrimonious relationship between the two began all over again with Magee's query as to why he was in court since ". . . according to the opinions of the Second Appellate Court, that was taken from me by the Sheriff's office . . . the case judgment was reversed . . ." But that was not a dismissal, and Magee had to stand trial again, with Walker presiding.

Judge Walker appointed attorney H. Clay Jacke to represent Magee in the second trial. It might have been coincidence, but Jacke's first act when he appeared with Magee was to enter a plea of not guilty by reason of insanity. Judge Walker had indicated that he had doubts about Ruchell's sanity, and was considering having him examined by psychiatrists. Jacke, in entering the plea, coincidentally was confirming the judge's opinion of Magee.

Magee insisted that he did not want an insanity plea, and was told that the matter would be taken up after the psychiatric examination. He was examined by Dr. George Y. Abe, who reported on May 23, 1965, that "clinically, defendant appears to have paranoid tendencies, but not of sufficient degree that he can be considered psychotic and unable to use average judgment." The doctor also noted that, "defendant may not cooperate in the proceedings unless he has an attorney he feels he can trust."

The other psychiatrist, Dr. Karl Von Hagen, noted that Magee, "states that the plea which led to this examination, was made by his attorney and that he did not make this plea and would not talk about anything more."

Magee did not trust his attorney, who without notice had changed a perfectly simple not guilty plea to one of not guilty by reason of insanity. And then, Judge Walker, a man Magee had no reason to trust, told him: "I appointed Mr. Jacke purposely because I know the quality of service he gives as an attorney. I didn't just pick him out. He has practiced before this Court for a number of years and the Court has known him a number of years. He knows that I know of his quality of service and that is what I selected . . . I feel you needed a real good attorney."

Magee would have no part in it. He had already filed an application for a writ of prohibition with the United States Supreme Court, asking it to stop the trial. Magee's writ included all of the grounds that he had wanted included in the appeal to the state courts, which had not been included by the court-appointed attorney who had handled the appeals procedure. From that point on, the legal history of Ruchell Magee became bifurcated. There is a line of argument, writ writing, and so forth, issuing from attorneys in Magee's behalf. At the same time, Magee was creating his own legal record, appealing at every step of the way any act of his attorney or decision by a judge with which he did not agree.

Psychologically Magee became his own attorney at that point. He knew, or felt he knew, that there was some combination of laws and courts that would grant him freedom. He became convinced that no one, in particular, no attorney was qualified to speak for his freedom.

Magee felt that defense attorneys cooperated more with district attorneys and judges than they did with the client they were defending. Attorney Ernest Graves, in commenting on Magee's relationship with H. Clay Jacke, noted that the plea of 'Not Guilty by Reason of Insanity' was entered over Magee's express objections. He also noted that Magee unequivocally wanted a plea of prior jeopardy entered on his behalf which everyone (his attorney and Judge Walker) persisted in both pre-judging and ignoring, even though the defendant had been determined (by the psychiatrists) capable of understanding the nature of the proceedings against him and conducting his own defense.

"Whether the plea may ultimately be determined to be unfounded, does not change the fact that the attorney has a duty to enter requested pleas for a defendant, and the Court has the duty to receive them. It is clear that as both the judge and the lawyer opined that the plea would eventually be found defective, they ignored their respective duties to enter it."

Magee was entering into the state of mind which later caused him to adopt the name Cinque, after the famous Cinque who was captured in Africa in 1839, sold into slavery and placed, along with other slaves, on the slaveship *Amistad* en route to the New World. In midocean, Cinque led a slave rebellion which succeeded in capturing the ship. He thought he had won his freedom, only to discover that the ship landed in America, where slavery was legal and he was once again in chains.

Cinque was represented in court by John Quincy Adams, who accepted the premise of his client, that to violently oppose being made a slave was in keeping with American laws. Magee could find no such assistance. But he knew that Cinque would have pleaded his own case had there not been an attorney he could trust.

The Fourteenth Amendment granting equal protection under the laws and guaranteeing due process was not a part of the Constitution at the time Cinque's trial was held. But the Sixth Amendment, part of the original Bill of Rights, was. And it, in addition to mandating a speedy public trial by an impartial jury, established the right of an accused to have the "assistance of counsel." Cinque accepted the assistance of counsel, who conducted a defense along the lines suggested by his client. Magee was not in that position.

However inappropriate H. Clay Jacke's act of inserting the insanity plea might seem, it is totally consistent with what has been done by lawyers and courts to erode the Sixth Amendment: "In all criminal prosecutions, the accused shall enjoy the right . . . to have the Assistance of Counsel for his defense." This is a recognition, long rooted in the common law preceding the Constitution, that a man has an inherent right to defend himself against harm, and consistent with that right, can employ appropriate means to do so. In a court of law an individual can choose to have an attorney to assist with his defense and can determine how to plead.

In practice, judges have maintained that an individual may either be represented by an attorney, or represent himself, although self-representation has been treated by the courts as though it were a privilege rather than a right. This violates the very essence that is man's spirit, namely the assumption that the individual, when faced with peril to his life or liberty, is the best qualified person to decide how that peril should be faced.

The right to self defense in Magee's case, and the tenacity with which he has asserted that right, is one of the problems that he has with the courts. His defenses have been treated as incompetent, therefore the basic right to defend himself has been abrogated.

In the final analysis, a man stripped of the right to defend himself is a man being prepared for slavery. Every person who goes to prison as the result of incompetent or indifferent legal representation, in a situation where he had no wish for the attorney representing him to conduct the case, has been reduced to a slave. Magee's resistance to the notion that he was not qualified to defend himself becomes one of the more important aspects of the Angela Davis case.

A pattern had been set which persists. Magee has consistently acted as his own attorney, filing papers with a variety of courts and legal jurisdictions. He has taken pains to make allegations that are different in many respects from those made by attorneys covering the same situation.

The reaction of the courts to Magee has been equally consistent. In the main, his pleas have not been taken seriously. But, although there seems to be a general conviction that he is incompetent, the courts have responded to those motions he has made, which, if granted, would eliminate a right or privilege, or otherwise hamper his own case.

What has been clearly demonstrated in Magee's relations with the courts, is that they have little tolerance for anyone considered to be wasting their time. For example, had Magee pleaded guilty to a lesser offense, there is an excellent possibility that he would not have been sentenced to life. Plea bargaining is based on the premise that an individual who does not waste the time of the court has demonstrated some penitence, and is sentenced accordingly. But, an individual who insists on pleading not guilty, and forces the state to try him, runs the risk of having the book thrown at him.

After incarceration, the only possible area for redress of grievances, the only place of appeal for a prisoner, is the courts. Prisoners get to know and appreciate the power of the courts, and seek their help in getting out of prison. "You don't really know what the law is all about until you get inside," one ex-convict explained. "Then you find out there are two parts to the law. The first part says they can give you so much time for such and such an offense. That's the part you knew before you were sent up.

"The second part says that they have got to do it right. That part becomes the inmate's bible. After you get inside you find out that a piece of the law is on your side. And every prisoner's faith is that some court, somewhere, will find out that he was not put away right, and cut him loose." [2]

As a result jailhouse lawyers have been credited with a number of successes. The jailhouse lawyer is actually a writ writer, a self-taught expert in law who picks a case apart and sends off appropriate appeals. Magee's contribution to the literature of incarcerated writ writers is monumental. Most of his prodigious output has been applied to his own situation. But he has involved himself with the cases of other inmates, particularly those cases which require some sort of class action. Most jailhouse lawyers come from a milieu which is of the streets, the cafeteria courts, and years of imprisonment following convictions that were obtained because these men could not afford competent legal service. To many, a good lawyer is as unlikely as a kindly warden or a humane prison guard.

Prison lawyers have no need for intermediaries. They stand alone before justice, clothed only in the thin fabric of their legal scholarship acquired behind the walls, knowing that while law often does not protect, it can occasionally get a wrong corrected and put a man outside those walls.

Jailhouse lawyers are not liked by prison officials, who consider them troublemakers. Attorneys find them irrelevant. Judges treat them as annoying examples of jailhouse madness, and those of the public who have been conditioned to believe that every man in jail is guilty, and that legal technicalities serve only to set guilty men free, see jailhouse law practice as the desperate attempt of prisoners to find a loophole in the law which sent them to prison.

Prison employees differ about Magee. Some say that he is a terrible prisoner, others find his conduct almost beyond reproach. But the disagreement seems directly related to the guard's respect for Magee's obsession with the law. There is general agreement that Magee is fairly easy to get along with as long as no one attempts to separate him from his law books and legal papers.

In 1968 Magee was part of a class action filed in Federal District Court seeking an order forcing the San Quentin mailroom to forward all legal mail without restrictions. Brought on behalf of

[2] Daniel DeWitt in interview with author, March, 1971.

"hundreds of California State prisoners," in an attempt to guarantee the constitutional rights, "to petition the United States Government, the right to communicate with attorneys seeking legal aid; the rights to communicate with lawful organizations for legal aid within the laws and limits of the United States codes and Courts; the right to be free from oppressive, arbitrary and capricious action; as secured by the First Amendment to the Constitution of the United States; and last but not least, the right to be free from cruel and unusual punishment, inflicted upon the plaintiffs by the defendants as hereinbefore described." [3]

At the time there were approximately 1,415 black prisoners in San Quentin. The names and numbers of more than 900 were attached to the complaint.

The court action itself did not bring the desired relief, but prison regulations were subsequently altered so as to provide freer access of prisoners to their lawyers and to legal materials. The changes were brought about by a combination of administrative fiat and legislative pressure from a number of lawsuits filed in the state courts. The discovery of the class action suit by inmates constitutes a threat to prison keepers that goes far beyond the legal implications of the particular lawsuit. Knowledge of the law is being disseminated to a general prison population.

The impact of a few favorable decisions, notably the California decision in the sixties recognizing the Black Muslims as a religious group, and requiring the prison system to allow Muslims to worship and to read their paper *Muhammed Speaks,* have prompted inmates to seek collective court decisions. These actions, in turn, have led to the strengthening of the prison movement, where, through strikes, work stoppages, and occasional riots, prison officials have been forced to grant minimal concessions.

Jailhouse lawyers created another threat to the prison system through their constant correspondence. They began to attract the attention of people outside the walls, some of whom were lawyers. As a result, a certain amount of information was smuggled out of prison with lawyers acting as the contact. Manuscripts, letters, descriptions of prison conditions, political tracts and so on found

[3] Daniel DeWitt *et al.,* Motion for Interlocutory Injunction, February 19, 1968.

their way out of prison. In response, prison officials began to isolate "revolutionaries," placing them in the adjustment centers, and also began to monitor more rigidly the activities of writ writers.

Magee went in and out of the adjustment center at San Quentin a number of times. In February of 1970, he was one of several signators to an affidavit attesting that San Quentin guards had tear gassed Fred Billingslea to death.

Billingslea, who had recently been returned to the prison population after hospitalization for psychiatric reasons, died following a tear gas attack. The guard who fired the tear gas was John Matthews, the same officer who five months later, claimed to have shot several people in the van. Magee was one of several prisoners who attempted to contact people on the outside to alert them to the fact of Billingslea's killing. They feared that without publicity the prison would list the death as due to natural causes. In the course of this effort, which included letters, affidavits and appeals for help to investigate Billingslea's death, Magee made an attempt to contact Angela Davis' mother.

Billingslea died on February 25, 1970. On March 2, 1970, James McClain was arrested and charged with stabbing Edwin K. Irving, a prison guard. McClain went on trial for assault. The trial ended with a hung jury. One of the factors in the trial was the eye-witness identification of McClain by his gold-capped front tooth. Ruchell Magee also had a gold-capped front tooth, and he was also in the vicinity of the stabbing.

Soon after McClain received the hung jury verdict on his assault trial, Magee received an order denying his petition for a writ that had been filed in relation to the 1965 trial. The court took the position that Magee had not raised any constitutional questions, and also made a point of mentioning that the reporter's "transcript of petitioner's second trial . . . shows petitioner made repeated outbursts during trial and was several times admonished and removed to a holding cell. On one occasion petitioner was returned to court with handcuffs and a muzzle and on another occasion later in trial with handcuffs only. We have carefully examined the transcript and find that the measures taken by the trial judge were not improper under the circumstances."

Magee's writ writing was interrupted the following week as he worked with McClain in preparation for McClain's retrial. This trial ended with Magee the only survivor of the group of four black men who left the Marin County Civic Center on August 7.

A Marin County Grand Jury indictment against Magee was returned September 4, 1970, and on September 10, he was arraigned before Marin County Superior Court Judge Joseph McGuire. Instead of being taken to a courtroom in the Marin County Civic Center, Magee and fellow prisoner, Luis Talamantez, an adjustment center inmate accused of assault in a separate case (who subsequently became one of the San Quentin Six[4]) were arraigned in a makeshift courtroom in San Quentin prison.

A recreation room at the prison had been set aside so that for reasons of security, Marin County Judges could hear cases at the prison instead of in the Civic Center. The first hearing was held on August 24, 1970. San Quentin inmates protested the move by staging a work stoppage. Picket signs sprouted outside of the prison on trial days, with a number of organized groups complaining to the courts that the hearings were being held in an illegal setting.

Judge Wilson, who was then the presiding judge of the Marin County Superior Court, said that only pre-trial hearings would be scheduled at the prison and only on an experimental basis. "It's a good time to try it" was Wilson's observation, an oblique reference to August 7.

The practice was discontinued, but in Magee's case Angela's arrest guaranteed that he would be tried in the Civic Center, even if trials continued at the prison. Angela, as his co-defendant, had no relationship to San Quentin and could not be made to stand trial there.

Magee's legal position was that he would not be tried by any of the Marin County judges because of their close association with the late Judge Haley. The judges had decided to disqualify themselves from hearing the case, but they also decided that they could properly handle the procedural pre-trial matters.

Judge McGuire appointed Henry Ramsey, a black attorney from

---

[4] Six San Quentin inmates charged with murder and assault in connection with the death of George Jackson, three inmates and two San Quentin guards on August 21, 1971.

Berkeley, California who teaches at the University of California in Berkeley to represent Magee. Magee would not cooperate with him. He insisted that the Marin County judges were without authority to make any record in his case. His position had been backed up by a removal petition which he had filed in the local federal court.

The concept of removal to a federal court was established in the recognition that blacks in southern states often could not get a fair trial from local judges. Federal law allowed a defendant to file an application for removal in those instances where the defendant was convinced that the state courts would act in a prejudicial manner. The law is very clear when it comes to removal. The mere filing of a removal action temporarily relieves the state court of all jurisdiction in the case.

If the federal court decides not to accept jurisdiction the case is remanded to state court. The removal statutes require that the federal court specifically remand the case back to state court in writing, a procedure that has not always been followed in Magee's case.

San Quentin guards, who are not known for their delicacy, found it necessary to drag Magee into the San Quentin courtroom for the September 10 hearing. "I object to this whole KKK trial, I have no other statement," Magee yelled as he was brought into the room. He did participate to some extent. He told Judge McGuire, "I was drugged into the courtroom. I was choked and thrown into the car like a dog. The prison guards killed the judge and I want to present this to the people."

The next appearance was just as stormy. "Mr. Magee is getting railroaded before he goes to trial," Magee insisted to the 50 sympathizers who had come to the trial. The court was immediately cleared and Magee was threatened with a gag.

Magee insisted that he did not want Henry Ramsey to represent him and the case was continued until September 29, when Clinton White, another black attorney, was appointed. Magee called White "a Tom working for the power structure. You'll kill me with Mr. White." White, on the other hand, said that he would maintain Magee's right to have counsel of his own choosing. Magee insisted that he wanted to represent himself. Judge McGuire ruled that he was incompetent to represent himself, a procedural ruling that has hung over Magee's defense ever since.

White felt uncomfortable in his role, and in October asked Judge Joseph G. Wilson to name him as legal advisor. The Marin County judges were rotating in hearing cases at San Quentin, apparently having decided to share the handling of the procedural pre-trial matters in Magee's case. Magee managed to raise enough hell about Marin County judges officiating so that they decided to appeal to the California Judicial Council. The CJC, which is headed by the Chief Justice of the State Supreme Court, supervises the activity of California judges. It assigns judges to cases where a local judge has been successfully challenged, and also assigns judges to conduct hearings where a judge has been accused of prejudice toward a particular defendant. Magee had filed charges against Judges McGuire and Wilson claiming prejudice. Much of what he had to say dealt with the relationship of the judges to Judge Haley. But Magee was also contending that because of his history in the state courts, and the necessity of those courts to stand by previous decisions, the case should be moved completely out of state jurisdiction.

On November 1, 1970, the judicial council appointed Appeals Justice Winslow Christian to hear Magee's complaint of judicial prejudice. A hearing was scheduled for December 22. Clinton White filed a request that he be removed from the case which was acted upon favorably. A white attorney, Leonard Bjorklund, was appointed over Magee's objection and the December 22 hearing was held.

Judge Christian disposed of Magee's claim of judicial prejudice in a matter of minutes. But, he went a step further, and without any warning declared that he was going to hold a competency hearing on the spot. Actually, there must have been some warning, as the prosecution was ready to prove that Magee was indeed incompetent. Their prime evidence was two sets of IQ tests. The first, alleging that Magee had an IQ of 75, had been submitted by prison authorities in Louisiana, who had determined in 1956 that Ruchell Magee was not fit for any occupation other than laborer.

The second IQ of 86 had been extracted from Magee in 1963, after being sentenced to prison in California. The IQ scores are not surprising. Magee says that he did not begin to read seriously until after his imprisonment, when he became obsessed with the need to fight for his own freedom. Since IQ tests are to a large extent reading tests, it is understandable that Magee might have scored low on them. But there is another factor.

Until fairly recently the official line binding prison officials, penologists and criminologists together, was that convicted felons, as a class, were of sub-normal intelligence. Prison officials, at least in California, have since modified that line. Now the typical inmate is described as, "a 27-year-old elementary, or high school drop-out (the median education level is 7th grade) with normal intelligence, who has virtually no sustained work-experience (neither skilled nor unskilled). He is an individual who was not able to function in reasonable harmony with his environment (sic). He needs training, guidance, and help in order to return to the community as a useful citizen." [5]

Ignoring the question as to the validity of tests in measuring intelligence, IQ tests administered in prison are given under the worst of all possible conditions, and cannot, by any stretch of the imagination, reflect a true picture of an inmate's intellectual potential.

Justice Christian accepted the IQ tests that were proffered, and then proceeded to ask Magee a number of questions, some dealing with fairly obtuse sections of law, in the ostensible attempt to determine whether he was capable of representing himself. The law governing self-representation merely required that a defendant understand the charges brought against him, the possible penalties for being convicted on those charges, and the defenses available to him. Christian's questions did not deal with that aspect, and he pronounced Magee to be incompetent.

Angela was arraigned the following day, December 23, and the two co-defendants met for the first time on January 5, 1971, when both were brought into the Civic Center. Magee was brought in chained and handcuffed, the cuffs attached to a chain that was

[5] California Department of Corrections pamphlet describing Soledad Prison.

wrapped around his waist. Several armed San Quentin guards sat within two feet of him during the procedures.

Judge Wilson was presiding and suggested that pleas not be entered until March, when he expected an outside judge to be brought in. Magee was hauled out of court immediately after announcing that he would not cooperate with his court-appointed attorney, Leonard Bjorklund, who at this point had had enough of Magee and had asked to be removed from the case.

Another complication was introduced in the case when it was discovered that Federal Judge Samuel P. Conti had denied Magee's petition for removal in December. But Conti had not remanded the case to the state court; instead he denied the petition on the basis that it was not accompanied by an appropriate filing fee. Filing fees are not normally required of prison inmates insofar as they are usually impecunious by virtue of being in prison. But Conti insisted the fee was required in this case. The Marin County judges accepted the statement that Magee's petition had been denied, and in doing so ignored his protest that the case had not been handled the way that the removal law stated it must be done.

Two attorneys, Robert Bell and Robert Carrow were then assigned to represent Ruchell Magee. The two were Marin County attorneys who had worked together on other trials. Carrow, a conservative Democrat and ex-Mayor of Novato, a small town in Marin County 15 miles north of San Rafael, contrasted sharply with Bell, who had been part of the legal saturation of Mississippi in 1964, when teams of lawyers went south to document, for the record, black oppression under southern law. He was part of the Neighborhood Legal Assistance program in Santa Rosa, California.[6]

Bell was not part of that group of radical California attorneys who vibrate between political and drug cases, and who have adopted

---

[6] Santa Rosa is noted as Luther Burbank's horticultural breeding grounds, and the burial place of Mammy Pleasant, a black woman who raised the position of running San Francisco whore houses to a high art. Mammy Pleasant is considered by black historians in San Francisco to be the mother of civil rights activism in the city. She lost a case against a San Francisco trolley company brought because in 1892 a conductor would not let blacks ride on his car. It was not recorded whether the presiding judge was one of her customers.

the language and rhetoric of revolution. But he was there, giving the power sign, exchanging revolutionary handshakes and saying "right-on" with the best of them. Rosencrantz and Guildenstern they were; Carrow, tall, correct, smoothly erudite, having perfected a style of injecting irrelevant banalities into tight legal arguments, and Bell, a thoroughly persuasive man who seemed at all times on the edge of an outbreak of indignation over somebody's oppression.

Only one judge, Leonard Ginsburg, who was the first to supervise Magee's trial following its separation from that of Angela Davis, recognized that it was impossible to put Magee on trial and have him totally represented by an attorney. Magee insisted on being an active part of his defense in court, and consistently raised hell whenever he was denied this status.

Bell and Carrow entered the case, talked a few times with Magee and decided that their best role was as legal advisors. Magee insisted that they resign from the case completely. So, as part of the ritual which began every session, Magee had both of them move to be relieved of the case, and failing that, to be given the status of legal advisor to a self-representing Magee. It was not really a ritual to Magee, but judges quickly reduced the request to that.

In March 1971, after Bell and Carrow's motion to become legal advisors was denied, Angela's attorneys argued at length that the trial should be moved to larger quarters. Judge Wilson, who had presided over San Quentin sessions, denied the motion, and proceeded to explain that legal tradition required that the trial be held in a courtroom. (The only larger quarters available were not courtrooms.)

The judge settled back to deliver a lecture based on the symbolism of the courtroom, the placement of the judge, witnesses, defense and prosecution as the meaningful product of centuries of legal evolution—"there is tradition . . ."

"Take me out of here man, I don't want to hear any more of this sickness," said Magee, and he seemed sincerely disgusted. He was convinced that if a shred of what Judge Wilson was saying about noble traditions was actually true, that he would be on the street, and not an imprisoned defendant. His removal was reported as a disruption, which it really was not. He knew from having been dragged into a makeshift courtroom in San Quentin, before this very judge, that tradition wasn't the reason Judge Wilson was turning down the request.

Wilson was not present at the next session. The Judicial Council had acted and appointed Judge John McMurray, a retired 70-year-old judge from Inyo County, a county largely inhabited by sheep and hunters, bounded on one side by Death Valley and on the other by the Sierra Mountains. McMurray listened patiently to Bell and Carrow, allowed them to withdraw from the case, and then reappointed them, apparently a technical move to avoid any taint of an appointment by a Marin County judge. "They'll have your interest at heart," he explained to Magee.

Magee, however, refused to participate, even to the extent of pleading not guilty. McMurray tried to win him over. He asked about his formal education, his experience with law. And, after Magee had told him of graduating from the 8th grade in Louisiana, McMurray appointed the attorneys. "I'm not doing this because I think you have subnormal intelligence, but because I think you need all the assistance you can get."

Magee argued for about ten minutes. There he sat, chained around his shoulders, his hands locked to his waist, and the chain which ran around his waist attached to a swivel chair, which in turn was bolted to the floor. The sight of the chains was bad enough, the sounds were eerie.

In the mornings, before Magee arrived, there would be lengths of chain laid out on the plush blue rug next to the chair that had been affixed to the floor in order to receive him. When he was brought in, already with a waist chain, guards clinked his chains until he was secured to the chair. And every time he moved the sound of link falling on link echoed through the courtroom.

Magee would argue, swiveling back and forth, with his hands held chest high, locked in the position that a fighter with fast hands prefers to box from. He insisted that he had a federal removal petition pending, and that the state court could not act before the federal courts did. He charged McMurray with appointing attorneys without proper legal authority.

"State officials, white racists are trying to murder me under color of law . . . I cannot accept your appointment and anything you appoint is over my objections . . . If I am denied I have no alternative but to seek relief in the federal courts, although I know the justice is about the same." When his plea was denied, Magee demanded of the guards, "Take me out of here!"

As the guards were unchaining him, Magee looked at Angela, and told her that the proceedings were rigged. "Your attorneys are just trying to put on a show. He answered my plea," Magee said with an expression of disgust, as he used his head as a substitute for an index finger to indicate the judge.

Magee and Angela Davis had not been seeing matters in the same way during the several conferences they had previously had. Magee's position was that he, and everyone else, knew that Angela was innocent and was being framed. He maintained that he had evidence which could prove Angela innocent. Certainly the fact that he was the only survivor of the incident, and was in a position to testify first hand as to the existence or non-existence of a conspiracy, indicated he had some evidence.

Magee insisted in these conferences that state judges would all arrange procedure so as to facilitate a conviction. He maintained that the creation of any kind of record in the state court was a waste of time, and that their mutual defense tactic should be to concentrate on efforts to get the case removed to federal court. Angela and her attorneys disagreed. Magee's outburst at Angela was designed to bring to her attention again the treatment he was receiving.

It was inevitable that Magee would have serious differences with the defense attorneys. He had never known an attorney who went all out for a client, and he was basically suspicious of attorneys whom he saw as yielding to the fascism of judges at important moments. Another aspect of the difficulties between Angela and her co-defendant was that Magee had considerable experience with written law, but practically none with the practice of law. Magee, in steeping himself in case law, had not been exposed to the fact that most cases do not appear in the law books, and that those which do, do not reflect the day to day struggle in the courtroom.

There was also the problem of the Angela Davis defense, which was built on the ability to command specific kinds of legal expertise for limited periods of time. At the very time that Magee was challenging Judge McMurray, the Angela Davis defense was trying to have motions heard to dismiss the indictment or have Angela released on bail.

At that point Magee had tied up the case in legal knots. Although Angela's lawyers could not go along with him on the wisdom of basing the case on a removal to federal court, they did not oppose his actions in open court. Furthermore, Magee was doing yeoman work in challenging judges—work that Angela's attorneys did not have to do. Had Magee not been indicted along with Angela they would have had to conduct a fight to eliminate the judgments of all Marin County judges from the record. As it stood, Magee made that fight unnecessary. It was an uneasy liaison, but one that Angela's attorneys could live with.

Magee left the court that day, and Mike Tigar, one of Angela's defense attorneys, argued that the indictment should be dismissed. But the next session, March 17, Magee was back, with more documents. He filed documents at every court session, and often in-between sessions. Spectators and participants began to understand that every court session would begin with Magee filing papers and having a dialogue with the judge. This time, Magee addressed the court on the question of being represented by Bell and Carrow. He also brought along an affidavit he had prepared in both his and Angela Davis' names, seeking to disqualify Judge McMurray on grounds that he was prejudiced.

There wasn't much that Angela's attorneys could do about the challenge. Their preference would have been to probe at McMurray and find out what he might do for the defense, and after extracting the most they could expect, then try for another judge. But Magee had jumped in with a full bag of challenges:

"You have been dismissed from this case. In order to proceed you will be driving over my rights and the United States Constitution," Magee told Judge McMurray. His assault practically pushed the elderly jurist off the bench. McMurray had come from retirement, living in a county where the fishing was good, traffic jams non-existent, and defendants much less aggressive.

McMurray looked at all that paper, gauged the kind of legal problems the documents posed and retired for a two-and-one-half hour session in his chambers. Judge Conti had muddied the waters.

Instead of remanding the case as demanded by federal law, he had sent a second removal petition back claiming the motion denied for failure to pay fees. So, McMurray was facing possible complications with the line of appeals on the removal action. In addition, before he could settle into the case, McMurray had to deal with a legal challenge concerning his personal bias.

After an hour in chambers, Albert Harris walked out, his face the color of a Marin County sunset. McMurray had decided: "I am prejudiced. I would have a great deal of difficulty with Magee in Court." Magee's comment was that the judge was "a very cunning man . . . he has a good point." McMurray had been appointed to handle the pre-trial phase of the case with the expectation that another judge would be appointed to handle the trial. He realized that the issues involved would result in "judicial chaos" if one or more judges handled the pre-trial, and he apparently had no heart to provide the judicial continuity. McMurray came back on the bench, looking more tired than when he left, and announced that he was disqualifying himself.

Angela's attorneys were bothered. Thus far they had been unsuccessful in having any of their important motions heard and ruled upon. They were anxious to get a ruling on bail, so that Angela would either be released, or they could be filing appeals on bail denial. There was more than legal timing involved. The political activity outside the courtroom was directly dependent on the decisions made, and activity engaged in inside the court. Since Angela's case was not progressing there were no court-related issues around which supporters and potential supporters of Angela could rally.

Immediately after Judge McMurray announced his decision to step down, Howard Moore, Jr. requested that the judge consider the motion for bail before adjourning court.

"I'll object to any proceedings at this time; it's a violation of my rights." Magee slipped in his objection before McMurray had an opportunity to respond. The judge responded more sternly than he had at any point during the two sessions at which he had presided. "You have been heard and you have prevailed, Mr. Magee, I refuse to act further."

"Step down," said Magee, the triumph unmistakable. Judge

McMurray had him removed from court and then said: "I refuse to act further, court is adjourned."

Angela's attorneys were even more upset when they found out who McMurray's replacement would be. It was Alan A. Lindsay, a Superior Court Judge from Oakland. Lindsay had been a Deputy District Attorney in the Alameda County District Attorney's office from 1945 to 1951, following his graduation from law school at Boalt Hall of the University of California. During this time he was a lobbyist for the Peace Officers and District Attorney's Association, seeking laws that would facilitate the arrest, detention and conviction of suspects.

He then spent a year on the staff of a California Commission on Organized Crime, and left that to be an executive assistant in the US Department of Justice, Criminal Division. Lindsay went from that to private practice at a time when he became vice-president of Lucerne Milk Corporation, which distributes through Safeway, and he also served on the Oakland Board of Education. He was president of the Board when serious attempts were made to integrate Oakland's schools, and to improve the educational opportunities for poor and minority students. Lindsay resisted every one of them.

Governor Reagan appointed Lindsay to the Municipal Court in April 1967. The Governor elevated him to the Superior Court in May 1969, where Lindsay served mainly as a Juvenile Court judge. So, the co-defendants were faced with a conservative judge, with a background in law enforcement, who was both a capitalist and a double Reagan appointee. And on top of that, Lindsay had no experience as a judge on the criminal bench.

When Judge Lindsay took his seat on April 1, 1971, there was a 35-page document challenging him that had been prepared by Angela's attorneys. They accused Lindsay of being a "racist appointed by Governor R. Reagan . . . who has demonstrated a long history of prejudice . . . his whole sphere of life is so outside the experience of that associated with the life of Angela Davis and her co-defendant that he is totally incapable of making a fair determination of the motions put forth by the defense. . . ."

They wrote of his policy as president of Oakland's Board of Education, and included an affidavit from a black lawyer who had represented Oakland's NAACP before the Board of Education. ". . . Under Lindsay, over 5,000 minority group children were housed in portable classrooms while only 1,000 white children used temporary buildings. Black schools were five times more crowded than white ones, and all six all-portable elementary schools served black children. The least experienced teachers were assigned to schools serving minority group children and the per capita expenditure was lower at minority schools than at white ones."

Angela's attorneys said that since "the relationship of judges and district attorneys frequently is in fact, or is viewed to be, close and sometimes indistinguishable," Lindsay, who had been a prosecutor, was not the one to judge "a black woman, a revolutionary, a communist . . . a critic of racist, oppressive unconstitutional practices in law enforcement, the judicial process and penal correction existing in the United States in general and in the State of California in particular."

The political end of the defense moved rapidly also. NUCFAD releases on Lindsay stressed that the appointment "illustrates the prejudice inherent in the judicial system." They pointed out that he had been in the Justice Department during the McCarthy era, and excoriated the judge on his record on the Oakland Board of Education.

"[Lindsay's] judicial qualifications are equally bad. His bench experience has been mainly in Oakland traffic courts and juvenile halls, with a special 90-day stint trying adult felony cases . . .

"Who can believe that a judge with the record of Judge Lindsay, who has almost no experience in the handling of major felony cases, was designated to sit for any reason other than to impose his biased philosophy in the conduct of this case? Not the defendant. Not the people." [7]

The object of all this scorn was a smallish, dark haired, mild mannered man, who spoke in a high voice that sounded as though it had been subjected to elocution lessons in order to overcome a lisp. His appointment to the case was for 90 days, a period of time

[7] NUCFAD press release, April 1, 1971.

which could be extended providing he took charge of the case and moved it along. To Lindsay this was an opportunity. This was his first big case, a trial that would go down in history, and he wanted in.

"I am now and always have been unalterably opposed to racial prejudice and segregation of any kind whatsoever," he stated in a 23-page answer to Angela's allegations. Magee had also submitted a list of charges but Lindsay chose not to respond to any of them. This led Magee to observe that Lindsay "chose only to answer Moore's objections and/or avoid confrontation with true issues."

Lindsay said that, "the allegations concerning my services on the Oakland School Board are based on fragmented assertions, opinions and conclusions which do not bear upon the issue to be determined." His response to the challenge read like a set of instructions to the judge who would hold a hearing to determine whether or not he was prejudiced. He pointed out that a hearing was not necessary, implying that he, as a judge, was leaning over backwards to give the petitioners due process. Albert Harris supported him in this contention. He filed a memorandum saying that Magee alleged no facts and Davis alleged no relevant facts. Therefore, in order to expedite the case in the name of the people, he found that a hearing was a waste of time.

There was a hearing of sorts. Justice Winslow Christian, who had ordered Magee restrained in December while ruling him incompetent, was assigned to rule on Lindsay's qualifications. Magee attempted to challenge Christian's right to rule in the case. The judge would not hear it. He ignored Magee's contribution to the challenge, and, thus, limiting himself to the proposition that the disqualification motion came only from Angela Davis, could find reason to prevent Magee from issuing a challenge, or even consulting with Attorney Robert Bell.

Christian's decision was based on Lindsay's response to the challenge. Lindsay, in addition to pointing out that he as a judge could have dismissed the challenge, produced a higher court decision stating that a judge could be dismissed for bias only if the complainant could make a case of being personally affected. The decision essentially would support an argument that even if a judge were proved to be a racist, that he could only be disqualified if the petitioner could demonstrate that the judge's racist actions affected him. "No knowledge, experience or opinion on the part of a judge can give rise to bias or prejudice, so as to disqualify him from hearing a case unless it results in hostility or ill will."

Lindsay also quoted a California Supreme Court decision made in 1916: "We fail to see how the appointment of a judicial officer by the Governor would even have a tendency to cause the former to adopt all the latter's prejudices and to decide cases not according to law, but in a manner which he might think pleasing to the appointing power." Well, that might be so, but it is no secret that presidents and governors appoint judges whose approach to the law parallels theirs.

Lindsay answered three of 29 allegations, and dismissed all of the others as "argumentative, and conclusionary." The 29th allegation threw him a little, as it was based on an affidavit by attorney John George, who had battled with Lindsay over the problems of blacks in Oakland's schools for a number of years. George's affidavit included a number of specific facts, which could be substantiated from other sources.

To this charge, Lindsay admitted that he had been on the Board of Education and that George appeared before it on numerous occasions. "I do not have sufficient information to admit or deny the allegations; however they are irrelevant . . ."

Christian found "no substantial basis for believing Judge Lindsay entertains prejudice or bias," and the question was settled in half a day.

The afternoon session that day was stormy. Bell and Carrow had tried a new tack to get out of the case, namely, the filing of a notice of substitution. Normally, as long as the retiring attorney and his client agree on who is to replace him a judge automatically allows a motion to substitute to go through. But in this instance, Bell and Carrow sought to substitute Magee, a stratagem that did not get past Lindsay. The problem was that the hearing had been called without any notice. Howard Moore, Jr. said that he had been notified at 2 p.m. the previous day, that there was to be a 9 a.m. hearing the following day. Bell and Carrow said that the only reason they were in court was that the judge's clerk called them and threatened to take sanctions if they did not appear.

The two attorneys were in the courtroom, seated in the spectators' section, when the afternoon session began. They were taking the position that the notice of substitution was a routine matter, and that Ruchell Magee, sitting at the defendant's table, had become the lawyer of record.

"I would like to say we tried to show conspiracy between Harris, Wright [Donald Wright, Chief Justice of the California Supreme Court and the person who had appointed Winslow Christian to hear the challenge] and you, judge," Ruchell explained. He said that the Department of Corrections, specifically Warden Nelson and several correctional officers, had been the subject of a civil complaint by him claiming attempted murder. Lindsay didn't interrupt, and Ruchell moved on. He accused Marin County judges of appointing attorneys who were legally disqualified, and said that one of the attorneys, Leonard Bjorklund, had offered him a judicial bribe to get evidence which Harris did not have.

Ruchell had literally blown Bjorklund off the case. When he could not persuade the attorney to withdraw, Ruchell, backed up by a San Quentin inmate, Leo Robles, charged that Bjorklund had offered Ruchell a deal, in which he would be set free, in exchange for information which would convict Angela. Judge Wilson had dismissed the allegations as completely unfounded, but Bjorklund did not care at that point. He realized that his usefulness in the case had ended and petitioned to withdraw. Lindsay was facing a problem. He wanted some lawyer to represent Magee, and knew that the only way it could be done was to force a lawyer to do it. For the time being, however, he let Magee talk.

Albert Harris objected to Magee making any more statements. "He may prejudice himself," explained the prosecutor. Ruchell was incensed. "Don't you protect Magee! Mr. Magee will protect Magee." Ruchell then continued, only to be interrupted by the court clerk, who read a list of the documents Magee had filed, and attempted to inform the judge of the progress of petitions that had been lodged in other courts.

Lindsay had had it. He ordered the attorneys up front. Carrow asked for a two-day continuance, so that the issue of whether they could be compelled to represent Magee or not could be settled. Friday, April 23, was requested because that was the day when their attorney, Henry Ramsey, would be free.

Lindsay refused to grant the continuance, and ordered Bell to sit next to Magee. Magee argued that because of the removal petitions the court had no jurisdiction, but Lindsay prevailed. He referred to Judge Conti's latest ruling. Judge Conti had decided that Magee's petitions were "legally frivolous." Conti therefore ordered that he could not file any documents without first having them cleared by the trial court, thus effectively blocking Ruchell's strategy of appealing to the federal courts.

"The documents are frivolous because I'm black," responded Ruchell. Everybody in the courtroom was mad except Lindsay, and most were bothered by him. Magee knew when to be silent and watch the proceedings. Howard Moore, Jr. jumped to his feet, drawing himself up high enough to dominate the judge. Moore took up where Magee left off.

"Yes, your honor, there are reasons to suspect a conspiracy. The clean bill of health you just got came too easy. I'm called at the last minute to a hearing held without additional argument, to be a participating witness to a hollow form. You judges just made up your minds and did it. We were dealt with in such a high-handed slave condition allowing the defense attorneys to sit there, as in a game of musical chairs."

Moore pointed out that Judge Lindsay himself, before being automatically anointed by his fellow judge, said that, "A trial must not only be fair, but the defendant must feel he is being treated fairly."

"What are you asking us to do, beg the court to deal fairly with the law, and those procedures designed to protect? It's a very simple proposition, judge. We had ten days from yesterday to file with the California Supreme Court, and you and I know that most appeals are a waste of time. This whole thing, from indictment to fast shuffle hearing this morning has nothing to do with justice, and we want you to relate to that. We'd like Mr. Harris to relate to justice. Everybody knows that if the prosecution were really interested, you could dismiss these charges on his recommendation."

"All I'm asking," he concluded, "is that white people respect their own law."

Harris would not argue with Moore. He was concentrating on Magee. He did not care about the disqualification hearing—that question was settled. He wanted to shut Magee up. Albert Harris and Ruchell Magee understood each other as only total adversaries can, and Harris was determined to flay Magee every step of the way.

He started with Bell and Carrow, saying that it was in the spirit of wanting to "protect" the defense attorneys that he opposed their "purported substitution" motion. He hinted at dire consequences awaiting Bell and Carrow in some court up yonder, when it was discovered that they openly maintained that a San Quentin convict was equal in legal capacity to trained attorneys.

That was Robert Bell's cue to stand up, fists clenched, to demand that Harris not protect him.

The prosecutor brought up Magee's IQ, referring Lindsay to the list of judges who had found the defendant incompetent, and giving "evidence of Mr. Magee's educational attainment."

Carrow and Bell spoke up, calling Harris' statement misleading, insisting that there had not been an adversary hearing.

The courtroom reverberated, with lawyers complaining, reading portions of past transcripts aloud, accusing each other and the courts of unfairness and generally performing. Much of the energy put into the conflict was fueled by the antagonism of Magee and Harris for each other.

Magee told Harris he was reading from a false transcript, and insisted emphatically that the prosecutor read the proceedings of another day. Judge Lindsay was trying to take control of the situation, but the assembled were insisting on being heard. While the judge was trying to talk about the authority of lawyers, Magee was insisting that he, Lindsay, was driving over removal petitions. Harris tried to establish that the petitions were incompetent when Magee erupted: "Pig, shut up!"

Harris was stunned, surprised, totally stopped in his attack. He stood there, hands at his sides and looked across the circular courtroom to Magee. "Pardon me?"

The courtroom was silent. Magee's command had interrupted the contentious rhythm without generating direct hostility. The judge, all defense attorneys, the spectators, and Harris knew that however shocking Magee's words, they were directed at a man who was conducting himself more like a street brawler reaching for concealed weapons, than an attorney, and that Ruchell's challenge of him had been at that same level.

"What else can I do except protest in front of the people?" Magee explained. "That monkey is standing up there telling lies. I haven't had my say, my say is in that affidavit."

Harris verbally backed away from Magee, and began talking of Bell and Carrow's responsibility. "Harris has deliberately lied again," said Magee, and proceeded to blast back at him once more.

"There's no law that requires a defendant to be competent or deemed competent," Bell and Carrow summed up. "We choose not to participate in the sham of defense." They demanded a full hearing to determine Magee's competence.

Lindsay finally took command of his court and delivered a few rulings. He told Bell and Carrow that he could not accept their offer to substitute Magee as an attorney because he was bound by prior decisions ruling him incompetent to represent himself. He then turned around, and in a reflex common to judges, gave something to the defense.

He vacated the order sealing the grand jury transcript, meaning that now there was more that NUCFAD could talk about outside the courtroom. But the question of Magee's representation was not settled. Bell and Carrow obviously wanted to drop out, and Lindsay had to solve that problem.

A week later Carrow and Bell were in court again, insisting that they would not represent Magee, and that the notice of substitution simply meant that he would represent himself.

"I do not represent this man, I am not going to represent this man and perhaps we should discuss what sanctions will be invoked if I do not represent this man," intoned Carrow. "The circumstances have made it impossible to establish the attorney-client relationship in this case."

Ruchell Magee was absolutely livid, and submitted a written preemptory challenge to the judge which Lindsay would not accept. Every defendant in a criminal case has an absolute right to eliminate one judge, just by filing a preemptory challenge. After that judges can only be removed for cause. But the first one was fair game for any defendant that wanted to get rid of a judge.

Lindsay wanted no part of the challenge because he was not sure whether this was some legal trick of Magee's. There was record of a prior preemptory. Also there was the question of the validity of a preemptory challenge issued by a defendant who was deemed incompetent.

At that moment Lindsay gained a new insight. He then fully understood Judge Conti's actions: "If you don't accept a writ, you don't have to act on it."

"You are driving over my rights. You are using the law to silence me. It's a conspiracy to murder Ruchell Magee," shouted the injured defendant.

Howard Moore, Jr. rose again to point out to Lindsay that once more he had proven why he should have been disqualified. Lindsay was trying so hard to remain judge that he had a challenge for cause dismissed, and then ignored a preemptory challenge. Moore asked for time to appeal Christian's refusal to disqualify Lindsay, offering to go to the State Supreme Court if necessary. The judge refused, and adjourned the session.

Two days later Bell and Carrow were in court with Henry Ramsey. Lindsay was willing to give up on the two attorneys, but he was not prepared to allow their motion of substitution to prevail. Lindsay demanded, and subsequently received, a new motion that Bell and Carrow be relieved of the case, and postponed the matter for a week.

In doing so he refused another bail request for Angela.

Lindsay was ready at the next session. He had been to a judge's workshop over the weekend and had picked up a lot of information; in fact he had solved his problem. Lindsay informed everyone that he had found a decision, people vs. Jones, in which a judge had been found in error for allowing a previously adjudged incompetent to represent himself. Harris leaped forward with the papers from Louisiana giving Magee an IQ of 75 so that Lindsay could avail himself of the opportunity to go down in history as the third judge in the trial who had adjudged Ruchell Magee incompetent.

Lindsay had reached a decision. Somewhere along the line he had decided that he was the judge, and that judges not only made up their minds, but they told people about it. He was now demanding that everyone, particularly Magee, listen to the judge.

"Listen carefully and quietly," he instructed Magee, who was charging on with an impassioned argument designed to dismiss Carrow and Bell from the human race.

"I assure you that I will listen carefully to everything you have to say."

Magee looked up at the judge, decided this time he was very serious, and shut up. Lindsay explained that he would release Bell and Carrow, an order that was being prepared. Then he questioned "who, inside, or even outside the state, can give you effective counsel?" Lindsay said that he had made a list of 25 attorneys, made informal contacts with others, all in the search for an attorney who could truly represent Magee. "I found the man," said Lindsay, not as a judge ordering compliance, but with the air of a community resource person seeking to share a reason to rejoice with his constituency.

By coincidence, this attorney, Ernest Graves, had already figured in the record of Magee's trial. Graves had been called on by Henry Ramsey at the time that Ramsey was the court-appointed attorney for Magee, to witness the details of a disturbance that had occurred in the San Quentin courtroom.

Lindsay said that he had decided that Graves might be the right attorney, and had gone to his judge's workshop in Los Angeles a day early so as to have time to meet with Graves, whose offices were also in Los Angeles. He had brought the entire public file to Graves, arranged for the attorney to meet with Magee, and now wanted the latter to agree to accept Graves as an attorney.

Magee had temporarily reached the limits of resistance, and accepted the appointment.

At the next session, on May 10, Lindsay set out to make the record clear. He reaffirmed his "absolute impartiality and lack of prejudice," complaining that he was the only person in the courtroom "who, without due process of law, can be deprived of the privilege of establishing the falsity of such a charge." He then moved on Magee, saying that the documents he submitted to the court were "confused and ineffective . . . [revealing] unfitness and incapacity to defend himself." On behavior he said: "I simply find very clearly from the record and from watching his deportment that Magee does not have an intelligent conception of the consequences of appearing without counsel, and that he must be represented by counsel."

Lindsay was easing in control. He had Magee represented by an attorney, and he had accepted Harris' offer, and was documenting for future judges his determination that Magee was inept.

Magee rose to the challenge and charged Lindsay with making a record detrimental to him: "I don't have no attorney, I AM the attorney," asserted Ruchell, establishing for Lindsay's benefit that he could go along with procedure as well as the next man, but that he knew what he was doing, and that no lawyer, or legal process, was going to deter him from acting in his own behalf.

During all of this Magee had been arguing with the Davis forces. He was insisting that even if the attorneys did not agree with his overall tactic of depending on removal to federal court, they should support his removal actions so as to get the best possible mileage out of this novel mode of legal defense. Angela and her attorneys had decided to go along with Ruchell, but the relationship was far from amicable.

On April 23, Ruchell had sent a letter to Angela, which he also sent to both San Francisco dailies and *The Pacific Sun,* Marin County's somewhat alternate press. The reporter on *The Pacific Sun* most interested in Ruchell was Alice Yarish who had filed a suit in Superior Court, challenging the San Quentin-imposed restriction keeping the press away from Ruchell. Alice found herself out of favor with Ruchell following her filing of the action. There was Magee, struggling to overcome the idea that the state courts should make any decisions that affected Ruchell Magee, and Alice Yarish files an action in a court which he refuses to recognize.

The San Francisco Examiner refused to print the letter until it was authenticated by a handwriting expert. Imagine, the newspaper of Ed Montgomery, scourge of the left, which directly receives evidence that Ruchell Magee and Angela Davis, co-defendants, are at odds, and they refuse to print it for fear of lack of authenticity.

Ruchell brought to Angela's attention the fact that he, Ruchell, her co-defendant, had a claim on her political and legal considerations. Ruchell called Angela and himself "victims of a clique of shyster lawyers out to convict us." He made no distinction between judges, presidents or defense attorneys. His premise was that lawyers—members of that professional class which draws up guidelines for rulers—were both corruptible and corrupt.

He particularly jumped on Sheldon Otis, a Berkeley attorney, who had impressive experience in trying difficult cases, many of them political. Otis was, and is, a well-respected member of the activist-oriented bar, but Ruchell said of him: ". . . maybe he isn't a CIA, but it's no doubt he's an FBI." Ruchell also said that Otis visited him prior to Angela's arrest, and had prior knowledge of it.

"Otis had to be involved in some way with law enforcement. He offered to represent me, before you were arrested," he addressed Angela.

"I will prove and show that nobody made any escape attempts, . . . trying to free the 3 Soledad Brothers . . . We, me, McClain and Christmas was going to tell that which we told those 12 jurys, and expose some more to the world the conspiracy between the California Judicial and prison system, murdering and enslaving innocent people . . . Yes Jonathan was going to tell why he brought those guns in court—but he was killed before we reached the radio news station . . . Angela you're being framed for something you know nothing about. Only those guns are being used as a tricky way to tie you into this slave case and deceive the people to believe that the case is about something other than what it is all about, murder and flagrant racist slavery . . . You are being tried in a lynch law court . . . These shysters are playing games, cold, rotten games, above your knowledge, Angela. Have you heard of the Angela Davis Corporation? Second only to the Ford, Chase Manhattan Bank and other chief capitalists. In short you're being pimped, honey . . ."

"Fire those pig lawyers before they strengthen more fraud

against you and the people will know the truth and free you. Now I've told you what to do—and how to do it . . . don't keep being deceived by lies framed in kind words."

Angela was not going to give up competent legal representation and throw herself in with Ruchell Magee. Tension between Magee and the Davis forces became apparent in court. Ruchell continued to argue about removing the case to federal court, and virtually forced Howard Moore, Jr. to announce to Judge Lindsay that Magee was correct in his insistence that the filing of a removal action deprived the state court of jurisdiction. Ruchell simply cited two cases decided on appeal in 1967 and 1968, which supported his position. The winning attorney in these cases was Howard Moore, Jr.

Ruchell was keeping his attention on the main goal, and that was to get rid of Lindsay. At every opportunity he castigated Lindsay, calling him biased, prejudiced, a trampler of the rights of defendants. All the while, he proffered his handwritten preemptory challenge. Lindsay initiated discussions around the question of whether Magee could file a preemptory. A defendant has only one such challenge, and Ruchell had filed a challenge against Judge McGuire the previous December. McGuire had stepped down, but the court was uncertain whether the judge had done so in response to the challenge.

There was also the problem of whether the court could accept a writ prepared by a defendant who had been declared incompetent, and who had been provided with an attorney. Ruchell insisted that his competence would not become an issue until Lindsay was disqualified. As to the attorney, Ruchell insisted: "the court has appointed an attorney for the sole purpose of preventing me from disqualifying you."

Graves suggested that the problem could be settled easily, by Lindsay appointing Magee to act as his own attorney in a special hearing that would consider only the question of Magee's preemptory. Graves further argued that the preemptory challenge was a privilege of the defendant, and although such a challenge is usually handled by an attorney, it rests exclusively with the defendant.

Albert Harris found himself on Magee's side. He agreed that the right to disqualify a judge preemptorily was a personal right. He also advanced the argument that the McGuire disqualification could not be considered the result of the proper use of a preemptory challenge as Magee did not have an attorney at that time. The prosecutor was trying to get himself out of a dilemma. If he argued that Magee had used his challenge, he would at the same time be asserting that a man he found incompetent, could on his own affect the legal record of the case. And Harris did not want that. He insisted that Graves, as Magee's attorney, sign Magee's writ, an action which presumably would show that Graves was a party to the action.

But Graves would not have it. In every court appearance Graves preceded his remarks with a disclaimer. He would explain that he was appointed to represent Magee, but that everything he did was over Magee's objection. He said that he had not advised Magee to use the challenge, and in fact might disagree with its use at that point in the trial. Graves suggested that perhaps there were two preemptories available. One which was the right of the defendant, and another, in those cases where a competent attorney had determined that a defendant had used his precious preemptory unwisely. Lindsay had had enough trouble without trying to deal with Graves' novel approach to the preemptory challenge.

Here was Ruchell, whom everyone, prosecutors, judges, and a couple of Angela Davis' attorneys, agreed was incompetent, succeeding session after session in raising legal complications that effectively kept the trial from going forward. Lindsay reluctantly decided that he had no choice but to accept the preemptory challenge.

There had been six judges in the case, and except for a brief argument for bail, Angela's attorneys had not managed to get one thing accomplished.

Next came Richard Arnason, a judge from Contra Costa County, a sprawling mixture of farms, industry, suburbs, and retirement villages. Arnason came from a large family in North Dakota, where he worked on the family farm through high school and on somebody else's farm through college. He became a lawyer in 1945 after graduating from law school at Boalt Hall of the University of California. In 1963, while a law partner of Jerome Waldie, a Democratic Congressman, Arnason was appointed a Superior Court Judge by Democratic Governor Edmund G. Brown.

Arnason did not have any of the stigma of being a prosecutor, one of the more popular routes to a judgeship. He was not known as a particularly liberal judge, but he did have a reputation for fairness and more important for all parties concerned, he was very highly regarded as a student of the law.

Ruchell immediately challenged this new judge by filing a writ claiming prejudice. Arnason countered the Magee brief in three hours with a four page reply denying prejudice. He found Ruchell's charges "irrelevant, argumentative, preclusionary and are statements of opinion and should be ignored or stricken from the record . . . The defendant Magee can and would have a fair and impartial trial if conducted before me."

Albert Harris also attacked Magee's filing, claiming it to be incompetent and alleging no facts.

Arnason accepted the Magee challenge, saying he would have the matter heard before another judge.

By this time Howard Moore, Jr. had had it. He demanded that Angela be released immediately. My client is "illegally held . . . locked into a proceeding that never gets started. She has been in jail 194 days and has not had an opportunity to argue for bail."

Ruchell reminded Moore that "Miss Davis' co-defendant is also illegally held." Magee again insisted that Moore support his removal action. You're just "putting on a show, demanding dismissal, knowing that the judge and Harris won't go for it," said Magee. Then he softened, saying that if Moore wanted to argue for bail and dismissal there was a way which would not prejudice Magee's removal strategy. He delivered a lecture on habeas corpus, and recommended to Moore that if the attorney really wanted to do something he would file a writ of habeas corpus and have the arguments for bail and dismissal argued in the hearing accompanying the writ. That way, as Ruchell explained, the Davis forces could get their arguments in, and the case could move forward.

The following day Justice Christian, for the third time, ruled that a judge was not prejudiced, leaving Arnason free to preside over the case.

Magee was losing his control. He had no more preemptory challenges and his challenge for cause had been denied. Angela's attorneys were no longer deferring to his removal petitions, feeling that in doing so they were damaging their client's right to have arguments heard in her behalf. The only move which Ruchell could make was to try and get rid of his attorney. On Thursday, May 27, Judge Arnason announced that he would hear arguments from Angela's attorney dealing with the dismissal of the indictment, the question of co-counsel status for Angela, and the question of bail.

Before the arguments could get under way Ernest Graves, tall, white haired, with a bushy moustache, looking like a movie version of one of His Majesty's officers in India, addressed the court.

"Mr. Magee has asked me to make a presentation to the court . . . He has asked me to relieve myself from the case, he has asked me to declare a conflict . . . He wishes the court to recognize the fact that I am not permitted to or shall I be authorized to argue any of his motions; that his position is that this court has no jurisdiction . . . and that the very fact of my appointment and my attempting to do anything on his behalf is giving the appearance and the facade of fairness to his position, and that he seriously rejects it . . .

"I will state this: that he earnestly and carefully argues the facts with me. He presents to me a coherent reason why he feels that my mere appearance in the courtroom constitutes jeopardy to his position . . . I wish the record to reflect, and continuously to reflect, that I have never had, and do not represent to this court that I ever have had, the slightest bit of concurrence or agreement in anything I have done by Mr. Magee. And that everything I have done, or said, is absolutely over his opposition . . .

"I don't know what the court will do, but I will state this: that it is certain that I have not visited Mr. Magee while he is in his present custody over in the prison. It is certain that we have not conferred, and it is certain that he does not wish to confer with me about the preparation or what is going on in the state court which he holds is absolutely nothing more than a fraud and a conspiracy to kill him."

Ruchell said that he wanted to speak before the court made its order. He pointed out that Justice Christian had not filed his response, that the Justice's prior refusal to disqualify Judge Lindsay was illegal. Ruchell called Graves' appointment "illegal and erroneous," and said he had filed more papers in federal courts trying to stop the proceedings. He asked for time to file for a writ.

Arnason said that he had been relying on the prior appointment of Graves which he found proper. He allowed that Ruchell might have a point, but that his position would have to go into the record at a later date.

"This is similar to a story my mother once told me about the king of old who granted a pardon after the prisoner's head was chopped off," responded Magee.

Arnason smiled, and told Ruchell that he had no more legal options. Ruchell blew up:

"You're a bunch of fake phoney stinking dogs . . . You know what I want to expose."

He turned and spat on Graves who was seated about two feet to his left.

"Your honor, at this time you're railroading me to the gas chamber and at this time I feel that I can do anything I want to do . . . You're not a judge to me, you are no more than a Ku Klux Klan."

Magee was removed and after a brief recess the session resumed. A very distressed Howard Moore, Jr. told the judge that "what I've witnessed here weighs very heavily on my client and myself." Moore informed the judge that there had been differential treatment afforded Angela and that he could only assume that it was based on the difference in background and education of the two defendants. He reminded the court that although Angela's motion to disqualify Judge Lindsay resulted in a totally inadequate hearing, that at least she received something called a hearing. Magee, however, after filing essentially the same disqualification notice, had not been given the courtesy of a hearing. Moore affirmed his basic support of Magee's position, explaining that he had asked for the hearing on the motion to dismiss for that day because Michael Tigar, who was to argue the motion, could not be there the following week.

Arnason instructed Tigar to begin his argument. Ruchell had been brought back into the court. He sat, chained, both feet close together, swiveling left and right, obviously agitated. Just as Tigar began to speak, Ruchell yelled, "Graves!," spun his chair around 45 degrees, and kicked Graves with enough force to knock the attorney to the floor. "I tried to make it legal. Any other way I can't. This is a kangaroo court and all you lousy stinking dogs is dragging me over into this court. Moore? Moore needs to be killed, him and all them shithead lawyers. You are a bunch of phoney stinking dogs."

Magee then directed his anger to Harris: "You lousy son of a bitch, you know what I want to expose and you still bring this shit in here. You're going to get it you punk son of a bitch . . ." Ruchell was again taken out of the courtroom and a brief recess was announced.

"Your honor, do you think the record should reflect what occurred here the last few minutes for whatever purposes it may ultimately bear any significance on?" asked Harris.

"Oh I think the court can handle that situation. We will proceed with the arguments," replied Arnason, coolly.

He had obviously regained both his composure and his breath during the recess, for when Ruchell tried to send Graves into orbit Arnason took off from the bench as though an army was after him. Even judges get nervous.

Graves was not hurt. Ruchell's blow had landed on his shoulder. During the recess Graves explained that there was no need for an apology from Ruchell. "He had every right to do as he did," asserted the attorney. He said that he understood Ruchell's frustration at being part of a process in which every attempt he made to defend himself and present arguments had been blocked.

A leaflet, signed Black Mothers United for Action, was circulated a few days later, titled: "The Legalized Conspiracy to Kill Ruchell Magee." It stated: "Mr. Magee took the only recourse left to him. He kicked the 'defense attorney' very unpolitely after his legal rights had been grossly shoved aside as if they had no merit. This caused only a halt for a short time in the 'proceedings'; it did not stop the whole show for a day . . . The judge overlooked both the kick and the statement of fact and politely pushed ahead with the show."

Graves was still the attorney of record, the sixth person to have been assigned to defend Ruchell.

At the following session, on June 2, Judge Arnason explained that he was halting the pre-trial procedures in deference to Ruchell's filing of removal petitions. Arnason had discovered a case in New York State where a drug conviction had been reversed because the defendant had been found guilty after refusing to plead. The defendant's refusal was based on the fact that a removal petition was pending, and ultimately this insistence led to the reversal. "There's too much merit to this case to build a prosecution on a reed that might not stand up due to a jurisdictional challenge."

"The Court has serious doubts and considerations as to its jurisdiction," Arnason explained, and recessed until that afternoon so that he could look into a removal petition which Ruchell had filed May 23. At the same time he announced that on a motion by Angela's attorneys he was prepared to hold a hearing for bail, in a separate habeus corpus proceeding—precisely the proceeding which Ruchell had suggested almost a month before.

Howard Moore, Jr. said that he had heard Ruchell's argument, and through research discovered that Ruchell Magee had provided him with the very remedy he needed. He absolutely had to have the opportunity to argue that the indictment should be dismissed, as the first of a series of arguments geared toward getting Angela out of jail. At the same time, he had no desire for conflict between Magee's legal position in that court and that of Angela. The habeas corpus hearing could be held technically separate from the trial involving Angela Davis and Ruchell Magee, therefore the argument for dismissal could be entered, in a court setting which posed no legal problem for Magee.

While the habeas corpus proceedings didn't cause Magee to react, prosecutor Harris did. For reasons difficult to relate to Harris' argument against dismissal of the indictment, the prosecutor chose to refer to Magee's legal filings as "semi-illiterate documents." Ruchell graced the remarks by calling Harris a "hog mouthed dog," and reminding the prosecutor that, "I'm not an advocate of a degenerate system." Harris kept claiming that the state was ready to try the case and that he wanted the pre-trial phase expedited. He did not agree with Judge Arnason that Magee's attempts to remove his case to Federal court deserved any further attention. He opposed any further delay, saying that Ruchell had filed more than 20 to 30 petitions with the courts, and at least one with the United Nations. The prosecutor suggested that perhaps Judge Arnason would consider severing the cases so that Magee could continue to wander around the courts, while the Davis matter was settled.

Actually, there had been at least one conference between Magee and Margaret Burnham in which the question of severance had been explored. The Davis defense was leaning toward severance. They had tried to effect a common defense, but could not accede to Magee's position that a basic defense tactic was to attempt removal to Federal court. Angela's attorneys were convinced that the case would never be accepted by a Federal court, and further, even if they succeeded in getting there, that their tactical position would be weakened.

The defense was counting on two items to help in their preparation and conduct of the case. First, there was discovery of the items of evidence that the defense could, through court order, compel the prosecution to give up. California has one of the more liberal discovery practices, and the move to federal court would result in a situation where the court's approach to discovery would be less generous than in California courts.

The other key to defense strategy was the voir dire of the jury. In Federal court the jurors are questioned by the judge, rather than by opposing attorneys. To go to Federal court would mean that the defense automatically gave up the in-depth questioning of prospective jurors which enabled them to get the best of all possible juries. Questions designed to reveal whether a prospective juror harbored deep-seated prejudice would not be allowed. At best, the federal judge would direct a question asking whether an individual was prejudiced. All too often the only people who answer this question affirmatively are those who want to get out of jury duty.

Politically, Angela's attorneys could not publicly assert their feelings that separating the case might be a good thing. "The public position of Miss Davis," Howard Moore, Jr. told the court, "is that she would not move for severance except for unforeseen contingencies such as illness. We do not want to be in the position of being isolated from Mr. Magee." But Moore was not closing the door either. Any party can sever, he explained, and then demanded that Harris state the position of the state.

Harris straddled the issue, talking as though he were both for and against severance. They were jointly charged, he concluded, therefore they should be jointly tried.

The defense position was that the case could be severed only on a motion by one of the defendants. Graves agreed that he wanted a united front. Judge Arnason felt that the court actually did have the power to sever the cases. The judge, in bringing up the question of severance, said that he was disposed to grant Magee a limited delay until the federal court acted on his removal petition, and was also disposed to sever the cases. But, "If everybody is going to resist severing, I'm not going to take it on my own."

Although argument about federal removal was at the core of the inability of Magee and Angela to resolve their legal differences, there was another problem attached to a common defense. Ruchell did not want to be tried directly for his part in the events of August 7. Ruchell's basic contention was that he was illegally enslaved, and therefore was justified, by an application of the 13th Amendment of the US Constitution, to do anything possible to alter his enslaved state. He offered to save the county of Marin $1 million, half of what Marin County officials were then estimating as the cost of the trial, if he could not prove, by beginning with his 1963 conviction, that he was illegally enslaved and deserved to be set free.

Graves was moving toward attempting a re-trial of the earlier conviction for reasons that had nothing to do with Angela. Ruchell was charged with violating Penal Code section 4500, which mandated a death penalty upon conviction. The charge of murder made the death penalty option. Penal Code 4500 applied only to a prisoner serving a life sentence. If the earlier conviction could be erased, then Penal Code 4500 would have no bearing on the case. He urged Arnason to appoint another attorney, Ernest English of Los Angeles, to gather material relevant to the "strange strange retrial of 1965." To everyone's surprise, Magee agreed to accept English.

That investigation never got off the ground as relations between the co-defendants were becoming increasingly difficult. The prospect of reviewing Magee's 1963 and 1965 convictions did not particularly appeal to Angela's attorneys. From what they knew of August 7, they felt that there was an excellent chance of Ruchell being found not guilty of the murder, and further, that they could get the kidnap charge dismissed. Their position was that kidnap was not a reasonable charge insofar as the hostages were taken as a natural consequence of an escape attempt. Perhaps conspiracy would be a bit more difficult to handle since Ruchell had implied in his letter to Angela that a conspiracy existed.

There was no claim by the prosecution that Ruchell had any prior knowledge of the aims or particulars of the conspiracy with which he and Angela had been jointly charged. But in his April 23 letter he told Angela of another purpose of August 7. The group was headed for a radio station in order to directly expose conditions in prisons. How Angela's attorneys might have handled that letter in a combined defense was never developed. The differences in approach to the case between Ruchell and Angela were too basic to be accommodated in one trial.

On June 30, Judge Arnason called for a six-day recess in order to give the defendants time to iron out a "slight legal disagreement" which surfaced when Magee demanded that proceedings again be stopped while he filed still another removal petition. Magee warned Moore in court not to "put on no arguments. I want the record just as it is now. If you do I have no alternative but to believe you are a pig, working with pigs working to railroad me and your client."

A recess was called where the attorneys, Angela, and Ruchell conferred. Afterwards Angela received permission to address the court and emphasized her solidarity with Magee, "despite efforts to picture us as different types of people. The only real difference is that he was caught by the system at the age of 13 and I was not caught until the age of 26. We are both black, born into a racist society, and are bound through blood because we have refused to acquiesce in the oppression that exists against us."

An accommodation was worked out between Ruchell and Angela. Magee had insisted throughout that his failure to have the case removed to Federal court was in part due to Angela's unwillingness to go along with him. He persuaded the Davis team to move for removal. Part of his logic was based on the differential treatment he had experienced in the way the courts handled Angela as opposed to what he had come to expect from judges. Ruchell advised Angela that he was sympathetic to her situation—sitting in jail while his attempts at Federal removal kept her legal efforts in limbo. The agreement was that Angela would seek removal into federal court, and if that effort failed, he would agree to sever the cases.

The removal petition went to Judge Conti. Angela's attorneys anticipated this and asked that he be disqualified from handling the case. Conti had said that he intended to deny Angela's motion in the morning, on Friday, July 9. Angela issued a statement saying that if Conti heard charges against his own actions it would be "leading directly to unfairness or the appearance of unfairness."

Judge Conti was basically unreasonable. He had remanded one of Ruchell's petitions to state court previously, not by following the procedural form, but by ordering Judge Lindsay to proceed with the case, threatening to come to Marin himself to get things going. He rejected the Angela Davis affidavit accusing him of prejudice, remanded the Davis petition back to state court (this time using the proper procedure) and continued his order restraining Magee from filing further petitions with the Federal court. Initially, Judge Conti included Angela Davis in the order, but rescinded this at the request of Albert Harris. "Such an order would prompt her attorneys to file another petition for her, which would then set up a test case which might be removed to an out of state jurisdiction . . . I do not want to be involved in a test case."

That was the end of the association of Ruchell and Angela as co-defendants. When Judge Conti remanded the case Angela's attorneys requested that the two co-defendants be severed, so that they could each pursue separate legal approaches to their defense. The request was granted. Moreover, Ruchell agreed to waive his right to trial until the Angela Davis trial was completed, or after six months. He was then taken back to San Quentin.

Although Ruchell Magee was no longer part of the trial he had affected it considerably. In his rough, often profane, and always direct way of approaching the legal process, he had demonstrated the capacity for unfairness in the application of procedures purportedly designed to guarantee fairness. "There must be law and order to protect people," Ruchell explained in an interview given at the time of the severance. "The law must be obeyed, but it can't be obeyed by one and disobeyed by another."

Ruchell Magee was used to standing on his own, and was prepared to continue doing so. The only faith he had was in himself, and in his ability to command the fundamentals of the law. All other items of faith—in country, in public institutions, in religion, had left him long ago.

"The only Jesus for a black man today is a man like Jonnie Jackson. He's a hard driving black man with plenty of soul to recognize the time of day. He wasn't talking black, he was acting black —just like I am going to do from now on."

6 : The Leading Lady II

On July 8, 1971, Angela Davis met George Jackson for the first of three conferences connected with her defense. The last meeting was held Monday, August 16, 1971.

"I'm totally intoxicated, overflowing with you and wanting you more than ever before. An hour and a half since the last embrace. You're in your cell, I'm in mine . . . ," she wrote just hours after the first all-day meeting.

Angela and George had greeted each other warmly, physically, with hugs, kisses, protestations of love, and expressions of wonderment that both of them, behind bars, would have an opportunity to be physically next to each other.

Defense attorneys admitted that the work session was handled somewhat inefficiently because of the necessity of the two to exchange personal remarks not related to defending Angela against the charge of being part of a conspiracy formed to free George from prison. But work did get done. After it was all over, Angela began to write. She jotted down random thoughts, related her experiences in the jail, and, after making the brief appearance in Judge Conti's court on July 9, where the joint removal petition had been rejected, she recorded that fact. Angela was writing a diary, in letter form, which was to change the character of the prosecution against her.

On July 23, she completed the 18th page of this document and got it off to George Jackson: "I'm glad we saw each other when we did—it makes me realize that I have not always been as alone as I feel at this moment."

The letter was smuggled into San Quentin as Angela was still not on George Jackson's mailing list.

On Saturday, August 21, all hell broke out at San Quentin. It ended with George Jackson dead, along with three prison guards and two inmates.

Prison officials reported that Jackson had been visited by attorney Stephen Bingham, who brought a briefcase and tape recorder into the visiting room. Bingham left the room once to buy cigarettes.

When the visit ended Jackson was taken back to the Adjustment Center, San Quentin's prison within a prison that is overwhelmingly non-white. There he was supposed to have removed a gun from his hair, threatened a number of unarmed prison guards, and killed Frank DeLeon, the guard assigned to skin search Jackson. Somehow, Jackson managed to open the 26 cell doors of the Adjustment Center, which are usually opened only half an hour a day. Other prisoners joined with him, in what was projected as an escape attempt. Two more guards and two inmate trusties were killed. The death weapons, it was said, were razor blades embedded in toothbrush handles.

How many of the prisoners were supposed to have been in on the alleged break was not made clear. John Larry Spain was the only one, of the six charged in connection with this incident, who was described as attempting to escape.

Essentially, prison officials were saying that George Jackson hid a two pound gun and a clip of ammunition in an Afro wig and smuggled them into the prison. Supposedly they had been provided by Bingham, and had been hidden in his tape recorder. Since that time San Quentin officials have provided their own tape recorders when a recorded visit with a prisoner has been allowed.

Reporters at *The San Francisco Chronicle* bought a gun and a wig, and failed to get the two to work together. They tried to smuggle the gun, hidden by the wig, past a desk a few feet from the starting point. The wig wouldn't fit over the gun, the gun couldn't remain balanced, and the reporter couldn't walk in anything resembling a natural stride. Jackson was supposed to have walked hundreds of yards accompanied by a guard who noticed nothing unusual.

Each of the San Quentin Six, charged with murder and conspiracy as a result of August 21, Fleeta Drumgo, Willie Tate, David Johnson, Luis Talamentes, Hugo Pinell and John Larry Spain, have reputations as revolutionary organizers in prison.

Drumgo was a Soledad Brother. Tate and Johnson had joined
Magee to write an affidavit charging a prison guard with the murder
of Fred Billingslea. Luis Talamantez with a reputation as a prison
organizer of Chicanos was awaiting trial for assaulting a fellow
prisoner. He was acquitted in February 1972. John Spain was sent
to the Adjustment Center in November 1970 when Prison officials
decided that his detailed diary of prison life amounted to "Inflammatory Literature". Hugo Pinell, who said guards had threatened
to kill him, charged Soledad Prison officials with offering him a
parole if he would testify against the Soledad Brothers particularly
George Jackson.

Alan Mancino, a white inmate of the Adjustment Center on
August 21, has claimed that guards tried to get him to testify against
the San Quentin Six. He filed a $450,000 lawsuit against San
Quentin's warden, associate warden, medical officer and correctional officers:

"Said claim arises from the following circumstances: On
August 21, 1971, about mid-afternoon, Defendant Doe . . . beat
claimant with axe handles and clubs, kicked claimant and shot
claimant in both legs while claimant was forced by defendants to
lie face down on the ground without any clothing on, with his
wrists behind his back and his ankles handcuffed to his wrists.
After said defendant shot claimant he was forced to remain lying
there bleeding and medical attention was withheld from him and
denied to him. Defendants after leaving claimant in that condition for approximately one hour or more picked claimant up by
the chains and carried him approximately 40 feet, where they
slammed him face down on a metal table with wheels. Defendants
then . . . operated in the hospital upon claimant while he was
still trussed and chained and refused to remove said truss and
chains until after part of the operation had been completed. During
this operation, claimant was denied any medication at all and
specifically denied any medication for pain.

"Defendants then took claimant to the medical cell for condemned prisoners, placed him in the cell, left him for approximately
ten minutes and then came into the cell, put a cloth bag over
claimant's head, and while he could not see and was strapped down
and could not move his legs in any way, proceeded to beat claimant

in the head and threatened his life and refused him any medical treatment whatsoever, including any medication for the pains suffered during the operation and the shooting, thereby torturing claimant Mancino until he made the statement that he was coached by defendants to make.

"Defendants kept claimant Mancino in this condition without medication until this coached statement was reiterated by claimant. Claimant then received one injection of Demerol. Claimant had been promised medication if he made the coached statement. Although while being tortured claimant was promised medication if he made the coached statement, after he reiterated the coached statement, claimant was kept incommunicado for approximately one week and received no other medical attention, even though he was in extreme pain and bullets remained in his legs. Defendants then transported claimant in an unmarked car to a prison in Carson City, Nevada, wherein he was kept approximately one week without medical care and kept incommunicado at the orders and under the direction of defendants. Defendants then kept claimant incommunicado at the prison at Carson City, Nevada, under the threat that if he made 'any waves', defendants would perform certain acts that would endanger not only claimant's life but the lives of claimant's family."

Mancino said that he was in fear for his life, was in fear for his relatives' lives and was in fear that he would never get out of prison if he made any comments at all regarding the acts perpetrated against his person by the defendants on August 21, 1971 and after. He was told that the names and addresses of his relatives would be given "to other people of a race different from his own," if he "made any waves." Mancino swore out his affidavit after being paroled in May, 1972. He said that prior to being released he had been transferred to Nevada State Prison for safekeeping. There is an apparent arrangement between California prison officials and those of Nevada to house particular California prison inmates in the Nevada facilities. One of the witnesses against the Soledad Brothers had been transferred to Nevada after he had been selected as a witness.

Angela was totally unaware of the happenings at San Quentin. She had been visited August 21 by Bettina Aptheker Kurzweil,

Howard Moore, Jr., and Barbara Ratliff, a law clerk for the defense. Moore heard the news on his car radio just as he was arriving in Berkeley, 30 minutes away from the prison. He immediately returned to San Rafael, went to Keaton's Mortuary and satisfied himself that the body there was George Jackson's, and returned to the jail to notify Angela of George's death.

Angela did not hear any of the details. What could be added to the information that George Jackson had been shot to death that could have impressed her? She knew all she needed to know. George was dead, and that aloneness of which she had been partially relieved had returned, this time trebled with the intensity that accompanies the death of a companion.

"An enemy bullet has once more brought grief and sadness to Black people and to all who oppose racism and injustice and who love and fight for freedom," Angela wrote. "On Saturday, August 21, a San Quentin guard's sniper bullet executed George Jackson and wiped out that last modicum of freedom with which he had persevered and resisted so fiercely for eleven years . . .

"The Jackson family must be saluted. Their grief is deep. In little more than a year, two of their sons, George and Jonathan, were felled by fascist bullets. I express my love to Georgia and Robert Jackson, Penny, Frances and Delora.

"For me, George's death has meant the loss of a comrade and revolutionary leader, but also the loss of an irretrievable love. This love is so agonizingly personal as to be indescribable. I can only say that in continuing to love him, I will try my best to express that love in the way he would have wanted—by reaffirming my determination to fight for the cause George died defending. With his example before me, my tears and grief are rage at the system responsible for his murder. He wrote his epitaph when he said:

" 'Hurl me into the next existence, the descent into hell won't turn me. I'll crawl back to dog his trail forever. They won't defeat my revenge, never, never. I'm part of a righteous people who anger slowly, but rage undammed. We'll gather at his door in such a number that the rumbling of our feet will make the earth tremble.' "

George Jackson's death made his property available to the prosecution. On August 21, before George Jackson's blood was dry, at a time that his cell was in complete disarray and the prison had not yet had time to absorb the fact that a number of people had died, Spiro P. Vasos, a fingerprint expert for the California Department of Justice, went to the prison, to cell number 1AC6, George Jackson's last residence, and removed four cardboard boxes, all that remained of Jackson other than his body and the memory of his existence. On Monday, August 23, the date of Angela's statement, George Murray, an investigator on Harris' staff, went through the boxes, "to look for any evidence which might link Angela Davis to George Jackson." Albert Harris was also in Sacramento, examining those items which Murray had screened for him. The one which created the most interest was the 18-page diary-letter. It was read, examined for fingerprints, placed under black light to determine whether erasures could be detected, or possibly if invisible ink were used, and was transferred into Albert Harris' possession.

The document became evidence. It was transformed into the basis of the prosecution argument—it became the evidentiary rosetta stone which helped to translate the monumental pile of information Harris possessed about Angela, her comings and goings, her writings, her beliefs, into a theory of what August 7, 1970 was all about. Harris decided that the raid on the Marin County Civic Center was indeed conceived to free the Soledad Brothers. But, the motive was not political, or rather, politics were secondary to Angela's basic reasons for involving herself in the planning and execution of the act.

"Her motive for aiding and abetting Jonathan Jackson and conspiring together with him—the reason that she did this was passion, simple human passion, a passion for George Jackson, the Soledad Brother, a passion that knew no bounds, no limits, no respect for life, not even the life of George's younger brother," was the way Harris put it to the jury. Harris was ready to go to trial—a year after the event for which Angela had been indicted and ten months after she had been placed in jail.

In September, Georgia Jackson went to court to unsuccessfully sue for the return of all her son's property.

In October, the San Quentin Six were arraigned two courtrooms away from the Marin County site of the Angela Davis trial. The six were brought in one at a time chained and shackled. All of them complained that San Quentin officials prevented free access to attorneys and that they had been beaten and mistreated by San Quentin guards since August 21. But, possibly because they were charged with complicity in the killing of the two guards and three prisoners who died along with George Jackson, Judge McGuire paid no attention to their complaints. Attorneys in Marin County who routinely handle cases originating in San Quentin insist that a working relationship exists between Marin County judges and San Quentin officials which results in a complete inability of the judges to accept as valid any complaints given them about illegal or unreasonable treatment inmates receive at the hands of prison guards.

A change of venue had been requested by the defense and in November Judge Arnason decided that Santa Clara County was the best county available. Perhaps it was. But Santa Clara County was far from the defense choice. They would have preferred the trial to be in San Francisco County, which has a substantial non-white community. It is one of the few population centers in America where there is a higher percentage of blacks in the satellite cities than there is in the urban center. Oakland, for instance, with half the population of San Francisco has approximately the same number of blacks. But San Francisco, from the defense point of view, would produce the best of all possible juries. The city was also the headquarters for the defense efforts.

The defense really didn't expect to get San Francisco, and NUCFAD was prepared to prove any trial site other than San Francisco as unreasonable. They had the facts and figures and were prepared to issue a press release detailing the disadvantages of any other choice Stockton was one of the cities considered.

"Stockton, California, is a small town in the San Joaquin Valley," said the prepared press release. "Its life is 'Agribusiness'; its population is almost completely white. Ironically, James McClain (one of the Black convicts killed on August 7 at Marin) was sentenced to San Quentin while still in his teens by a Stockton judge, convicted by a Stockton jury—but not a jury of his peers. Angela Davis, a Black woman Communist, certainly cannot expect a jury of her peers in Stockton, California."

Stockton might have been unfavorable, but there were compensations. The domination of agribusiness meant that there were a fair percentage of blacks, Filipinos and Chicanos, who were theoretically available for jury duty.

A lumbering town in Northern California close to the Oregon border was also on the list. There weren't any minorities there who could be counted on to understand the issues from a non-white perspective. But again, things weren't all bad. While it was politically conservative territory, their citizens understood about guns. They might not have approved of Angela Davis—black and revolutionary—with guns, but they would have to accede to the principle. After all, most households there had weapons. Unexpectedly, however, for reasons connected with the life style revolution which is going on, there was a number of colonies of young whites living in that part of the state who were fairly well educated, politically radical and quite willing to work on Angela Davis' behalf. In fact, there were 30 or 40 of them, who after settling in Northern California and sorting their politics out, joined the Communist Party.

Santa Clara County, its principal city San Jose, was chosen, and NUCFAD wrote: "Santa Clara County was the scene of California's last real lynching. Santa Clara County has a 2% black population (the same as Marin) and a history of racial struggle culminating in a series of recent, brutal murders of young blacks by San Jose police. Another recent community fight involved an attempt by local rednecks to have Prof. Jack Kurzweil of San Jose State College fired because of his membership in the CPUSA. Last year, 13% of Santa Clara County voters registered with George Wallace's American Independent Party. State Prosecutor Albert Harris has assured the people that Angela Davis can get a fair trial in Santa Clara County, when it is absolutely clear that Angela cannot get even a jury of her peers in Santa Clara County. In fact, Angela's chances of getting even one person of color on her jury in that county are statistically insignificant."

The defense brought in a sociologist, Jerry Paige from the University of California, Berkeley, who testified that prejudice against communists was pretty intense there. Paige submitted a six-county telephone survey to back up his contentions. Another UC professor, who had worked at San Jose State College, testified that his experiences in San Jose convinced him that Santa Clara residents have a "distrust and fear of the outsider and of ideas and conditions that imply change." A black fundraiser for Nairobi College, an all black educational effort positioned immediately north of Santa Clara County, said that he found businessmen in Santa Clara County unwilling to donate funds for Nairobi College, "as long as those niggers are raising hell in colleges."

The testimony didn't change any decisions. At 6 a.m., December 2, 1971, Angela was transferred from Marin to a jail in Palto Alto, a city in the north of the county where Stanford University is located. She was handcuffed and placed in an unmarked car along with two Marin County Deputy Sheriffs and a matron. Behind was another unmarked car, with two more Marin deputies and Santa Clara Undersheriff, Thomas Rosa. She was placed in what Santa Clara Sheriff's press release writers chose to describe as a "two room basement suite." Sheriff James M. Geary said that the facility was chosen because only minor modifications were needed to meet detention requirements. He said that the area had two adjoining six-by-eight-foot cells, and a fresh air exercise area, and that: "Miss Davis will be allowed to mix with other female prisoners if she so desires."

Angela described her accommodations differently. She said that the jail in Palo Alto was generally used as a short term holding facility and was not equipped for long term prisoners. There were no provisions for feeding prisoners on a regular basis and her food was brought to her cell. Her two cells were windowless. One cell, approximately six by eight, had padded walls and a hole in the center of the floor that served as a toilet. The other had a bunk and a more traditional toileting arrangement. Angela would spend as much time as possible in one cell, and then, for a change of pace would go into the other cell. Opportunities for exercise were limited to one-half hour outside her cell at night.

Albert Harris was negatively impressed. As long as Angela was confined, he made references to her accommodations in jail in the most shocked and sometimes indignant tones. Sure, he knew she hadn't been convicted, and yes, he was aware that she had been granted the right to represent herself. But two cells? "Why she has the only private office in a county jail in California, in fact the entire country." That was too much for Harris.

A few days later Howard Moore, Jr. told a group of about 500 demonstrators at the courthouse in Palo Alto that, "we will continue to fight for a change of venue until we have no more fight to fight." But even at that point he knew that the venue fight was over. The day that Angela had been transferred to Santa Clara County, Governor Reagan signed a bill sent over by the legislature one week before which would have the state pay the cost of the Angela Davis trial to Marin and Santa Clara Counties. It was estimated that Marin had spent $350,000, and that Santa Clara might spend up to $1 million.

Moore suggested that, "the best place we can hold the trial is at 103rd St. and Central in Los Angeles, but I don't think we will get that." He was being facetious, that was a part of Angela's stomping grounds in Los Angeles. His remarks were made at a press conference where he angered a couple of reporters, saying that San Jose reminded him of a southern town. When pushed by them to explain what he meant, Moore talked about the city's physical characteristics and its southern ambience. But both the reporters and Moore knew that there was more to it, and the reporters were challenging him to call the town racist or prejudiced in print, possibly so that San Jose could have a chance to prove it.

San Jose does have a southern ambience. All the signs were there: the suspicious scrutiny when entering an office building, the casual conversation in a department store, initiated by someone who turns out to be security, the fields which are still within city limits, where brown and black workers, supervised by whites, picked vegetables from the rich soil. There were the rental car concessions at the airport, where black customers found they had to produce more credentials or references than in other cities.

All that Moore was saying was that little psychological adjustment was necessary for a black from the south to understand how to get along in San Jose. At the time the trial was being transferred to San Jose, a black scientist, John Henry Smith, was killed by a San Jose policeman for reasons that had more to do with the policeman than his victim. Smith was sober, well dressed, unarmed and not belligerent. He did want to know why he was being stopped by policemen. Community pressure resulted in a trial for the policeman, Rocklin Wooley, who was acquitted of involuntary manslaughter by an all-white jury. A friend of one of the policemen involved with Wooley was on the panel of potential jurors for Angela's trial. He was not selected.

"We seem to see everything differently," Harris suggested, in commenting on the defense charge that Angela could not get a fair trial in Santa Clara County. "Certainly the black population in Santa Clara County is about the same as Marin. I'm sure the black persons in the county will be amply represented in proportion to their numbers . . . how many will be on the jury is a matter of chance." He estimated that the trial would take four to six months and that there would be about 110 state witnesses. "No," he said in response to a reporter, "that's not an unusual number, the Manson case had 84 state witnesses." Another reporter pointed out that there were four defendants rather than one in that trial.

The question of bail was still uppermost. Much of the defense effort, both in the courtroom and through the political campaign, revolved around the question of releasing Angela. The bail issue, garbed in a number of legal arguments, had gone from Judge Arnason to the California Supreme Court.

In January, 1972, a hearing was held in San Francisco before Federal Judge William T. Sweigert. Angela was represented at this appearance by Anthony Amsterdam. Amsterdam had argued against the death penalty before both the California and United States Supreme Courts. He also prepared and presented Earl Caldwell's argument on freedom of the press before the US Supreme Court. Amsterdam regularly writes briefs and legal memoranda for cases which interest him that contain substantial questions of constitutional law. He makes his living and spends most of his time teaching constitutional law at Stanford University.

Amsterdam summed up the defense's position about lack of compelling evidence to keep Angela in jail. He pointed out that Harris had presented 17 cases supporting his no bail argument: five involved persons who were present when the crime was committed, six either knew of the crime in advance or had picked up a suspect with a smoking gun in his hand, four helped plan the crime and two of them had been in continuous criminal activity. Amsterdam argued that a criterion for denying bail was the conviction that a verdict would be sustained on the uncontradicted evidence which resulted in indictment. "I have never seen a case where the verdict was sustained on such weak evidence," he concluded. Amsterdam went a step further, saying that the practical test of a capital crime was the real prospect that the death penalty would be applied. There have been six women on death row, all of them triggermen, he emphasized, insisting that the judge recognize that even in the event of a conviction, the chance of Angela being sentenced to death was minuscule.

Angela spoke on her own behalf. She argued that bail had been granted in capital cases throughout the country, and that her denial was proof to some observers that the reason was political rather than legal. She shunted aside the argument that no bail was a requirement of the California constitution with the observation, "whether its policy has been action or inaction, the government has used the constitution to maintain a racist status quo . . . If this court does grant me bail, it will be a victory for all those trying to rectify what is left of democracy in this country."

Harris said that Angela's case had been treated the same as other capital cases. "Eleven state and four federal judges can't be wrong," he argued, "and they all effectively denied Angela bail. If California judges have kept her in violation of the law then they ought to be removed," he thundered, apparently upset that Anthony Amsterdam could imply that she was improperly jailed.

"Judges can be wrong without being impeached," was Amsterdam's rejoinder.

Harris cited a letter from Thomas Jefferson saying that if bail was wrongfully granted the Judge should be jailed. "The law makes it necessary that she remain in custody. She's in jail under excellent conditions. She has been given the best treatment. She has a typewriter and a radio and both are against the rules."

Sweigert's interest in the argument dealt more with the length of time the case had been pending than with the legal issues surrounding bail. Harris attempted to detail a listing of the kinds of defense actions that had caused the time lag, including mention of Magee's removal petitions.

"But the petitions only took one or two days," observed the elderly jurist, "I handled one or two of them myself."

He denied bail, but noted in doing so, "It could be plausibly argued that any judicial system which in addition to precluding bail . . . also requires or permits such cases to drag almost interminably, comes arguably close to denial of the right to speedy trial, denial of due process and, perhaps, even cruel and unusual preconviction punishment . . .

"The fact that Miss Davis may have contributed to or caused the delay is not a convincing explanation . . ."

The trial was imminent. Santa Clara County had built a secure courtroom, complete with a new jail facility for Angela connected by a tunnel to the courtroom, and was going to bill the state for it all. The defense complained that the length and nature of the trial had exhausted their financial resources. Howard Moore, Jr. citing legal expenses as between $5,000 and $15,000 a month, suggested that the state should finance the defense, "in order to equalize the opportunity."

NUCFAD released a statement saying, "The defendant cannot possibly raise sufficient funds to sustain a defense over such an extended period of time.

"While counsel for the prosecution are assured of a regular income regardless of how long the trial lasts, counsel for the defense must go uncompensated . . ."

Ed Montgomery and *The San Francisco Examiner* produced an "informed source" who said the Communist Party had used Angela Davis' case to raise a lot of money. "Unfortunately, very little has filtered through to her legal defense fund."

NUCFAD responded, blaming the *Examiner* and other papers for spreading "false and unsubstantiated rumors." They outlined legal costs, saying that a total of $60,000 had been spent thus far for attorneys' fees. In addition there was a $15,000 annual cost for staff salaries, and NUCFAD was in debt $10,000.

Governor Reagan had the last word. He called Angela's request for taxpayer funds for defense "utterly ridiculous." Then he suggested that if Angela wanted the state to pay that she should "throw herself on the mercy of the court." Some chance! The legal team had solidified, all pre-trial appeals had been exhausted, a defense strategy agreed upon, and they were looking for justice, not mercy.

Doris Walker, a veteran of 20 years of courtrooms and a long history of political battles, had entered the case in September. She and Margaret Burnham did much of the interviewing of prospective witnesses, as well as plotting the outlines of some of the specifics of defense. Mrs. Walker is small, with greying hair, in that not quite elderly mode of existence that one associates with experienced kindergarten teachers. Even her speech, slow but not drawling, precise in pronunciation, with a voice that easily falls into an inquiring inflection, induces attentiveness, much like a talented elementary school teacher uses her voice to get her educational program over to her students. But she is a lawyer with a hell of a lot of fight, and she threw it all into the case.

Angela was acting as her own attorney. Judge Arnason had given her the privilege in June, after it was certain that she wasn't going to fire her attorneys, and that the case would possibly be severed. It's doubtful that Arnason, or any collection of judges, would have wanted to preside over a case in which Angela Davis was allowed to represent herself, and her co-defendant was denied that privilege.

She contributed to the courtroom maneuverings sparingly, and to the extent that her co-counsel status was meaningful in the courtroom Angela acted like a well-behaved client. But her status as co-counsel was important.

There is a great deal to be said for the defendant as attorney, which goes far beyond legal arguments about the meaning of the "assistance of counsel for his defense." Part of the defense of every person is the fact that he is that person, and makes an impression on those who judge, directly related to the person he is. Part of the verbal pageantry of a trial is the abstraction of the witness chair. In theory, people are judged on the evidence and the evidence alone, but only when there is an overwhelming amount of evidence, or when there is none. Where evidence is contested, where versions of events are being contrasted, where an ordering of the evidence involves an assessment of the witnesses, factors other than the evidence influence the decision. A good witness is a convincing witness, and quite often persuasiveness is more a matter of demeanor than information.

The jury looks at the defendant throughout the trial, searching for a hint of who that person might be, a clue, rooted in judgments

about the probable personality of the defendant, to guess whether
that configuration of personal traits is capable of committing the
crime charged. That's a real part of judging, and no legalistic for-
mulations dealing with decisions based on the evidence, and the
evidence alone, will eliminate that element in human beings judging other human beings.

It's not unreasonable to suggest that an accused should have the
opportunity, if he should want it, to display more of what he
stands for to a jury—not in special pleading, but by conducting
himself as he must, as his nature directs him, when defending
himself against any serious threat. It is not necessary that every
defendant charged with every crime be an active part of the defense,
the courtroom strategy. But that decision should be made by the
accused in consultation with his attorney.

Angela had style. Gold embroidered, translucent, full-sleeved
blouses, maxi skirts with long slits buttoned to determine the length
of leg that shows, flouncing short-skirted prints, leather skirts, and
an ever present stole, brought attention to her. She spoke warmly,
usually with conviction, and occasionally with indignation.

Angela conducted part of the argument on the motion that the
state pay the costs of the defense. She knew that there was no way
that a judge in California would authorize a $300,000 expenditure
to an accused, so that she could sustain four attorneys, wage a long
legal battle, and maintain a barrage of information to the public.
Governor Reagan wouldn't put up with it.

Angela knew that Arnason was not about to volunteer for
scrutiny by Governor Reagan, yet tried to get home the meaning
of the state action. The State of California had passed legislation
which recognized the inability of counties to afford certain kinds of
criminal trials. Since the state, the accuser, can frame charges in
a way that conviction is assured unless large sums of money are
spent for defense, its first willingness is to pay for convictions.

Angela suggested that the law requiring the state to pay the
tab for lengthy trials should be interpreted as authorizing the
financing of her defense. The public defender's office had been
suggested by Harris, just in case she decided to take the Governor's
recommendation seriously. Angela charged that members of the
state apparatus had conspired to kill her.

"We contend Governor Ronald Reagan played no small part in this conspiracy. We intend to subpoena Ronald Reagan, call him, and put him on the stand and ask him to explain how he abetted and aided this conspiracy."

Angela said the state of California is to blame for the existence of the charges and is "using all of its myriad forces against me." As to the public defender, she considered it a part of the judicial system. "There is the fact that I simply couldn't trust the Public Defender's office . . . I know that they have participated in the railroading of thousands of my brothers and sisters . . . In fact, I distrusted the judicial system so much that I left the state . . ."

Leo Branton, Jr., the fourth attorney, had been brought in to replace Sheldon Otis. Otis had left the defense team in the fall, in an attempt to avoid publicity surrounding some personal problems which might have had a negative effect on Angela's chance for a fair trial. Branton, who practiced in Los Angeles, had years of experience in California courts, and had developed a devastatingly effective courtroom presence. He had started out as an actor, and went to law school when acting jobs became too hard to find. He never abandoned the world of acting. Branton acted in court, and had a practice based in the world of entertainment and theatre. He represented Nat Cole and Jimmie Hendrix, and had produced a Los Angeles production of James Baldwin's first play, "Amen Corner."

He had represented the Panthers, members of the Communist Party, and was in the enviable position of being able to choose his cases. When he was invited to be a part of the Angela Davis defense, he put his office in shape for a long trial, managed his regular business by commuting between Los Angeles and San Jose on weekends, and for four months took over a large part of the Angela Davis courtroom work.

The first request Branton made when entering the case was that the trial be televised by satellite to the rest of the world. Arnason didn't seem to take that motion seriously, but Leo Branton, Jr. did. Branton challenged Judge Arnason, thread for thread, for the title of the sharpest man in the courtroom. Branton was supersharp, white on white ties, deep vented Edwardian coats, Italian cut suit, and colors, lots of colors, mainly in the shirts.

Judge Arnason went for Branton's approach to clothes, Branton's demeanor in the courtroom, Branton's knowledge of law, in fact, Arnason went for Leo Branton.

Arnason said he admired Branton as a complete lawyer, an attorney whom he confidently felt could perform as a prosecutor or a judge. Arnason felt that all of the attorneys connected with the trial were exceedingly competent, and had singled out Branton as being a notch beyond the others.

Howard Moore, Jr. said that he could never accuse Arnason of being unfair, but that after Leo's entry into the case, the judge seemed more fair. Arnason didn't jump through any hoops for Branton, but he did seem to be a bit more accommodating to the defense in minor decisions which tended to make things a little easier for them. By then the mass movement in support of Angela had been developed. Undoubtedly Leo Branton, Jr. did impress Judge Arnason, but the judge could not help but be impressed by the parallel effort outside the courtroom which brought letters, telegrams and telephone calls to his desk in protest or support of specifics related to the trial. He was constantly being reminded that every decision he made was being observed by a multitude of people.

The courtroom defense combination was impressive to look at. Four women and two men, arrayed around two tables pushed together to form an L. Branton would generally sit with his back to the audience, facing the judge from the end of the table closest to the prosecution. Howard Moore, Jr. would more often be at the other table, facing the jury. The seating arrangements for any day shifted, depending on what the attorneys were doing that day and which of them had to consult with whom.

Margaret Burnham tended to sit facing the jury and at the end closest to the judge. This seat was less convenient for getting up to address the court, something which Miss Burnham seldom did. She's an effective advocate and judges have discovered that at least one soft, deep brown, small and rounded attorney could hold her own against their occupational compulsion to run the show. Margaret, who started making appearances for Miss Davis in New York, handled some of the pre-trial examination of witnesses testifying about Santa Clara's method of selecting jurors, with emphasis on the discriminatory effects of the process. Doris Walker more often sat beside or near Leo Branton, Jr. Angela and Kendra Alexander generally sat somewhere in between the attorneys. They were a colorful group on a variety of levels: their multi-hued and attention-getting clothing, the variations in skin color, their individual modes of attentiveness to the proceedings, ranging from intense to casual, and the fact that they all seemed fired by their own self-assured animation. And truly, one of the reasons the defense seemed so colorful was that the prosecution was so colorless.

Occasionally there were one or two state investigators, but for most of the trial it was Albert Harris and Deputy Attorney General Clifford Thompson, who sat representing the people. Harris is just shy of being stocky, escapes being short by two inches, has short clipped, greying hair rigidly restrained from finding its natural curl, and a kind of sincere, bumbling manner.

"You wouldn't be prejudiced because Miss Davis has four attorneys and the people are just represented by Mr. Thompson and myself?" Harris once asked a potential juror with a perfectly straight face. Here is a man with the resources of the most populous and wealthiest state in the union behind him, making sure a juror understands that both sides are really equal, even if there are four of them and two of us, and meaning every word of it.

Harris was the prosecutor for the people, who stood stolidly, legs slightly apart, and appeared sincere. He'd apologize because he wasn't as literary as some defense attorneys, seemed slightly overwhelmed by detail—"You never know exactly where to start. But I think that it will make a little more sense if we start on August 7," explaining to both judge and jury that his function was to help them reach a decision. He is one of the more important people in the Attorney General's state-wide apparatus as head of the criminal division, but in court, Harris projected himself as a hard working people's attorney who couldn't be sure about a lot of details, but was clear on the larger picture, Angela's guilt.

His assistant, Cliff Thompson, is comparatively young, tall and broad shouldered. He's described as brilliant, a hard worker and a good attorney, skilled in researching legal particulars. He and Mike Tigar—who, with longish hair, a totally mod approach to dress and a radical approach to law, is almost a direct opposite of Thompson—were classmates at Boalt Hall and jointly produced the school law review while sharing academic honors. The difference in physical appearance between Thompson and Tigar was essentially superficial. What stands out when comparing the two is the assistant prosecutor's tolerance for racism.

Howard Moore, Jr. and Angela Davis walked out of court one day in an angry reaction to Thompson's racially linked constructions. This was in June, in Marin County, where Thompson was arguing against a defense motion for an evidentiary hearing to explore the ways in which the Marin County Grand Jury selection system eliminated blacks. The two left at the point that Thompson was insisting that the presence of one black man on the Grand Jury [the second black in that body's entire history] represented black over-representation in proportion to their numbers in the county. There are only 2% blacks in the county, he explained, and 5.5% blacks on the 19-member panel.

Howard left his seat. "I'd like to be excused, because this kind of racism is very upsetting."

"I'd like to leave myself," Angela said, and the two spent the rest of the session talking to each other in the holding cell.

The walkout was inspired by an earlier comment in which Thompson, in comparing the qualities needed in a petit juror as opposed to a grand juror, stressed the need for intelligent, well educated people as grand jurors. The obvious implication of his remarks was that it was hard to find blacks in Marin County who had the intelligence and education necessary to qualify them for Grand Jury membership.

Thompson lost this argument, incidentally, and an evidentiary hearing, in which Marin County judges were subpoenaed to testify about the criterion they used to select potential Grand Jury members whom they recommend.

Thompson routinely denied the charge that he was racist, while arguing in defense of practices that systematically exclude minorities. Thompson has an arrogance that is masked somewhat by his straining for the sincere way of addressing people so perfected by his boss.

He cross examined Ralph Guzman, Ph.D., a University of California professor, who had been director of the Peace Corps in Venezuela and Peru, has written several books, and is a leading authority on all aspects of Spanish-American life, Chicanos in particular. Dr. Guzman had conducted exhaustive research into names, to make certain that the euphemism "Spanish-surname," used to authenticate non-discrimination against Chicanos and Puerto Ricans and Latinos, were honest. Dr. Guzman was testifying about the lack of Spanish speaking people on juries, noting that: "We did not find any instance, anywhere, where Chicanos are registered to vote in proportion to their numbers in the population." This was part of testimony on behalf of the defense, showing why Angela was likely to end up with an all white jury.

Thompson, exhibiting signs of the "my maid told me so it must be so" syndrome associated with certain kinds of expertise on racial and ethnic matters, tried to tell Guzman, through questioning, that the term "Chicano" was a pejorative used by Mexican Americans to describe militants. Guzman informed him this was not true.

Harris and Thompson worked well together, and although they were built entirely differently, somehow in their quiet greys and blues, their assumption of the total correctness of the prosecution position, and in their autonomic defense of all law enforcement agency actions, they seemed to be one and the same person.

Before the trial began, Margaret Burnham argued that the methods used to select a jury in Santa Clara County tended to exclude the poor and the non-white, classes of people who would understand Angela's situation and be better capable of judging her guilt or innocence. The Panther 21 in New York were acquitted, she argued, because there were a sizeable proportion of blacks on the jury who understood the problem of police agents running around the black community acting as provocateurs.

She referred to the Detroit trial of James Johnson, who shot and killed his foreman in the middle of a speedup on the assembly line. There were 46% blacks in Detroit, many of whom worked in the assembly plants, some of whom were on the jury. They could understand his "not guilty by reason of insanity" plea, based on the contention that the conditions on the job drove him mad. Johnson was acquitted. She described the percentage of non-whites on the jury panel as "outrageous" and asked that a new list be drawn up that was based on the licensed drivers in the county rather than the registered voters. "Miss Davis should not be tried by a jury hobbled with the stumbling block of racism."

"The concept of peer group representation is anathema to American concepts," Thompson replied. He explained that a 10% disparity between the number of non-whites in the county, and those represented on the jury panel, was entirely reasonable.

All of this was skirmish, the court battle was yet to come. Judge Arnason listened to it all; he denied a change of venue motion, turned down the request that Angela's attorneys be paid by the state, dismissed the challenge to the trial jury panel selection system [while assuring that 18- to 21-year-olds would be on the panel], refused the defense request that the prosecutor turn over any information in his possession that dealt with prospective jurors, and set the trial date for February 28. By that time the jail facilities being built for Angela in San Jose would be ready. But Angela never stayed in that jail.

On Friday, February 18, the California Supreme Court declared that the death penalty violated the California Constitution. According to everyone, including the Prosecutor, this made Angela eligible for bail. Harris argued that Angela should not be released for 30 days, the time it took for the Supreme Court decision to become final. Judge Arnason disagreed, saying that no useful purpose would be served by keeping Angela in jail for an additional month. She was released on $102,500 bail February 23, under heavy restrictions. She had to live in San Jose, in a court-approved residence, restrict travel to the six San Francisco Bay Area counties, not travel by air, report weekly to a probation officer and not attend any meetings or rallies without express permission of the court.

There had been a number of protests about the elimination of the death penalty which led to Angela's release. When Evelle Younger became aware that the California Supreme Court was going to rule on the question of capital punishment, he asked the court to delay its ruling until the US Supreme Court had ruled on the same question. The court ignored him. Then, after the ruling, Younger asked the US Supreme Court to delay the effectiveness of the California decision, until it announced its decision. The court refused to do this. Younger then asked the California Supreme Court to reconsider its opinion and was rebuffed again.

It turned out that Younger had anticipated that the court might rule against the death penalty and had attempted to get Justice Marshall McComb, the oldest member of the court in both age and years of service, as well as the most conservative, to utilize Younger's wording in the formation of a hoped-for dissenting opinion.

"I respectfully request your Honor to consider incorporating our petition into an opinion . . . in view of the vital importance of the court's ruling to the public and the public's need to be fully informed of the various ramifications of the decision."

McComb did not acknowledge the letter, and never wrote a dissenting opinion. Younger, however, continued fighting for the retention of the death penalty. A drive to restore the death penalty headed by police officers and prison guards was given support by presidential advisor Robert H. Finch, who had been Lt. Governor of California during Reagan's first term. Finch suggested that the penalty be kept for slayers of prison guards and criminals who kill during the commission of a felony. Younger wrote the initiative measure which was placed on the November ballot and which won. An interesting feature of the proposition was that its language forbade any court to rule in the future on the constitutionality of the death penalty.

If Prosecutor Harris had won his argument and convinced Arnason not to release Angela for 30 days, the trial might have been completed with her in jail. By striking down the death penalty, the California Supreme Court made a man named Juan Corona also eligible for bail. Corona was charged with killing 25 itinerant workers. His attorney filed an application for bail just days before Attorney General Younger asked the Supreme Court to "clarify" its decision as it applied to bail in what had been capital cases.

The court essentially upheld the Troia decision, an 1883 California Supreme Court decision which denied bail to those accused of capital crimes "where the presumption is strong or the evidence thereof great." The court said that while it had outlawed the

death penalty, it had preserved the law allowing judges to deny
bail in those cases once punishable by death.

The bail question was back in Judge Arnason's hands as the
court had upheld the constitutionality of a law which he had
previously cited as the reason for not granting Angela bail. Arnason
had told Angela in June 1971 that the only reason he did not
grant bail was that the law prevented him from doing so. He
didn't expect a higher court to change the law. Faced with the
fact that the court's clarification of their death penalty ruling had
not changed the law, Arnason had to decide what he was going to
do.

Albert Harris had predicted that if Angela were freed on bail
she would never be seen again. "When she is released she might
as well be given an air travel card along with her possessions."
Harris fought hard to keep her in jail at a point when it was
obvious that she was entitled to be let out, and was ready to move
to have Angela's bail revoked. The only reason he did not was that
his superior, Attorney General Evelle Younger, told him not to.
What happened? It was Younger's department that was trying its
best to convict Angela.

Why he took this position is a matter for speculation. The defense committee's official stand is that the mass movement that
was built around Angela paid off in the matter of bail. They said
that Judge Arnason and the Attorney General's office was del-
uged with thousands of letters, telegrams and phone calls demanding that Angela be freed.

There was one report that Leo Branton, Jr. called an old political ally in Los Angeles who had some influence with Evelle
Younger and persuaded him not to disturb the orderly process of
the trial by demanding that Angela be returned to jail.

Detractors of Angela Davis on the left thought they detected
a clear political deal. They reasoned that the case against her was
pitifully weak, and was designed as a safety valve to bleed off
political energy from the general struggle for liberation. Under this
theory, the posture of the state was to keep Angela in apparent
peril, but not to go overboard. This group was particularly incensed over Angela's move separating her trial from that of Ruchell
Magee.

Magee, they said, was a relative unknown and a man whose defense involved much more of a basic challenge to accepted due process than those issues raised by Angela and her attorneys. Angela, they explained, because of her politics, was obligated to maintain the legal connection with Ruchell Magee that the state had originally imposed on her. It was easy for Angela to demonstrate the bankruptcy of the state's case against her. It was her political duty, therefore, not to separate herself ideologically from Jonathan Jackson. A political defense would mean that Angela asserted Jonathan's right to do what he did, but would declare herself innocent of complicity with the act. Since she was not complicit with Jonathan she could not be so with Ruchell, and she, therefore, should have placed all of the resources at her disposal in the service of Ruchell Magee.

Whatever the case, the release of Angela on bail was one of the turning points in the trial. She was free to participate fully in the legal defense and also in the political campaign waged around her plea of not guilty. She was free to pursue her case, but with the release on bail, questions about her relationship to Ruchell Magee, Jonathan Jackson and politicians who have the power to pull strings, began to plague her.

7 : Casting Call

Cast completion began February 28, 1972, the first day of jury selection. The prospect was for an all white jury, with women in the majority and low income persons all but eliminated. The possibility of blacks being selected was dim. There was only a 2% black population in the county and they had registered to vote in smaller numbers than whites. Similarly, few Mexican-Americans could be expected to serve. Santa Clara County had approximately 18% Chicanos, but they comprised no more than 8% of the registered voters.

There was a chance that people under 21 would serve on the jury. Judge Arnason had ordered that the 15,000 to 20,000 18 to 20 year olds who had been registered to vote be included in the list of registered voters screened for jury duty in the case. At the time of his order in December, 1971, no one under 21 was legally eligible to serve on a jury. But, the law extending the vote to 18 year olds, which coincidentally made them eligible for jury duty, would be in effect by the time a jury was selected.

The defense had challenged the practice of selecting jurors from the voter registration lists. They introduced testimony which included a comparison of five high average income election precincts with five with low average income. It was discovered that 12,375 people in the richer areas produced 56 prospective jurors. By contrast, the five low income areas, though having 2,000 more people, contributed only 16 possible jurors. This, and other related facts, were not considered by Judge Arnason to be indicative of discriminatory selection processes.

A panel of 175 people were notified to report to a two room jury assembly area that was equipped with closed circuit television. One hundred and sixteen showed up. Most of the others were covered by letters from doctors, lawyers or employers explaining their absence.

Jury selection was expected to take up to two months, with the possibility that it would require even more than the record five months which had exhausted a list of 5,000 potential jurors in the Bobby Seale case in New Haven. Arnason was prepared to avoid, if at all possible, such a time-consuming selection process.

He carefully scrutinized every written request that a person be excused from serving, and demanded from most of those who appeared in court asking to be excused, some document supporting their claim that medical, financial or other severe disadvantage would attend their serving on a jury. Arnason also refused to dismiss any potential juror for cause unless that person specifically declared that he or she could not judge the defendant fairly. A measure of the character of the jury panel can be gathered by the fact that only the defense found reason to challenge any of the potential jurors for cause. Not one of the approximately 70 people who were questioned in court gave the prosecutor any reason to challenge them because he thought they were biased against the state's position.

None of the possible jurors admitted to being racially prejudiced, or suggested that their ability to judge Angela fairly might be inhibited by their knowledge that she could be described as a black militant and called herself a revolutionary. But, when it came to communism, a significant number of those interviewed said that they couldn't judge a communist fairly.

Leo Branton, Jr. and Howard Moore, Jr. handle themselves with the authority of men who are accustomed to convincing women to have confidence in what they say. They have developed two different styles of courtliness bordering on a promise of gentle seduction which gets them over hurdles with many of the women jurors they have to deal with in court. Neither of them had any success in convincing a number of potential jurors, particularly the women, that they ought not hold Angela's membership in the Communist Party against her.

Jurors were examined in two stages. The first was an individual interview to determine whether the prospective juror had been so affected by pre-trial publicity that they could not discard previously

held opinions and judge the case according to the evidence presented. That phase was completed when 12 tentatively accepted
jurors were in the box. At that point they were questioned in depth
about any prejudicial attitudes they might have.

Albert Harris maintained that Angela Davis was on trial for
kidnapping, murder and conspiracy, and not because of her political affiliations. He therefore objected to jurors being questioned
about their attitudes toward communism and communists, particularly in the first phase of the selection which dealt with pre-trial
publicity. He was overruled, but even had he not been, it would
probably have been impossible to prevent the display of anti-communist opinion which was exhibited.

Howard Moore, Jr. for instance, quizzed a very attractive 22-
year-old electronic worker dressed in a red, white and blue mini-
skirt. At the beginning she seemed fairly liberal and easygoing. She
listed *Playboy* among the magazines she read, to the laughing approval of some of the men in the courtroom, who apparently would
have preferred the juror to be part of their reading material.

No, she didn't have racial prejudice. She told Moore that she
watched Flip Wilson on television and enjoyed him immensely.
Angela Davis? Yes, she'd read about her in connection with August
7. Also had heard of her before "when she was in Los Angeles
teaching." When asked whether Angela's party affiliation would
affect her decision in the case, the young lady admitted that it
might make a "slight difference." She was against communism, but
her feelings were weak. Howard probed a little more and extracted
the opinion that, "They want something different from the normal
way of life for me," and that her ability to judge a communist
could, possibly would, affect her judgment in the case.

Moore then asked Judge Arnason to dismiss the juror for cause
and had the request denied. Prosecutor Harris, who had no objection to an anti-communist being on the jury, then asked "Do you
feel as you sit here today that you can undertake and perform this
duty fairly?" "No" was the response. Her anti-communism would
be in the way. She was excused.

A retired trucker was tentatively passed for jury duty. "Did your
exposure to what you read or saw in the media lead you to form
an opinion about Miss Davis' guilt or innocence?"

"I didn't form any opinion on anything." He'd just glanced at the papers and paid no attention to it, "it didn't mean nothing to me." The trucker didn't know why Angela was fired from UCLA, but he did know she belonged to the Communist Party.

"Do you have any prejudices against communism?"

The trucker sat there, stolid, unyielding, with a scowl that had accompanied him in a thousand table stakes poker games and intimidated dispatchers seeking to send him on a run he didn't like.

"I don't like them!" His previous casual attitude was transformed almost into rage. "They ought to go back where they came from. I'm native born and I like this country."

"Would the fact that Miss Davis is a communist cause you to think less of her than other persons?"

"In that respect, yes."

"Mr. Waugh, why don't you like communists?"

Albert Harris objected and it was sustained, but Waugh was not about to stop.

"Why should I? You're talking all communist, you're not talking a murder trial . . . you can take it any way you want."

He later told Harris that Angela could get a fair hearing from him. The defense did not have to eliminate him because the trucker decided after sitting in the box for a day that he could not conveniently serve on the jury.

Seven women and five men were ultimately selected, most of whom expressed decided anti-communist feelings. They satisfied the defense attorneys, however, that their convictions against communism would not affect their ability to judge Angela solely on the evidence produced in court, based on the criterion set down in the instructions given them by Judge Arnason.

The prosecution and the defense insisted that they were searching for jurors who could give both sides a fair trial, but that is so much talk. The idea of a fair jury, held by both prosecution and defense, was a collection of 12 people who would deliver the verdict they were asking for. They each had a definite idea about the kinds of people they wanted, and did not want on the jury, and the opportunity to eliminate those they felt might judge adversely.

Although the death penalty had been declared unconstitutional, the concept of the capital crime had been left intact by the California Supreme Court. This meant that every trial involving an offense formerly punishable by death afforded both defense and prosecution 20 preemptory challenges, 40 opportunities to eliminate jurors that they did not like with no questions asked. This is in addition to those prospects whom they can convince the judge to excuse because of bias demonstrated during the voir dire.

A voir dire, the process of examining prospective jurors to determine bias, is used to do more than ascertain juror impartiality. Opposing attorneys use the opportunity of examining jurors to condition a jury to their point of view. In any vigorously contested case the attorneys will not settle for a jury until they are satisfied that the panel contains a couple of jurors with fairly strong personalities whom they can count on to fight for conviction or acquittal after the evidence is in. Their willingness to settle for the balance of the jury being fair and impartial is compromised by a determination to let no one serve whom they feel is totally beyond their persuasive powers.

Harris had a decided advantage. He knew that the majority of the jurors would be white, with better than average incomes and a predictable uneasiness about communism and violence. He could be certain that many of them, including those who owned firearms, would have feelings of apprehension about a black communist who called herself a revolutionary, and who owned two carbines, a shotgun and an automatic pistol. He knew that whites generally react negatively to more than surface probings of their racial attitudes and that most people are offended by a line of questioning which implies that they cannot be fair to a defendant. One of his tasks in examing the jurors was to capitalize on their uneasiness by stressing the virtues of the system of justice of which they were a part, implying that the defendant has less loyalty to that system than they do.

He did this by repeatedly assuring the prospective jurors that he didn't really question their ability to be fair, and by trying to demonstrate through his questions [and objections to the defense questions] that the defense was raising political and social issues in an attempt to avoid the fact that this is a criminal trial.

Harris had sought further advantage by arguing in chambers that the jury should be death qualified, meaning that jurors opposed to

the death penalty should be automatically eliminated. Death qualified juries tend to convict. The defense did not have much difficulty
in convincing Judge Arnason that a death qualified jury in a case
which could not result in an execution was totally inappropriate.

The defense sought advantage also, and managed to offset some
of the handicaps presented by having the case tried in Santa Clara
County. They mounted an effort to find out as much as possible
about the prospective jurors in advance of their being selected. A
team of six investigators, headed by an attorney from Detroit who
had been involved in a similar but less ambitious effort in Michi-
gan, investigated the first two venire panels, or about 350 people.

They checked the voter rolls for party affiliation, searched to see
if any of the potential jurors had signed petitions indicating a liberal or conservative bias, and looked for evidence of anti or pro
opinions on the war in Vietnam. Did the prospective juror live in
an integrated neighborhood? Had the panel member signed to have
the Peace and Freedom Party or the American Independent Party
on the ballot in 1968? Were they thought to be liberal or conservative in their political views? Were they active in struggles to introduce or eliminate bussing for integration? Was there anything about
their movements in the community that would help the defense
guess that they might be predisposed to be for or against Angela
Davis?

In addition, the defense utilized the services of five black psychologists who attended every jury selection session. "We could
not have selected this jury without this help," Howard Moore, Jr.
explained at an annual meeting of the National Association of Black
Psychologists, which met in San Francisco two months after the
trial had ended. Thomas Hilliard, one of the psychologists involved,
read a paper describing the process they went through. Both Moore
and Hilliard seemed to be advising black psychologists that they
could play a professional role in the courtroom by helping attorneys
sharpen their skills in jury selection.

The psychologists watched all of the prospective jurors, the associations they made with other panel members, and the way questions were answered. In some instances the questions asked by defense attorneys had been provided by the psychologists. "Our belief
was that a juror's voting is influenced not only by the court evidence

and his own attitude," Hilliard explained, "but by the interaction of his personality and the group dynamics in the jury room."

Defense attorneys made the final decision to accept or reject a juror, and some of those decisions were reached without any consultation, but they made those decisions from a more informed base than they normally would have had.

This defense program contributed greatly to the speed with which the jury was chosen. The defense settled for a jury at the point that they were convinced that the remainder of the panel contained so many poor risks that they would be well advised to go with what they had.

The defense obviously knew what they were doing. Approximately 40 people were questioned at some length during the nine days it took to select 12 jurors. A number of jurors were eliminated for cause, and the prosecutor used three preemptory challenges and the defense two. About 30 interviews and four days were required to choose four alternate jurors. Here the prosecutor used two preemptive challenges, while the defense had five of the panel excused for cause and used six additional preemptive challenges.

The entire selection process, while relatively short for a trial of this nature, was intense, fiercely combative and conducted on a variety of levels. Angela's attorneys, in addition to probing for attitudes which betrayed the possibility of racial or political prejudice against Angela, were intent upon impressing prospective jurors with the presumption of innocence that envelopes a defendant. They would stress the fact that it was the prosecutor's job to prove Angela guilty, and not their job to prove her innocent. All prospective jurors, however favorably disposed toward Angela they seemed, were severly challenged when their answers implied that they expected Angela to explain about her guns, her reason for leaving California, her relationship to either or both of the Jackson brothers, or any other matter.

Harris, on the other hand, would emphasize the nature of the charges, make certain that the jurors had no reservations about reaching a guilty verdict based on circumstantial evidence and extracted a promise from each of them to give the state a fair hearing.

Howard Moore, Jr. and Albert Harris conducted symbolic battle with each other on a chalkboard which both of them used to illustrate their positions. It started with Harris diagramming the charges against Angela, explaining such terms as conspiracy, aiding and abetting, rescue and escape. Moore erased some of the diagram, drawing broad stripes which he said represented the presumption of innocence which the prosecutor had to erase with convincing evidence. After a time, Harris obliged the defense attorney by erasing part of Moore's chalk line and reconstructing his diagram.

As the questioning of jurors proceeded, each of the attorneys seemed to settle down to using half the board. But then Moore moved over to Harris' side of the board. He had been using the words "frameup" to describe the prosecution case, and drew a rectangle around Harris' diagram saying that the presumption of innocence framed the charges.

Harris resorted to an eraser, then Moore added the word "GUESS" in large letters immediately above the charges. The prosecutor responded by saying that he was certain that the jury would not have to guess at the verdict and could easily find the defendant "guilty," a word he then wrote across Moore's latest addition.

At the next opportunity, Moore expressed his belief that the jury would find his client not guilty, and placed the "not" in front of Harris' "guilty." Harris then withdrew from the competition, assuring the panel that he was not going back to the board. And for the rest of the trial he wrote not one word.

This battle of the chalkboard was extended over three days, during which time the struggle over jurors became downright contentious. The trips to the board, while obviously a part of the serious business of examining jurors, provided each of the attorneys with an opportunity to get a point across, while relieving some of the tension caused by their competition.

Several people whom Harris hoped would be on the jury had been excused because of prejudicial statements or confessions of an inability to judge Angela Davis fairly. He had also been helpless in preventing a prospective juror whom he wanted from withdrawing.

Robert E. McCarty, the Assistant Manager of Corporate Taxes for the Southern Pacific Transportation Company, where he had been employed for 31 years, seemed an ideal prosecution-prone juror. His anti-communism was properly restrained. McCarty felt that a communist could legitimately teach students (an opinion not shared by many of his fellow panel members). But he said that the communist should stick to teaching mathematics, engineering or some other exact science and should be barred from teaching philosophy, economics or political science. He expressed the opinion that communists were a threat to America, that there were situations where he could not separate the threat he felt communism posed to the nation from a sense of personal threat, but he persisted in saying that he could give Angela a fair trial.

McCarty responded to a question dealing with August 7 with the observation that he was amazed that it was so easy for armed people to get into a courtroom. He said that he felt that the perpetrators should be prosecuted and punished to the full extent of the law, and then quickly added, "only after a fair trial."

"I have to say that Miss Davis in my opinion is innocent until we—she's proven guilty . . . When she departed the state I had my doubts . . . They were not convincing doubts."

Moore maneuvered McCarty into shouting "Free Angela" three times at the top of his lungs, a performance which in retrospect probably shocked Mr. McCarty. He showed up the next day with a letter from Southern Pacific saying the company could not guarantee his salary beyond two weeks.

"After 31 years?," Harris was unbelieving, but he was really not in a position to challenge decisions made by Southern Pacific.

The struggle for jurors settled down to a battle involving three people: Howard Atkinson, a semi-retired contractor; William Hotaling, a manager for IBM, and Janie Hemphill, a black housewife.

Moore was doing his best to have Atkinson disqualify himself. Leo Branton, Jr. was working on Hotaling, and Harris had the job of eliminating Janie Hemphill. Atkinson, a large, well-manicured, self-assured man, was the first of the three to be questioned. He and Howard Moore, Jr. clashed immediately in the pre-trial publicity phase when Atkinson said that Angela had received too much publicity. Moore could not get Atkinson to define what he meant. He felt that if Atkinson explained himself he would expose attitudes which could lead to dismissal for cause.

Hotaling followed Atkinson, and was examined by Leo Branton, Jr. He had read that Angela had been fired, "something to do with the way she provoked people on campus."

"Did what you read about Angela Davis or the Communist Party cause you to form an opinion?"

"Yes . . . I think that anyone who is a member of the Communist Party is against the government of the US."

"Did it cause you to form an opinion that was adverse to Miss Davis?"

"Yes."

Hotaling admitted to Branton that he was prejudiced against all communists, and could not give Angela a fair trial. But when Harris asked him, "Could you decide solely, based on evidence produced in court?" Hotaling fell in line and stopped making prejudicial statements.

"I would base my decision on the facts," he declared. "He (Branton) kept using communist in all his statements, but the way you put it, I can."

Branton challenged Hotaling again: "Do you believe it is possible to unhear a sound?" Harris objected. "Maybe I should have said unring a bell," countered Branton. But the attorney did not persist in his questioning.

He later asked Hotaling: "Don't you believe that commies would cheat and lie and do anything to overthrow the US government?"

Hotaling said that he thought anyone who would take radical action, "commie or non-commie" would lie. But later he modified this opinion saying that, "just because a person is a communist doesn't mean that they are dishonest." Branton asked Arnason to excuse Hotaling on the basis of his "communists are liars" statement. Arnason took the request under submission, read the transcript overnight, and the next day denied the motion.

Arnason apparently couldn't stand the tension generated by the examination of jurors, particularly the casual acceptance implied by defense questioning that there would be no non-whites on the jury. The judge lost his usual urbane and assured demeanor, skipped over two of the waiting jurors, and instructed the bailiff to bring in Mrs. Hemphill. Then, realizing the mistake he had made, he rearranged the entire schedule for the sake of consistency, and left the two people he had skipped over to wait for an even longer period before being questioned.

Janie Hemphill, a dark, brown-skinned woman, was decidedly not radical. She came to court wearing a maroon coat with a patch on one of the lapels reading "Have a Good Day." She had three children, 10, 12 and 13, whom she felt would not create difficulty if she had to spend three to six months as a juror. She told Howard Moore, Jr. that, "I'm not very political or things like that," saying that she knew nothing of Angela Davis until her husband had brought her up to date a few days before, "and it didn't stick."

Harris wasn't impressed. He tried to convince Hemphill, through questioning, that she might be concerned during a long trial about her children, but Mrs. Hemphill insisted that the children could get along very well without her. All of the time that Harris was questioning her, Cliff Thompson, who normally sat quietly when his boss was working, kept trying to bring Harris' attention to some notes that were on the table before him. Harris ignored Thompson and Hemphill tentatively passed.

A week later, with six of the jurors who would ultimately judge the case temporarily seated, it became Hotaling, Atkinson and Hemphill's turn to be questioned in depth. Atkinson owned weapons and said he had no objection to communists doing the same. He said he regularly hired black carpenters and that he would rent to blacks if they paid the rent. Moore hammered away at Atkinson, who refused to give the attorney any reason to eliminate him without a challenge. While Atkinson refused to be more specific in his charge that Angela Davis received too much publicity, he qualified his statement by noting a problem in the general handling of the news.

"Mr. Atkinson, do you want to serve on this jury?"

"Not necessarily."

"It's his duty," snapped Harris, growing impatient with the questioning.

Atkinson said that he would not hold Angela's friendly relations with the Black Panther Party against her. He did not definitely link the Panthers with riots, but did associate violence and the Panthers. He said, with obvious satisfaction, that he no longer considered them a danger, because he thought that their weapons had been confiscated. He felt that communism was a system in which people work for the state, but that there were different kinds of communists. "Russia likes to control the world, the Chinese are something else again." He thought that Chinese communism had no ambitions outside China.

"How would you feel as a juror if Miss Davis did not take the stand?"

"I think I would want her to testify, to explain. I think I would like to hear her side . . . I might wonder why didn't she take the stand."

The questioning of Atkinson was ended.

Hotaling maintained his composure, but was extremely upset at Branton's unrelenting attack implying he was unfair. "I know myself better than anyone in this court," he said, "and I am able to judge this case fairly."

Hotaling regained a grip on himself and began answering questions in a way that Branton could not challenge.

"Do you believe she was a member of a plot to free the Soledad Brothers?"

"Not necessarily."

"Can you believe she genuinely believes blacks are in prison because of a racist judicial system?"

"I think some are there for that reason."

The answer didn't quite mesh with Hotaling's earlier inability to find racism in California. Branton asked Hotaling:

"Would you be satisfied to be tried by 12 black people with your state of mind?" Hotaling thought awhile and answered, "Yes, if they were fair minded."

"Would you be willing to be tried by 12 communists?" Hotaling couldn't hack that. He was willing to let one communist on his jury, if he were fair minded.

"You don't believe I can find 12 fair minded communists do you, and that's the guts of the issue."

"I'm not willing to have 12 communists try me. I want a jury of 12 fair minded people who have been questioned as deeply as you are questioning me."

"Would you be satisfied to be tried by 12 black communist women?" was Branton's relentless followup.

Hotaling just sat there, staring at the witness stand to the left of the jury box, imagining himself in there, projecting a black woman in his seat, and other blacks, looking like Angela Davis, filling up the jury box. The courtroom was silent for a long time. "I'd take my chances, yes," was the almost inaudible answer.

Branton unsuccessfully argued to Judge Arnason that Hotaling should be dismissed.

Harris, who had devoted perhaps two minutes to the questioning of Atkinson, was more brief with Hotaling.

"Could you accept the proposition that Angela Davis, then 26 years old, a professor at UCLA, a center of world-wide attention, a professor who had been to the Sorbonne and studied in Frankfurt, could you accept the fact that she could conspire with a 17 year old from Blair High School who had never finished high school, in fact never attended an institution of higher learning?"

Hotaling said he could, and his voir dire was completed.

The next day Howard Moore, Jr. gently questioned Janie Hemphill. He exchanger comments with her about picking cotton, and had her describe her life as part of a large family (five boys and four girls) who traveled over the southwest with their parents as migrant farm workers. She'd come to San Jose 17 years before, not long after her family had settled down near Fresno, the same area where Roger McAfee, a rich farmer who put up the bail for Angela, was living. Mrs. Hemphill represented the ideal juror to the defense. She began working when she was 12 years old in Arizona. She had been a short order cook, had worked in a sandwich factory, as a domestic worker and as a dishwasher, among other jobs.

The defense had previously complained bitterly because of the paucity of working people available to serve on the jury. Branton had demanded that Judge Arnason order jurors compensated at a rate greater than $5.00 a day, so that working people could afford to be part of the trial. The request was refused. Moore, in his questioning, was actually demonstrating how ideal such a juror might be. He asked about her family, whether it was close knit and had managed to stay together through all the difficult times they had experienced. Mrs. Hemphill said they had.

"You still believe in this country, don't you?"

There was a long pause before the answer, "yes."

She said she had no feeling toward communism and knew nothing about it.

"You won't be swayed by subjective factors, so as to show you are fair and unbiased you'll lean over backwards and convict Miss Davis?"

"No," was the response, and his questioning had ended.

Throughout the trial Harris had been referring to himself as "the people," and explaining to the prospective jurors that he represented the people of California. Branton had once grown tired of this approach, and reminded the jury that Harris was the representative of the Attorney General, and that "the people" was nothing other than a formal term. But the prosecutor began his questioning of Mrs. Hemphill by informing her that the term "the people" was descriptive, and another way of saying "it is the State of California that is charging Miss Davis."

Having firmly established that he represented the state, the prosecutor then quizzed Janie Hemphill about her reaction to the defense questioning of Atkinson and Hotaling. Did she feel resentment toward Moore and Branton because they asked difficult questions? No. It's their duty to ask those questions, they're just representing their client, Harris confirmed, and Janie Hemphill nodded in agreement.

The prosecutor moved a little closer to the jury box. He assumed, he told the prospective juror, that if she did not resent defense attorney questions to other jury members, that she would not resent the nature of his inquiry. Harris didn't deal with the question of race, and perhaps he should have. He had heard Margaret Burnham argue that the reason for a number of acquittals of blacks had been the presence of blacks on their juries. It would certainly have been a reasonable enough approach to determine whether Mrs. Hemphill, because she was black, would give undue consideration to Angela Davis.

There was a possibility that in exploring her racial attitudes, formed in a lifetime of hard work within the racist restrictions common to Oklahoma, Texas, Arkansas, and Arizona, where she had followed the crops for so long, he could imply that Janie Hemphill harbored deep seated prejudices of her own. He also might have chosen to question her superficially, and at some point in the future eliminate her from the jury. Instead, he engaged her, accused her of being prejudiced against the state because of an action that had been filed against her and her husband by the California Alcoholic Beverage Control Board (ABC).

Harris explained that in cases where a prospective juror was engaged in a legal controversy with the state, it was necessary that the prosecutor discover whether that disagreement would result in prejudice against the state. Mrs. Hemphill said that she knew of no legal controversy between herself and the state, thinking that Harris might be referring to a lawsuit brought by creditors. But Harris was after something else, and he came up with it, probably in the papers that Cliff Thompson had been trying to show him the week before, which he now handed to Mrs. Hemphill.

Harris is good. He has cultivated the lack of color almost to the point of virtue. He is sincere, not quite as informed as he'd like to be, but definitely in command of the larger picture. That's the image he projects, and to a large extent, the person he actually is. During the entire session with Mrs. Hemphill, Harris was sincerely apologetic, not quite in command of detail, desperately, almost painfully, trying to get to the truth of Mrs. Hemphill's possible prejudice toward the state.

Harris knew what he was going to do. He knew about Huey Newton, the Panther 13 in Los Angeles, Martin Sostre, the Soledad Brothers, and probably a host of politically oriented cases that have, and are being processed through the courts. Harris knew that neither the state, nor federal government, had reached the point where they were sure that a jury in a well publicized, politically oriented case, would convict. He needed all the help he could get, and he knew that none of it was likely to come from blacks. Mrs. Hemphill had to go.

Janie Hemphill has one of those faces which give no hint as to what she is experiencing emotionally. When she read the papers

Harris had handed her, her mouth changed shape slightly, her eyes slowly went back to Harris, and she understood what was being done.

The Hemphills had opened a beer and wine club in San Jose in July 1971. Mr. Hemphill had always made a living. He hung sheet-rock in the subdivisions that bloom in California like bacteria on a warm slide, and could always get a job that paid enough to support his family. But he wanted, and worked for, more. The beer garden, like the management of a liquor store sometime before, represented a step toward that something more. In September, San Jose police raided the place, and arrested Mr. Hemphill for running a gambling game. In December he pleaded guilty, was fined and placed on probation.

The Hemphills abandoned the club after the arrest. They had been losing money, and had reached the point where they could only afford to keep the club open on weekends, when business was best. The arrest cost them even more money, promised to cut business further, so they put a padlock on the door and walked away.

In the latter part of December, the Hemphills received a notice from the ABC to renew their beer and wine license. They ignored it, they didn't need a license when they weren't running a club. Meanwhile, the ABC had received a routine notice about Mr. Hemphill's arrest and conviction. They scheduled a hearing to determine whether the conviction, which also violated ABC regulations, should result in the revocation of the Hemphill's beer and wine license.

Mrs. Hemphill didn't know what her husband did about the hearing. She gave the papers to him and ignored the matter. The impression she left in court was that they did nothing.

Harris claimed that the hearing was still pending, which perhaps it was, three months after service, and that the ABC's notice of hearing constituted evidence that Mrs. Hemphill was involved in a legal contention with the State of California, and therefore was possibly prejudiced. The papers he handed her were a copy of the hearing notice, and an affidavit attesting that the notice had been served.

Mrs. Hemphill outlined the history of the club and her indifference to the hearing. She thought that they did not have a beer and wine license because they had not renewed. It had never occurred to her that the state was moving against something more abstract, their privilege to have a license. And even had that thought occurred to her, she wasn't about to go and fight for an empty privilege. If you didn't have a club, you didn't need a license.

Harris persisted. How could she be fair to the state when she was resenting the state taking away her liquor license. But we closed the club and didn't need the license. No! The state closed the club and you resent it.

Howard Moore, Jr. leapt to his feet, his beard bristling. Howard insisted that the proceedings should be held in chambers.

It was O.K. with Harris, he was willing to move to chambers.

But, Leo Branton, Jr. wasn't going for chambers. He maneuvered to keep the prosecution position out in open court. Branton, snapping his lean body like a whip, insisted that the damage had already been done.

"I resent in the deepest way possible the unforgiveable way Mr. Harris has attempted to embarrass Mrs. Hemphill. This is an example of white racism that we have to deal with."

There had been a white woman prospective juror who had a pending criminal case, who had been allowed to discuss her problems in serving on the jury in chambers. But there was something else, even closer to Harris, whose wife had been a victim of Nazi excesses in World War II. A Hungarian refugee, working in San Jose as a waiter, had a depth of prejudice against communists that would not allow him to be a part of the jury. His feelings were sincere, and Harris, who supposedly shared with the defense counsel compassion for those who feel they have been oppressed, and have the scars to prove it to the sceptical, was willing to spare that European the agony of a court room recitation of the personal reasons why he could not serve.

But it evidentially had not occurred to Harris that perhaps a black woman, caught up in a lottery which decreed that she, and no other black, be called to possibly judge Angela Davis, should be protected from an investigation of her personal life, which, even if it might disqualify her as a juror, should not have prompted gratuitous exposure.

Even if it did occur to him, Harris did not grant that black woman the protection of prosecutorial discretion. Janie Hemphill became part of this case. She was a juror whom the defense wanted. And he, the prosecutor, was in a position to demonstrate that middleclass Angela, with her impending Ph.D., and working class Hemphill, and her convicted gambler husband, were cut from the same cloth—blacks who run afoul of the law.

Branton was aware of the prosecutor's motivation, and was not about to allow the defense to provide an opportunity for Harris to correct an assumed mistake and run off to chambers, leaving the impression behind that he had lost his head in the heat of struggle and committed an unfortunate impropriety. No, tell him he's a racist, point out the consideration that had been afforded whites, and let Harris deal with it in open court.

Harris lashed back at Branton. "I deeply resent your remarks, as a lawyer and a human being." Then, the prosecutor tried to qualify his response. "I am entitled to determine whether this pending action will prejudice her against the state." He said that the previously excused juror had brought the criminal matter up herself, making it easier to handle in chambers.

Both Howard Moore, Jr. and Leo Branton, Jr. had worked, somewhat unsuccessfully, to eliminate two people through self exposure, whom the defense had perceived to be racists. In their failure to disqualify them they had exposed a much more basic and potentially persuasive source of racism in the courtroom—Albert Harris. What Harris was doing to Janie Hemphill, in public, was what they thought Hotaling and Atkinson would do to Angela back in the jury room. And Branton, acting for the defense, allowed him to go on.

There was nothing more to get out of Mrs. Hemphill. Harris went on asking her about the details of the service of the papers by the process server for ABC. Then, possibly suspecting that he'd shown too much power and not enough humility, he asked if Mrs. Hemphill could understand his concern about the need of the state for a fair trial.

"I guess so."

He had to move her now, Harris had to work for the equivalent of a response from Hemphill which could justify his defense that, "well she didn't complain about me calling her nigger, she knew that my heart was pure, and so I don't see why you have any right to criticize me. Mrs. Hemphill understands, even if you don't."

But she did not anoint him with oil of Uncle Tom.

Harris tried logic. "That's been done by Mr. Moore and Mr. Branton any number of times and now it's my turn to do it." Hemphill said she understood, but wouldn't say she could agree with it. Harris then insisted that the evidence of possible prejudice was obvious. "The state has in effect taken your license," giving Mrs. Hemphill a chance to at least say she was aware of his racist tactics.

"I don't think they have a connection," she said, once again completely placid, her battle behind her and only the wait ahead until Harris removed her from the jury, ". . . if you could explain it to me."

Harris went through a long explanation about how the Attorney General represented all state agencies, and that if a matter came to court in an action involving the state, that the Attorney General's office would be there, and therefore he couldn't be too careful. "Do you think it was fair if you had a lawsuit against Miss Davis, would it be fair for you to sit on a jury?" He was paraphrasing Branton, still making comparisons, attempting to equate a racist act with an aggressive attempt to expose racism.

Hemphill could only expose how she felt. She looked at Harris as though she thought him a fool. There was no hatred, but also no pity.

Her expression went far beyond the judgmental. It implied total awareness that some racists are fools enough to believe that the powerlessness of blacks to avoid racist attack compels a necessity to excuse the attacker.

"Are you asking me if I could be fair?"

"Yes," said Harris, waiting for Hemphill to beg like Hotaling did for the attorney who perceived him as an enemy of his client to let him prove himself on the jury. He stood back and gave her a chance to ask him to let her in on his trial.

"For so many years I have had to blot so many things out of my mind that I can do this now." She was looking through Harris, notifying him that she could forget what he had done to her without effort. "I am a fair person," an assertion which grew completely out of her knowledge of herself. "There's a lot of things I've had to put aside in my life and look at both sides of the question."

"Are you offended?"

She wasn't offended, and Harris knew it. The ungraciousness, the clumsiness, the bumbling maladroitness he had cultivated as a technique had caught up with him. He really didn't know how to get out of this.

"I'm not offended, it has nothing to do with our lives."

"But that raid terminated your business." Harris was desperately clinging to the wreckage of the contrived legal construction in which he had expected Hemphill to get lost.

"But we're not in business anymore."

Harris had done his best, and he'd blown it. Hemphill couldn't have been plucked off the jury without notice. After all, she was the only black in sight. Harris was asking Mrs. Hemphill to play a part in her own victimization by expressing approval of him while he went about reducing her humanity.

Harris, in his questioning of Mrs. Hemphill, had demonstrated something to the jury which the defense could only have hinted at. The jurors could have rationalized Harris' inevitable preemptory challenge of this black woman as something he did in his best judgment. But, the six whites present, who would end up as jurors, recognized that Harris had delivered an example of the gratuitous racism visited constantly upon blacks.

Winona Walker, a retired librarian who made the defense nervous, a lady whose favorite nephew was a deputy sheriff in Washington, a woman who had insisted on her dislike of controversy, a potential juror who had the strength to take a position and never budge, patted Janie Hemphill on the back after the voir dire. Winona Walker, who had never been married, whose life had been spent in arranging books on shelves, who read children's stories in her off hours, had to reach out and touch Mrs. Hemphill and let her know that even an escapist librarian cannot get so much out of touch with humanity as to not recognize an act of brutality.

The prospective jurors were being asked by the defense to probe themselves, and discover whether they harbored racist reflexes that would reduce Angela's chance for a fair trial. The jurors who were in that room knew that they couldn't justify the attack on Janie Hemphill without accepting their own racist complicity.

If any of the jurors had the slightest doubt about how Harris felt it was eliminated when he questioned Ann Wade, a 28-year-old housewife who had spent much of her early life in Georgia. Mrs. Wade had read some of *If They Come in the Morning* just days before being called to jury duty. She told Howard Moore, Jr. that she thought the purchasing of guns would be evidence that a plot existed. The only feelings she had about the leaders of the black revolutionary movement, which she had gleaned from newspapers, was "that they wanted to raise black people up." Harris had questioned Mrs. Wade about the book, asking her if she knew that Margaret Burnham co-authored the preface with Angela Davis. He was corrected by Moore who said that Bettina Aptheker Kurzweil was the co-author. Harris accepted the correction and then insisted that Miss Burnham had contributed to the writing of the preface, adding pettiness to inaccuracy. Then Albert Harris stood up there in front of God, the judge, the court, and everybody, and demanded white loyalty of Mrs. Wade.

"You heard me described as a racist, a white racist here today."

"Yes I did."

"Do you believe that?"

She didn't have much choice in an answer. What kind of a question is that to put to a mild, suburban, polite housewife. How does one answer a question like "Do you believe I'm ugly?," or "Do you think I should bathe more often?" Most often these questions are put in a way that both avoids an argument, and the danger of hurting the questioner's feelings.

"No, I don't," was the reply.

Now Harris moved on to secure her white loyalty in the future.

"You will probably hear me described as a white racist quite a number of times if you sit on this jury. And if you hear it over and over again will you be more likely to believe it?"

In other words, if at a future point in the trial the defense charges that an act of his was racist, she was to believe the prosecutor, not the defense. Realistically, not many potential jurors will sit and tell the prosecutor for the State of California that he is a racist. So Wade told him, "No, I don't think I will."

"Do you feel a sense of guilt as a white person?" Harris was whipping a liberal in line, demanding another response.

"In some ways I do. I suppose that we all have some guilt." Harris stopped questioning.

On the following day, March 9, 12 jurors had been picked. Harris exercised his first preemptive and eliminated a divorcee who had exhibited a streak of personal independence, which coupled with a generally liberal outlook might incline her to identify with Angela. He grinned at the defense, apparently expecting them to be surprised that he had not given Janie Hemphill the axe. He wasted his grin. They didn't expect Mrs. Hemphill to go until almost the last. Besides, the defense was trying to get their own strategy together.

Although their intelligence was not as good as Harris', who could come up with any document concerning anyone which was filed in a state office, the defense had determined that most of the jurors they would consider reasonable had passed through.

They wanted to garner their 20 challenges, and to do that, they wanted another free look at a prospective juror. Preemptive challenges are like poker. You discard a juror and draw another one. Then the other side discards and draws one. If one side passes, the other side has the option of passing, making the jury selection final, or exercising another preemptive. The idea was to get Harris out in front with his use of preemptives, so that if selection got down to the wire the defense would control the final choices.

There was danger in this approach. Harris could simply pass and accept the jury. That would leave Atkinson and Hotaling on the jury, something that the defense, with the exception of Margaret Burnham, was not willing to do. She felt that they could win even with that jury, but Branton, who along with Moore, would be handling most of the trial, said no.

After a replacement for the eliminated juror was seated, Leo Branton, Jr. stood up, supersharp in his quiet duel with Arnason on the selection of striking shirts and ties. Arnason's dark blue shirt, with a wide red and white diagonally striped tie under his black robes, contrasted with Leo, dressed in soft purple stripes. "We accept the jury as presently constituted," and Harris' sphincter nearly went haywire.

Harris recovered from the shock. There was no way he could go with that jury. In addition to Janie Hemphill, there was a woman whose husband was a Stanford University graduate student.

"The challenge passes to the people," said Arnason.

Harris gathered himself together and dismissed the grad student's wife. Branton, interviewed immediately afterwards, said that if Harris had passed, "I would have dropped dead."

On March 14, a tentative jury which did not include Hotaling, Atkinson or Hemphill, who had been preemptorily dismissed the previous day, was accepted by both sides. Angela Davis told the court:

"As I look at the present jury I see that the women and men do reflect the composition of this county. There are no black people sitting on the jury. Although I cannot say this is a jury of my peers, I can say that after much discussion, we have reached the conclusion that the women and men sitting on the jury will put forth their best efforts to give me a fair trial.

"I do not think further delay in the jury selection process will affect in any way the composition of the jury, and because we have confidence in the women and men presently sitting in the box, I am happy to say that we presently accept this jury."

That last statement was somewhat inaccurate. The defense suspected that if they did delay that the jury composition would deteriorate. They were right, judging from the fact that it required an additional four days to pick four alternates, and that the defense used five of eight preemptive challenges, while having six people dismissed for cause. Harris exercised only one preemptive in eliminating an American Indian woman who administered the Indian Center in San Jose.

The jurors were: (1) Ralph DeLange, 38, a maintenance electrician who had once been a school teacher; (2) Nicholas Gaetani, 45, an accountant; (3) Ruth Ann Charlton, 41, a sales supervisor for a department store; (4) Mary Borelli, a housewife, whose brother had been a San Quentin inmate; (5) James Messer, 33, an Annapolis graduate and Air Traffic Controller; (6) Louis

Franko, 40, Mexican born and an IBM employee; (7) Michelle Savage, a student, who at 20 was the youngest juror to serve in California; (8) Rosalie Frederick, 44, an unemployed divorcee; (9) Mary M. Timothy, 51, a medical research assistant; (10) Winona W. Walker, 65, a retired librarian; (11) Ann B. Wade, 28, a housewife; (12) Stephanie L. Ryon, 22, a collection agent.

Robert Seiden, who at 70 was the oldest of the jurors, replaced Mary Borelli during the third week of testimony. That left three alternates, Barbara Deutch, a divorcee, Samuel Conroy, a mechanical designer, and John Tittle, 19, a student.

They weren't Angela's peers, but they were a cross section of Santa Clara County, minus excluded non-whites. There were no more characters to be cast, and the real show, People versus Angela Davis, was ready to begin.

8 : The Curtain Raiser

In his opening remarks on Monday, March 27, 1972, Albert Harris outlined the case against Angela Davis. "The evidence will show that the defendant knowingly and with criminal intent aided, promoted, encouraged and instigated by act and advice the commission of this crime—namely, the kidnapping of Judge Harold Haley and the other hostages . . .

"I'm satisfied that the evidence will show beyond a reasonable doubt the commission of each of these acts, although only the proof of one overt act is sufficient to justify conviction of the crime of conspiracy . . ."

"There will be no evidence offered by the prosecution over the next few weeks of the exercise by the defendant of her right of free speech and assembly under the First Amendment, except for certain letters that she wrote. There will be no evidence of speeches that she has given nor will there be any evidence offered by the prosecution of any rallies that she has attended. You will be satisfied that the case of the prosecution does not rest in any degree whatever upon the nature of the political views of the defendant, whatever they may be."

Harris was saying that he was not going to offer evidence in support of the first of 13 overt acts spelled out in the indictment. Overt act number one stated that on June 19, 1970, "pursuant to the above conspiracy and to carry out the objects thereof," Angela and Jonathan "participated in a rally at the State Building in Los Angeles and advocated the release from lawful custody of the said Soledad Brothers."

The second, third, fourth and seventh overt acts covered the four separate purchases of the weapons Jonathan brought to the Marin County Civic Center, and alleged that Angela had furnished him with the guns. Undoubtedly, if the prosecution could come up with evidence that she had "furnished" Jonathan Jackson with these guns, or any one of them, there would be reason to suspect a conspiracy between the two.

Overt acts five and six charged that Angela and Jonathan visited San Quentin, "where Jonathan P. Jackson attempted to visit his brother George Lester Jackson, one of the 'Soledad Brothers' whose rescue from lawful custody was one of the major objectives of the conspiracy as hereinabove alleged." Suppose the state was capable of proving that Angela accompanied Jonathan to San Quentin. Would that automatically make Angela Davis guilty of conspiracy? According to Harris, it would. The same could be said of the eighth overt act, which alleged that Angela and Jonathan were present at the Hall of Justice in Marin, "for the purpose of viewing the premises and planning the activities and crimes to be committed on the following day." Harris was saying that if the jury was satisfied that Angela had been present at the Civic Center on August 6, with Jonathan Jackson, that was sufficient to find her guilty of conspiracy.

His opening remarks had neither the force of law or the authority of evidence. They did, however, reveal prosecutorial thinking, and as such had an undetermined amount of persuasiveness.

The eighth to 12th overt acts, although including the words "pursuant to the above conspiracy and to carry out the objects thereof," made no mention of Angela Davis. These acts described the events of August 7 from the point that Jonathan entered the courtroom, to the time when Ruchell was alleged to have shot Judge Haley. The only fact contested there was the shooting of Judge Haley, and Angela Davis was not in a position to mount any defense proving that Ruchell did not pull the trigger. Certainly the prosecution couldn't mean that the jury should find Angela guilty if they were satisfied that those acts had been committed. Even if the jury found that overt acts eight through 12 were the result of a pre-existing conspiracy it does not follow that Angela was necessarily a part of that conspiracy.

Ruchell Magee, in his letter to Angela, had written of a plan to go to a radio station to expose the workings of the Department of Corrections. Overt acts eight through 12 would have been just as applicable in a charge of conspiracy which assumed Ruchell's version of the meaning of August 7 was the correct one.

The 13th overt act charged: "that on or about August 7, 1970, pursuant to the above conspiracy and to carry out the objects thereof and following the murder and kidnapping at the Marin County Civic Center as hereinabove alleged, the defendant Angela Y. Davis did purchase an airline ticket at San Francisco International Airport for Los Angeles and did depart from San Francisco and proceed to Los Angeles." The fact that Angela took that plane was easy to prove, but did that ticket purchase add up to conspiracy?

Harris described how Jonathan went into the courtroom and left with three prisoners and five hostages, carrying out "objective number one of the conspiracy—kidnapping for the purpose of extortion." The extortion? "Inducing the local law enforcement people to refrain from preventing the escape" and "to force the State government to release George Jackson and the other 'Soledad Brothers.' "

The plan, according to Harris, was to drive from Marin County to the San Francisco Airport, there exchange the hostages for the Soledad Brothers, and then take an airplane somewhere.

"The defendant rushed aboard a flight departing from the San Francisco Airport at 2:00 p.m. on August 7th . . . How did she get to the airport? When did she learn that the rescue scheme had aborted? . . . Did the defendant arrive at the airport immediately prior to her flight or earlier? Evidence will be offered on this question. It is enough to say now that the people will also offer into evidence a slip of paper that was found in Jonathan Jackson's wallet. On that slip of paper you will find the telephone number that referred to an out-of-the-way public telephone near the American Airlines counter at the San Francisco International Airport. You don't call a public telephone booth unless you expect someone to be there."

"Now while many persons were involved in this criminal enterprise, there is no surviving witness, to our knowledge, of the conversations by which the defendant expressed her knowledge and her criminal intent . . . Jonathan Jackson died on August the 7th. George Jackson, who was in the Adjustment Center at San Quentin, is dead. James McClain is dead. William Christmas is dead. Ruchell Magee is the only surviving participant of those events, and he too is awaiting trial.

"Thus, we must rely—and we will rely—on evidence of facts from which you can infer—you can reasonably infer, the necessary elements of rendering assistance, of knowledge of Jonathan Jackson's criminal purpose, proof of the sharing of the criminal intent of Jonathan Jackson, proof of the agreement or conspiracy with Jonathan Jackson to commit the crimes, and the specific intent to commit the crimes."

Harris outlined four elements necessary to establishing guilt through circumstantial evidence: motive, means, opportunity and consciousness of guilt. "The evidence will show beyond a reasonable doubt that all four elements are present here: One, that she had a powerful and compelling motive; two, that she had available under her control and in her possession the means by which the crimes were committed; third, that she had the opportunity to aid and abet Jonathan Jackson and to conspire with him; and, finally, that she made clear in no uncertain terms her belief in her own guilt by fleeing from the State of California on the day of the commission of the crimes . . .

"This teacher of philosophy is a student of violence . . . The Defendant does not live only in the world of books and ideas, but . . . is committed to action . . . is committed to violence. Her own words contained in letters to George Jackson that we will produce in court . . . will reveal that beneath the cool academic veneer is a woman fully capable of being moved to violence by passion. The evidence will show that her basic motive was not to free political prisoners, but to free the one prisoner that she loved. The basic motive for the crime was the same motive underlying hundreds of criminal cases across the United States every day. That motive was not abstract. It was not founded basically on any need, real or imagined, for prison reform. It was not founded on a desire for social justice. It was founded simply on the passion that she felt for George Jackson, and the evidence of that motive will not be circumstantial. You won't have to make any inferences. It will rest on the Defendant's own words . . .

"The evidence will show that the Defendant became involved in this conspiracy, the principal object of which was to free George Jackson, because she was deeply in love with him . . .

"Those words appear in a number of letters some of which were found in a search of her apartment in Los Angeles on August 16, 1970 . . .

"There will be evidence that on July 8, 1971, a meeting was arranged between the Defendant and George Jackson at the Marin County Jail . . .

"The evidence will show that the Defendant and George Jackson used this meeting, their only physical meeting that I know of, as an opportunity for a close passionate and physical involvement . . ."

Harris had no reason to know that Angela had met and spoken with George Jackson when he was on trial in Salinas, but he should have been aware that there had been two meetings with Jackson subsequent to the meeting of July 8, both of them held in the Marin County Jail.

"Over a month later, George Jackson died at San Quentin. Among his property was found a group of letters. These letters were written on a typewriter that Miss Davis had available to her in the Marin County Jail . . . The letters had been smuggled into San Quentin State prison . . . They may be embarrassing. But because they so clearly articulate the state of mind of the defendant and because they so clearly establish her relationship with George Jackson, it is our duty to have them disclosed in full . . .

"You will find, I think, from the letters, a willingness on the part of the defendant to do whatever she felt had to be done to free George Jackson . . ."

Harris discussed Angela's possession of the means to commit the crime, namely the four guns. Jonathan, he said, had accompanied Angela during some of the six occasions that she had bought either guns or ammunition. Mrs. Jackson, Jonathan's mother, also went along on one occasion and herself bought ammunition which fit two of the guns used.

His discussion of means also included money. "You will find that, on August 4th of 1970, the Defendant was in the San Francisco Bay area, that she cashed a check for $100 at the Security

Pacific National Bank in Oakland. On August the 5th she purchased the shotgun that was used in the commission of the crime. On the morning of August the 6th, that is the day before, Jonathan Jackson used two $20 bills for the use of the Hertz Rental van . . . and after the events of August 7th had concluded, Jonathan Jackson had 50 cents in his coat pocket, and he had a dollar bill stuffed in his shorts . . . In short, the evidence will show that practically everything that was used in the commission of the crime, practically every instrumentality and every physical item that was used was the property of Angela Davis."

Angela had the opportunity to conspire with Jonathan, explained the prosecutor. "The evidence will show an increasing tempo in terms of their close association as the days grew closer to August the 7th.

"Now, being together is only one facet of the evidence. Obviously, it is one thing for persons to have lunch together or to go to a show together or to do many things together. It is something different when two persons go to a gun shop or a pawn shop two days, less than two days before a crime is committed, and one of them purchases a gun that is used by the other in the commission of a crime . . ."

Harris outlined Angela's association with both Jonathan and his parents in the weeks preceding the crime. He mentioned Angela and Jonathan being stopped crossing into California from Mexico, July 30th, Angela's stay, along with Jonathan and Mr. and Mrs. Jackson in a Berkeley motel two weeks before. He said that "just three weeks precisely before August 7th—the defendant left the apartment where she had lived for some considerable time, and she moved into a new apartment . . . Jonathan Jackson helped her move into the apartment. We will present evidence that for the next three weeks the defendant and Jonathan Jackson shared living quarters in that apartment."

Harris dwelt particularly on the week beginning Monday August 3. "This was the day that James McClain went to trial in Marin County. On the same day, Jonathan Jackson together with his mother and Joan Hammer went out to visit George Jackson at San Quentin. And that night, the defendant left Los Angeles . . . and came to San Francisco. She was not to leave the San Francisco

Bay area again until August the 7th had become a bloody page in our history."

He placed Angela and Jonathan at San Quentin the afternoon of August 4th. "In the visitor's log for that day you will see that Jonathan Jackson wrote his own name in . . . and you will find the name immediately beneath it, which he wrote in, Diane Robinson . . . Later that day Jonathan Jackson borrowed the Volkswagen in San Jose." It was Harris' contention that Angela used this Volkswagen to drive to the San Francisco Airport on August 7th.

He said that Angela accompanied Jonathan to San Quentin again, August 5th, where she sat in a waiting room while Jonathan visited his brother for two hours.

"Later that day after the visit with George, the two of them went to San Francisco, and the defendant purchased a shotgun . . . she was accompanied . . . by Jonathan Jackson."

"The evidence will show that George Jackson was the only conduit or channel of information between Jonathan Jackson and James McClain. The evidence will show that these visits to George Jackson by his younger brother on Tuesday and Wednesday were for the purpose of planning what would happen on Friday, August the 7th."

According to Harris, on August 6th, Jonathan and Angela were seen at a Texaco service station adjacent to the Civic Center in the yellow van, seeking help because the van had developed battery trouble. After getting the car started, the two went back to San Quentin, where Angela stayed in the van, "probably to keep the motor running" while Jonathan visited his brother. "A San Quentin inmate will testify that he observed both Jonathan Jackson and the Defendant in the van as they left the parking lot at around 12:30 that day." At 2:00 p.m. Jonathan was again in the courtroom. Harris said that at about 10:30 that morning, prior to his appearance at the service station, Jonathan, dressed in a trench coat and carrying a blue briefcase, was seen in the courtroom. On the second courtroom visit he brought in a paper bag. Harris said that at 3:00 p.m., Jonathan appeared in the courtroom a third time, again with the trench coat and the blue briefcase.

"At about 7:45 that night, the night of August 6th, Jonathan Jackson signed the register at the Holland Motel in San Francisco

. . . the first motel that you will find, if you have occasion to drive from Marin County to San Francisco . . . He was accompanied by another person and he rented the room for one night." Harris said at another point in the trial that he had reason to believe that Angela was the person with Jonathan.

Consciousness of guilt, Harris concluded, was evident in Angela's hurried departure on a 2:00 p.m. flight from San Francisco. He outlined her path from California to Florida via Chicago and Detroit and her arrest, while wearing a wig and carrying false identification in New York City.

"We think that after you have heard the evidence, your insight into what the defendant did will be as keen as the vision of those who saw through her disguise in New York City. We think that the evidence . . . will show you why the crimes in Marin County were committed. We think the evidence will show you that they were committed because of the commitment of Angela Davis to George Jackson.

"We will show, I think, that the two people who cared most about George Jackson in the entire world participated in those steps, and we will go through them item by item . . . We expect that the evidence will cover everything that I have mentioned here today, and we expect that it will cover other matters that I haven't passed on."

Undoubtedly the two did care a lot about George Jackson. But Harris was overlooking the fact that George Jackson had a mother, a father and three sisters who cared for him with the same intensity as Jonathan Jackson and Angela Davis.

"We are satisfied that when you have heard it all . . . and when you have heard all of the evidence that is presented by both sides in the case, you will be convinced of the guilt of Angela Davis."

The defense had anticipated the basic outline of the prosecution's case, alleging that the escape attempt was the first step in a plan that would seek to exchange the hostages taken for the Soledad Brothers. They assumed that Harris had dropped the first overt act of the indictment in order to de-politicize the case, to avoid dealing with questions about constitutionally protected speech that were bound to be raised by the defense, while closing an area to the defense of explaining the meaning of the meeting of June 19, 1970. Harris did not want the defense to lay out the case of the Soledad Brothers in the Angela Davis conspiracy trial. But they had miscalculated.

Harris had dropped that part of the indictment because he didn't need it to prove his case. He was going to insist that Angela was motivated to conspire with Jonathan Jackson to free the Soledad Brothers, not because of politics, but instead, "the reason that she did this was passion, simple human passion, a passion for George Jackson, the Soledad Brother, a passion that knew no bounds, no limits, no respect for life, not even the life of George's younger brother."

Harris' opening statement had been weakened somewhat by objective events. It had taken all day for him to deliver his opening statement, and the morning portion detailed the events of August 7, as well as the prosecution assertion that the crime had been committed to free the Soledad Brothers. During the lunch recess, everyone received the news that the two remaining Soledad Brothers had been acquitted of the charges against them. Harris' afternoon presentation was delivered in a courtroom where everyone knew that he was claiming that Angela was instrumental in fabricating a plot to release men from prison who would, as it developed, be found innocent and in theory eligible for release from prison.

The psychological disadvantage of arguing that Angela Davis conspired to free men who would subsequently be proved innocent was somewhat offset the following day, when Angela was scheduled to make the opening statement in her defense. A jail break attempt, originating in the building adjacent to that where her trial was being held, delayed the trial one day.

Three men, Norman Lucas, Ted Guererro and Jacob Zitzer, reported to the jail infirmary when it opened at 8:00 a.m. that morning. There, at knife point, they took two hostages, Sue Kawamoto, 20, a medical secretary, and Alexander Safonoff, 31, an employee of the public defender's office. The men were being held in jail pending transfer to other institutions. Lucas, convicted of bank robbery, was headed for federal prison. Guererro was enroute to Vacaville, a state facility, because of a parole violation. Jacob

Zitzer, who had been booked under the name Chuck Williamson, had recently escaped from San Quentin, and had been arrested for robbery. The three, with their two hostages, began bargaining with Santa Clara County Sheriffs for their freedom, demanding a car to leave in.

Word of the escape attempt created a security emergency. The compound, where the trial was being held, was immediately shut down. About half the jurors were in the jury assembly room. The others were left standing on the steps of the courthouse, wondering what to do next.

Fewer than half of the news corps were in the pressroom. It was a very well attended press day—as everyone expected Angela to deliver the opening argument—meaning that perhaps 25 reporters found themselves locked in, as did a few spectators who had begun filing into the courtroom.

The prosecution and law enforcement officials had insisted throughout the proceedings that the elaborate security was designed as much to protect Angela as it was to defend the court from surprise attack. But security, which tends to be automatic, mindless and always with a purpose that has not been made quite clear, didn't move to protect Angela Davis. She and her attorneys arrived at the fence just moments after the general security alarm had been raised. The deputy at the gate would not let her in. Therefore Angela Davis, the cause of all this security and certainly the object of some of it, sat outside the chain link fence that had been erected in her behalf and wondered what was happening.

Two reporters representing *The New York Daily News* and the Associated Press somehow got into the pressroom after security had been declared. They managed to subdue the obdurate deputy with threats dealing with the United States Supreme Court, the deputy's immediate supervisor, who could not be reached on the walkie-talkie, and promises that they would not try to get out of the enclosure once they were allowed in.

In the pressroom, newsmen were uninvolved. There was the previous day to hash over, tentative leads to try out on fellow reporters, speculations to exchange about Angela's possible response to the prosecutor and complaints to make about the telephone company's penury in only providing donuts for the press corps on Mondays. When they finally realized that something was out of order they also discovered that they were locked in, with no more rationale being given for their condition than the word "security," which is advanced as a reason for every restriction by those who really believe that security comes from restricting the movement of people.

Angela went back to her attorney's office. All of the jurors, with the exception of alternate Tittle, were finally called into the courtroom and excused for the day by the judge. The Sheriff decided to de-secure the Angela Davis trial compound for the time it took to release the spectators in the courtroom corridor who had no place to sit but the floor, and the newspeople in the pressroom, who found themselves with no news to gather.

The newsmen were let out in time to discover that the escapees had proceeded with their hostages to the booking area in the basement, just adjacent to the exit leading to an automobile ramp. The roof of the building was covered with armed men. All around the front entrance to the ramp were men in civilian clothes who turned out to be off duty deputies. Some of them, who were rated as sharpshooters, carried high powered rifles outfitted with scopes. Others had shotguns.

A car, rumored to be the one provided for the escapees, was backed down the ramp. Officers, uniformed and otherwise, eased down the ramp also. Suddenly a sharp report, loud enough to be heard several hundred yards away, came from inside the building. The crowd which had been kept a distance away from the building, could see the obvious relaxation of the officers. The escapees had been captured. They had been negotiating with Captain Wesley Johnson, who was in charge of security at the trial, and negotiations broke down at the point that the prisoners demanded Johnson's gun and handcuffs. Johnson stepped away from the prisoners, and Detective Sargeant Robert Lees killed Jacob Zitzer, who was considered to be the leader of the escape attempt. The emergency was over.

Angela Davis came to court Wednesday morning having to deal with the unknown effects of the escape attempt on the jury. Much of the defense attorney questioning during jury selection had been designed to subtly disassociate Angela from August 7, to make certain that the jury did not reflexively associate her with violence. And then, literally on her doorstep, there was an escape attempt.

Judge Arnason, at the request of the defense, questioned the jurors about what they had seen, heard and read. After satisfying himself that the jury had not been negatively affected by the escape attempt, Arnason admonished them that there was no relationship between the escape attempt and the trial.

Angela Davis could then make her opening statement.

"The Prosecutor has the burden of proof upon him, and I, the Defendant in this case, need not say anything if I so desire," alerting the jury that they, in judging the case, should look to the Prosecutor for evidence of her guilt and not to her for evidence of her innocence.

"We say to you, members of the jury, that the Prosecutor's evidence itself will demonstrate to you that this case is no case at all . . . His case is based on conjecture, guess work, speculation . . . We do not dispute . . . that lives were lost and people were wounded . . .

"There are two separate issues involved here. There is the issue of whether deaths occurred and how those deaths occurred. Then there is the issue of whether I had anything to do with the occurrence of those deaths . . .

"But what must the Prosecutor show you about me in order to prove this case? . . . There are basically three things which he has to prove . . . that there was a plan predating August 7, that I had foreknowledge of a plan predating August 7, and that I took steps to deliberately promote the execution of that plan."

As the prosecution had made no claim that she was there on August 7th, there were only two issues which had any bearing: "whether I had knowledge of what was to transpire on August 7th and whether I did anything with the deliberate intent to promote those events . . ."

"First, let us deal with the evidence which the prosecutor intends to present in support of his contention that I had a motive to participate in the Marin County events."

She proceeded to comment on the first overt act of the conspiracy count, noting that she had been exercising constitutionally guaranteed rights on June 19, 1970. "This indictment provoked widespread concern . . . that I was a victim of political oppression. I ask you whether or not it would not be reasonable to infer that the prosecutor is aware that no fair-minded juror would convict me on the basis of such evidence. Therefore, he has said to you that he will present no evidence of my participation in the struggle to free the Soledad Brothers. What he has done is that he has transformed the character of this case.

"Now, he will have you believe that I am a person who would commit the crimes of murder, kidnapping, and conspiracy, having been motivated by pure passion. He would have you believe that lurking behind my external appearance are sinister and selfish emotions and passions which, in his words, know no bounds.

"Members of the jury, this is utterly fantastic. It is utterly absurd. Yet it is understandable that Mr. Harris would like to take advantage of the fact that I am a woman, for in this society women are supposed to act only in accordance with the dictates of their emotions and passions. I might say that this is clearly a symptom of the male chauvinism that prevails in our society . . .

"We say that the evidence will show that there's absolutely no consistent credible proof of what the precise purpose of August 7 was . . .

"We say that the evidence will not support the prosecutor's contentions. There will be absolutely no evidence to indicate that those who participated in the events of August 7 made concrete arrangements for the release of the Soledad Brothers. There will be no evidence that they specified a procedure for an exchange, nor will there be any evidence that they specified a place for the exchange to occur.

"Would a mere statement apparently uttered in passing, if it was uttered at all, be sufficient to convince you that the release of the Soledad Brothers was the purpose of August 7th?

". . . Members of the jury, you will see when testimony is adduced to this effect, that we sought out those kinds of activities which permitted us to involve ever greater numbers of people in the public defense of the Soledad Brothers. Testimony will make it clear that we felt that the influence of large numbers of people would help win them an acquittal and that they would be freed in that way from an unjust prosecution . . .

". . . We were correct in our understanding of the Soledad Brothers' case, for Monday morning as you sat here listening to the prosecution's opening statement . . . the twelve men and women who . . . had listened to all the evidence . . . against the Soledad Brothers . . . pronounced the two surviving Soledad Brothers not guilty . . .

"The evidence will show that every single activity organized by the Soledad Brothers Defense Committee was totally within the realm of legality."

She talked not only of her activities in behalf of the Soledad Brothers but of her activism in California beginning with her involvement with the Black Student Council and UC San Diego and ending with the Communist Party.

"I have been associated with various movements, not only organizations, I have been associated with the struggle to protect and extend the rights of working people, whether they be black or Chicano or Asian or Native American or white . . .

"In all of my activities . . . my goal has been to aid in the creation of a movement, a movement encompassing millions of people, indeed the majority of people in the United States, a movement which might ultimately result in a more humane socialist society."

Angela recounted her activity in support of Huey Newton, the Panther 21 in New York, the movement to free Ericka Huggins and Bobby Seale and the movement around the 18 Panthers arrested in Los Angeles in January 1970. There was also the Soledad Six case, similar to the Soledad Brothers insofar as it involved black prisoners charged with killing a guard at Soledad prison, in whose defense Angela had also been involved.

She outlined her friendship with the Jackson family as well as the parents of the other two Soledad Brothers, and linked part of the basis of her relationship with Jonathan to threats received at UCLA "after the controversy . . . surrounding my teaching position emerged."

On the weapons she said that: 'While I did purchase guns, I

did nothing to furnish Jonathan or anyone with the weapons which were utilized during the action on August 7 . . . You will become aware, as the trial progresses, that my experience with guns dates far back into my childhood. You will learn about the neighborhood in which we lived, where my parents still live today, and that it is called Dynamite Hill, our house being situated on the very top of the hill.

"Because of constant threats and actual incidents of violence which took place in our neighborhood, my father had to keep guns in the house. We will tell you in testimony about our fears and apprehensions that we might be the next victims ourselves of a racist assault. We will tell you about our close friends, including the four young girls in the church bombing in Birmingham who were struck down at the hands of racist bombers.

"You will understand that a black person who grew up in the south . . . guns were a normal fact of life . . .

"The evidence will show that my purchase of weapons was totally unrelated to any illegal activities and further, each time I purchased a weapon, I did it in my own name, and I gave my address and the place of my birth, and I ask you, members of the jury, whether this sounds like the kind of evidence which can be used to demonstrate participation in a conspiracy . . ."

Angela assured the jury that her gun purchases would be accounted for, and that the large purchases of ammunition would be explained by evidence showing that she did quite a bit of target shooting.

As to flight being evidence of consciousness of guilt, "this . . . reveals the absurdity of the Prosecution's case, for by this evidence he is attempting to transmute normal, everyday human conduct, namely, going to catch a plane, into evidence of guilt."

Angela admitted to dropping out of sight, because "I had reason to fear police violence, should I voluntarily submit to the authorities at that time. The evidence will show that, on many occasions in the past, Black and Chicano people and particularly political activists have been victims of police violence. The evidence will show that I had ample reason to fear unjust treatment by the courts of California, that I had reason to fear the prospect of many, many months of incarceration without bail, that I had reason to fear an eventual trial before an all white jury therefore, not a jury composed of my peers, and that I had reason to fear many other obstacles to my efforts to protect my innocence."

The Prosecutor "must shape his circumstantial case out of the ordinary circumstances of everyday life, and he leaves it to you, members of the jury, to supply the missing link which converts ordinary activity into criminal conduct."

She pointed out that the fact of moving in July 1970, did not automatically imply that she had anything to do with the conspiracy. Angela denied that Jonathan had lived in her apartment. She also attacked Harris' accounting of the $100 check cashed August 4. "He tells you about the $100 and, then, in his very next breath he says: 'Jonathan Jackson rented a van on August 6 and paid for it with $40, with two $20 bills.' And you are the ones supposed to put these two facts together . . . There will be absolutely no evidence that I gave Jonathan Jackson $40 to rent a van. This is not the only wild guess. It is not the wildest of guesses . . . If you are to arrive at the conclusion that I did supply guns to Jonathan Jackson, that I did participate in a conspiracy by purchasing certain weapons in the month prior to August 7, then you must guess, you must speculate, you must conjecture, you must surmise. On Monday, the prosecutor told you that he will present evidence to prove that Jonathan Jackson registered in a motel in San Francisco on the night of August 6. He said that Jonathan Jackson was with another person. If, indeed, he was with a second person, is there any evidence as to who the mystery man or woman was? I know, and the Prosecutor knows, that it was not I.

"Yet the inference is left hanging. You are left to guess, to speculate."

Moving on to the phone number found in Jonathan's wallet: "Was Jonathan Jackson supposed to call that booth? Was he supposed to stop the van on the highway and get out and make a telephone call to the airport or was someone supposed to be in a telephone booth? . . .

"Members of the jury, the evidence will show that the charges against me are the logical extension of the unlawful attacks which began with the actions of the government of this state and of the

Regents of the University of California when they unlawfully dismissed me from my post at UCLA."

She accused Harris of emulating the University of California Regents in trying to transform her from a citizen of the world of ideas to a violent activist. She said that her doctoral dissertation was on the theory of force, and that books with violence in the title, which Harris claimed proved she was "a student of violence," related to that dissertation.

Angela concluded: "We know, and we have the utmost confidence that your verdict will be a just verdict. We have the utmost confidence that your verdict will be the only verdict that the evidence and justice demand in this case. We are confident that the case will terminate with your pronouncement of two words—not guilty."

Opposing positions had been taken, and it was up to the jury, after hearing all of the testimony to decide exactly what that evidence added up to. The differences between prosecution and defense lay more with their interpretation of the meaning of particular facts, than in a dispute as to whether an event did or did not occur. They agreed that August 7 had occurred, and that books and guns which belonged to Angela had been found on the scene. There was no dispute about Angela's association with Jonathan Jackson, although the defense did deny that Angela had been with Jonathan during three visits to San Quentin and one to the Marin County Civic Center. Angela did not deny that she wrote letters to George Jackson, but disputed the meaning which the prosecution found in those letters.

And then, there was the question of flight. To Harris, Angela's act of leaving California, of disguising herself and adopting a false identity, was evidence of her guilty state of mind. Angela said no, her unavailability following August 7, was a decision born of fear, not guilt. Both sides agreed that the case encompassed a far reaching conspiracy. For the prosecution, the conspiracy was between Angela Davis, Jonathan Jackson and persons unknown. Angela insisted that the conspiracy was a product of official acts, a state inspired effort to discredit her and, therefore inferentially, radical politics.

Both sides had attempted to influence the jury during the selection process and with their opening statements. The truth or falsity of any of their assertions during these two phases of the trial were not an issue. Both prosecution and defense wanted to create a conceptual framework through which the evidence could be viewed, and by which a decision could be made.

All that was left to be done was to let the play proceed.

9 : Justice in the Round I

Maria Graham, one of the jurors who had been taken hostage, was the first of over 40 prosecution witnesses testifying to the events of August 7. Mrs. Graham, who had been wounded in the shooting, seemed nervous as Harris led her through a description of her experiences, beginning with the forced exit from the courtroom and ending with the terror and carnage in the van.

Harris, over the objection of the defense, asked: "Did he say anything about the Soledad Brothers?"

Mrs. Graham answered that she had heard Jonathan say, "We want our Soledad Brothers set free. We're going to keep these prisoners until they are set free." The witness said that she heard several shouts to the effect "free the Soledad Brothers" on the walk between the courtroom and the van. She told of getting into the van and sitting on the floor with her back to the driver. She remembered McClain asking Jonathan where they were going and Jackson answering, the San Francisco Airport. Mrs. Graham did not remember anything about the shooting, saying that she was busy trying to keep her skirt down. She did see Gary Thomas reach for a gun, "then I saw my arm flip up." This was the shot that severed the brachial artery in her right arm. Thomas's body fell over her and she heard him shout "for God's sake, please don't shoot."

Howard Moore, Jr. conducted the difficult cross examination. His main interest was in the statements Mrs. Graham said she had heard about the Soledad Brothers and her claim that Jonathan had named the airport as their destination. Mrs. Graham was adamant about the airport statement, but her testimony about hearing Jackson demand the freedom of the Soledad Brothers was weakened somewhat through questioning.

Mrs. Graham had made four separate statements to prosecution investigators over a year's period, and had never referred to Jonathan's courtroom demand that: "We want the Soledad Brothers free or we will kill the judge."

Mrs. Graham said that she had remembered that fact just the day before, when discussing her testimony with Mr. Harris. Moore insisted that she had been coached. "No one has even mentioned the Soledad Brothers to me," was her response.

"The truth is that before your conversation with Mr. Harris that you had no memory of hearing Jonathan Jackson or anyone else demand in the courtroom that the Soledad Brothers be freed."

"I hate to admit this . . . it reflects on my intelligence."

"But, nevertheless, Mr. Harris did influence you to recall something you had not remembered in four reports and several conferences going back over two years."

Moore's problem with Graham was that he had to get this woman who had undergone the ordeal of August 7, to relive and retell what had happened in the van without having her break down on the stand. He had cast some doubt on her ability to remember exactly when and where the statements about the Soledad Brothers were made, but he wanted to make clear that she did not witness any shooting in the van. The defense attorney's effort was directed more toward Ruchell Magee than Angela Davis. He was protecting a record that would be intact, when and if Maria Graham testified against Ruchell.

He led her through questioning to position herself in the bus. "You were packed in real tight?" Moore's voice had risen, conveying some of the feeling of hysteria which must have been part of that scene.

"Yes," she said, following Moore's lead perfectly.

The attorney sat on the floor directly in front of the jury box. The sight of Howard Moore, Jr., the eminently proper attorney, sitting on the floor, commanded the jury's attention. Mrs. Graham could have had convulsions on the stand, and the jury would not have noticed it. He took over Mrs. Graham's role, shouting her lines at her, recreating her participation himself; the jury was forced to listen, by watching him, for details of testimony which might neutralize the dramatic horror of her recitation. He carried her through an almost hysterical "I was too busy trying to keep my skirt down," to—

"You didn't see him take the gun," referring to Gary Thomas.

"Yes, he reached over me to take the gun."

"You didn't see him fire that gun yourself, you did not see anyone in that van fire a weapon at all."

"I heard guns and I don't know where. They were loud and close when the firing started. I can't tell you what happened after that."

Moore returned to his feet. He and the witness were off the hook. He was spared the necessity of grappling with a near hysterical woman, and, in trying to discredit her testimony, brand himself on the memories of the jury as an attorney hammering away at a witness who was trying to forget past horrors. She, on the other hand, would not have to cope with the material which the prosecutor hoped would influence the jury to vote against violence, and therefore against Angela.

Moore wanted the jury to reflect on the fact that the witness had nothing to offer from her experience in the van that could hurt his client. Graham, sitting in the van, facing Judge Haley, Ruchell Magee and William Christmas, did not see the shots fired which the prosecution claimed had killed Judge Haley.

Next was Norene Morris, another juror who had been present in the courtroom, but who had not been taken hostage. Mrs. Morris had written a report of what she had witnessed two days after the event and had not mentioned anything about the Soledad Brothers. She did testify that McClain had asked Jonathan Jackson for the adhesive tape with which he attached a sawed off shotgun to Judge Haley's neck. Harris had stressed this point as evidence of a preexisting arrangement between McClain and Jackson.

Doris Wittmer, one of the hostages, also had little to contribute to an understanding of what happened in the van. She had not heard the Soledad Brothers mentioned, and had spent all of her time in the van lying face down, desperately trying to keep the noise of gunfire from her ears by pressing her arms against them.

The prosecution's main witness to the fact that the freedom of the Soledad Brothers was the object of August 7, was James

Kean, a photographer for the *Independent Journal,* Marin County's daily paper, who took most of the pictures of the quartet of blacks, along with hostages, that were used in evidence. He estimated that he took up to 30 photographs in a corridor near an elevator, where the group, along with disarmed officers, stopped for a time. Kean said that just before the group entered the elevators McClain told him, "Tell them we want the Soledad Brothers by 12 o'clock." Kean said he asked him to repeat it just so there would not be any mistake, making McClain specify whether he meant noon or midnight. McClain, according to Kean, said he wanted the Soledad Brothers released by noon. Kean then wrote down "Soledad Brothers" in a notebook he carried.

Kean explained to Leo Branton, Jr., on cross examination, that he thought McClain gave him the information, having recognized him as a member of the press. Perhaps that was so. The photographer looks like any balding, middle-aged, and still slender except for some bellowing at the waist, man. Kean said he thought McClain wanted to get the message out about the Soledad Brothers, however he did not report this fact to police, despite the fact that he had worked closely with them in his 20 years as a newspaper photographer. Also, the slip of paper on which he had written "Soledad Brothers" had been misplaced.

Kean was followed by a group of police officers, including Dan Terzich, Police Chief of Mill Valley, all of whom had been in and about the corridor through which the group had traveled, and who had been disarmed by one or another of them. Captain Harvey Teague testified that he had heard someone in the group refer to freeing the Soledad Brothers, but wasn't sure who. Clifford Niederer, a police officer from Corte Madera, said he heard something, "to the effect that he represented a new revolutionary movement," possibly a reference to McClain who was reported to have told Kean, "take all the pictures you want, we are the revolutionaries."

Deputy Sheriff Theodore V. Hughes said that he heard two or three of the men shout clearly "Free our brothers at Folsom, free all our brothers." Hughes was the deputy who reclaimed his gun from the van and did not discover until the following morning that all of the rounds had been fired. One of the rounds from this gun apparently produced Judge Haley's chest wound. Hughes turned his weapon over to investigating officers, but no usable fingerprints could be taken from it.

The most important witness to this phase of the prosecution was Gary Thomas, who had lost the use of his legs because of a bullet wound in his spine sustained in the van. Thomas testified from a wheelchair, which was pushed in and out of the court by Deputy Sheriff Bowling, the only black among the 20 or so deputies who regularly worked at providing armed security for the trial.

Thomas recalled Jonathan's takeover of the courtroom, and described his forced exit from the building in company with the other hostages. He said that he heard McClain tell Sheriff Mountanos over the phone that, "We have the judge. If you don't do as we say we'll kill him and the other people." But he was emphatic in his inability to remember any mention of the Soledad Brothers. Thomas remembered a curious detail mentioned by Maria Graham. The two said that after entering the van, McClain began to drive. He then decided that it was too difficult, and changed places with Jonathan. Neither Thomas or Mrs. Graham could remember how the two men changed places, whether they shifted inside the van, or used the doors and walked around the vehicle. Thomas also testified, as did Graham, that the destination was the airport. But, where Mrs. Graham had attributed the naming of the destination to Jonathan, Thomas named McClain. Thomas also testified that as the van stopped, just before the heavy firing began, he heard a shot, and then one or two more. He could not say where the shots came from. He saw Jonathan withdraw his hand from outside the window with blood on it, and on the revolver he was holding. Thomas said he turned around in time to see Judge Haley's face dissolving from the force of a shotgun which Magee had fired. He then grabbed the gun which Jonathan had put down on the engine compartment, shot toward Jonathan, put a bullet in McClain's back, turned, fired toward Christmas, and shot Magee in the chest.

He tried to shoot Magee again, but the gun clicked, it was out of ammunition. "Magee stopped moving. I shouted, 'stop firing, please stop firing' . . . at about the same time I felt a sharp pain in my back. My legs gave out and I crumpled down . . . About

one inch of my spinal cord was shot away. As a result I am para-
lyzed from the waist down."

Branton's cross examination was based on the premise that
Thomas' memory of the August 7 events were blurred because of
his personal involvement with the late jurist. Thomas' wife, Maur-
een, is Judge's Haley's niece, and the attorney, immediately after
the shooting, had described his uncle as a saint. Branton theorized
that the bloodbath in the van started when an outside fusillade of
shots killed Jackson and McClain and that Thomas then took
McClain's gun and began to fire at Christmas and Magee.

"Because of your emotional state, you have been uncertain
of the sequence of events that day, haven't you?"

"That's a very broad question."

"Isn't this what really happened? Isn't it a fact that the first
fusillade of shots into the van killed both Jackson and McClain
and you grabbed the gun McClain was holding and you turned and
began to fire into the back of the van at Christmas and Magee.
And you hit Christmas and Magee and possibly even hit Judge
Haley?"

"No." In one of his earlier statements, Thomas said that the
weapon he had used had been taken from McClain.

"It's true isn't it that the only shot you know of being fired
inside the van by someone other than yourself is the shot you said
was fired by Ruchell Magee?"

"Yes."

"And it was in Magee's direction and Magee's direction only
that you fired shots, wasn't it?"

"No."

"Isn't it true that it was only after you hit Ruchell Magee
that the shotgun went off?"

"No."

"Did you hear the shotgun go off?"

"No."

"Isn't it true that the reason you didn't hear it go off was
because at the same time you were hit in the spine, the shotgun
went off?"

"No."

Thomas said that he could not identify the pistol he used.

Branton kept asking if it was McClain's, and not Jonathan's gun, which Thomas had used. Thomas said it was Jonathan's. Branton developed a few inconsistencies between Thomas' testimony before the Grand Jury, and that given at the trial. But generally, Thomas' testimony held, a fact which surprised no one, least of all the defense attorneys.

It was the Marin County Sheriff's Department which carried out the initial investigation, resulting in a situation where deputies often were testifying both to their own experiences as participants, and to their investigative efforts as policemen. It became clear that the excitement and confusion which existed August 7, had affected the professional competency of several of the officers.

Officers could identify who gave the order to cease firing, but no one could testify about who gave the order to start. Sheriff Mountanos, who figured heavily in the testimony, had not been called as a witness. It was the Sheriff who had taken the call from Judge Haley. He had then gone down to the court's floor, ordered several men to keep their pistols holstered, and was subsequently disarmed. Mountanos also had been in the parking lot at the time the shooting broke out. In press appearances in the immediate aftermath of the shooting, Mountanos had been exceedingly critical of the role played by San Quentin guards, who were apparently the only law enforcement officers who fired that day. The Sheriff's plan had been to allow the escape, but to order his men to follow the van, possibly with the help of helicopter surveillance, and to wait for an opportunity to rescue the hostages.

San Quentin guards, in firing, either contravened his orders not to shoot, or else were not aware that the order was given. The possible abrogation of authority by San Quentin guards was not made an issue at the trial. Defense attorney's interest in this phase of the trial was almost exclusively devoted to questioning the evidence gathered at the Civic Center which could possibly link Angela to those events. This evidence, however, had to be discussed within the context of all the evidence gathered. It developed that there had been a number of mistakes made.

It isn't particularly surprising that police officers faced with the enormity that was August 7, would not react as efficiently as they might under less disturbing circumstances. It is also a fact that some police officers are less efficient than others. The difficulty comes in the fact that the understandable confusion of August 7, somehow was translated into neatly labeled exhibits and properly filed away reports, which in no way reflected that confusion.

The autopsies, for instance, were completed in about four hours, according to Dr. John H. Manwaring, the doctor who performed them. That may very well be sufficient time to determine the cause of death for four people. The autopsies were performed, in part, in the presence of Fred A. Wynbrandt, the Chief of the Department of Technical Services, California's crime lab. Dr. Manwaring removed bullets or bullet fragments from the bodies, and handed them directly to Mr. Wynbrandt.

Nevertheless, a year later Manwaring found it necessary, after consultation with Wynbrandt and Eric Collins (a Deputy Attorney General who helped prepare the case) to reverse his opinion of the paths traversed by the bullets which killed Jonathan Jackson and William Christmas. Entrance wounds became exit wounds and vice versa. Manwaring's opinion about the cause of Judge Haley's death had also changed. At the Grand Jury hearing Manwaring testified that either one of two wounds sustained by Judge Haley could have caused death. At the Davis trial the doctor insisted that the judge's chest wound would not necessarily have caused death, and that the head wound was definitely fatal.

Howard Moore, Jr. was obviously annoyed with the doctor's testimony. Moore pointed out, through questioning, that Manwaring is a private physician, who has appeared in court only for the prosecution, except for a few drunk-driving cases. Moore's thrust was that Manwaring was a professional prosecution witness, whose autopsies are flexible enough to fit a prosecution theory about a crime. In this instance, the flat determination that the head wound killed Judge Haley would block any defense based on the chest wound possibly being the cause of death. Also, the reversal of the wounds in Jackson and Christmas matched better with the reconstruction of the shooting presented by Harris. Manwaring, incidentally, had conducted the autopsy on George Jackson, and had reversed his opinion there about the paths of the bullet several months after his original report, a change of opinion which made his final report coincide more closely with the cause of death as described by prison officials.

Ballistics tests had been taken, but not all the bullets could be identified. A slug taken from McClain's arm was described by Wynbrandt as being too large for a 30-30 (the caliber used by San Quentin guards) leaving the inference that McClain had been shot by Thomas.

Bullet fragments were passed around to the jury, as part of Harris' program to have them relive as much of August 7 as possible. It was only because Judge Arnason upheld a defense objection that Harris did not show the jury pictures of the judge's shotgun damaged face. There was a large mound of evidence, each with its number, but not all with meaning. A coil of wire and a bullet were submitted. They both came from Christmas' pocket and did not contribute to an understanding of what had happened in the van. There was a multiple exhibit, a slug which was taken from Ruchell Magee along with one taken from Gary Thomas. Six live bullets were introduced, a piece of plastic from a car that had been damaged by gunfire, and an expended shell that had been found on the sidewalk.

There's no question that a lot of shooting went on, but the guns that shot from outside the van were never examined. Several San Quentin guards testified to shooting, but their weapons had been returned to the armory and had not been subjected to ballistics tests.

Testimony of almost half of Harris' witnesses, and over three-fourths of the 200 pieces of physical evidence he had submitted, concerned August 7. He had to prove that a murder and a kidnap occurred, and that certainly could not be done without testimony relative to August 7. After this phase was completed, defense attorneys maintained that Harris had proven neither kidnap nor murder. Both Moore and Branton took the position that Gary Thomas did not have the gun assigned to him by the prosecutor, a position which challenged the bulk of the prosecution allegations dealing with who died and by what means. Their job as attorneys was only to raise the problems, not try to solve them. They were Angela's attorneys, not Ruchell's. Angela was charged with murder, not with shooting anyone, and August 7 was not the key to her defense. This phase of the prosecution case ended with Harris reading the Soledad Brothers indictment of January 16, 1970, charging the three with murder and assault. Branton then called on Harris to stipulate that George Jackson had been found not guilty after his death because he could not be present to defend himself, and that subsequently the two remaining Soledad Brothers were acquitted. Harris snappishly declined to have anything to do with Branton's proposal.

Coming up was a battle over the admission of evidence taken from Angela's apartment. The jury was sent away, and FBI man James McCord was questioned, in order for Judge Arnason to determine whether the evidence which he took from Angela's apartment should be admitted. The defense contention was that McCord had a warrant charging Angela with unlawful flight across state lines to avoid prosecution, and that the items which he took from Angela's apartment were not relevant to the subject of the warrant. Harris' position was that the warrant spelt out "correspondence, lists of names and addresses, photos of friends," and that "there's no room left to ascertain what was taken was legal." Perhaps Harris was right. Part of what was taken was introduced into evidence—two letters to George Jackson dated June 2 and June 10. There was a minor mystery about the letters, as they were photocopies. Angela knew of no photocopies of correspondence at her apartment, and there was no indication on the inventory filled out by McCord that photocopies had been picked up. Whatever the case, it seemed as though the FBI had gone into Angela's apartment and taken everything in sight that had something written on it.

The defense argued that since the letters were not material to Angela's crossing state lines that they should be suppressed as evidence.

A third letter was also the subject of this special hearing, one dated June 22, 1970, which was intercepted at Soledad Prison and taken from an envelope sent by George Jackson's attorney John Thorne. Raymond Kelsey, the mailroom guard, said that he discovered the letter in a routine search for contraband and turned it over to his superior Captain Moody.

The letters to George Jackson went directly to the core of Harris' case, his passionate conspiracy theory. The letter which went to Soledad included the words, "liberation by any means necessary" and "if I am serious about my love for you, about black people, I should be ready to go all the way."

"The night after I saw you in court . . . I dreamt we were together fighting pigs, winning, we were learning to know each other . . . We have to learn to rejoice when pig's blood is spilled . . . to learn how to set the sights accurately, squeeze rather than jerk and not be overcome by the damage" was written in the letter of June 10.

Harris wanted the challenge to those letters being introduced as evidence dismissed quickly so that he could present evidence to the jury according to his timetable. He had just finished inundating the jury with August 7 violence, attributed to Angela's planning. Now he wanted to get an extended picture of a violent Angela Davis across. He expected a fight over the admissibility of the letters, but he wanted it limited both in scope and in time.

The most vigorous objections of the defense were to the introduction of an 18-page document found in George Jackson's cell after he was killed. Spiro P. Vasos, a fingerprint expert working for the Bureau of Criminal Information and Identification (CII), and subordinate to Albert Harris, went into Jackson's cell on August 21, 1971, and took all of his property to Sacramento. Vasos testified that the cell was messy, with debris and blood distributed all over at the time he was there, just hours after Jackson's death. George Murray, an investigator for the Attorney General, told of going through the box on August 23, and giving the letters which he found to Albert Harris, and to Vasos, at Harris' suggestion, so that the letter could be examined for fingerprints.

A Marin County deputy, Mary Ann Brown, who worked in the Marin County jail where Angela had been confined, testified to sneaking into Angela's working cell after lights were out, taking a typewriter from there, and copying two pages of what turned out to be the 18-page letter taken from George Jackson's effects. The prosecution agreed to stipulate that the typewriter was taken at the request of Albert Harris and without benefit of a search warrant. The exemplar—the two pages which were copied—were also at issue, as they were being offered into evidence to prove that the 18-page letter had been typed by Angela Davis.

Branton argued against the introduction of the four letters along with the exemplar. He said that Angela, though in jail, had been allowed to represent herself. This meant that her workroom was in effect a law office, which the prosecution had unconstitutionally and unconscionably obtained.

He said the letter seized at Soledad should be suppressed because Angela was not charged with a crime in June, 1970, when that letter was taken. As to the 18-page letter, the seizure was illegal on its face, as there was no search warrant involved.

Harris said that he didn't care about the exemplar, as he could prove by other means that Angela wrote the 18-page document, but he insisted that all of the letters be admitted as evidence. Harris prevailed, Judge Arnason ruled that the exemplar would be suppressed, but that the other letters could be ruled into evidence.

That was just the preliminary skirmish over the letters. The attorneys were arguing inadmissibility because of the manner in which the prosecution came into possession of the documents. Arguments over their relevancy would come later.

Vasos had more to say about this evidence than the fact that he had carried it from San Quentin to Sacramento. He had been the state's fingerprint expert and had found 52 of George Jackson's fingerprints and one of Angela Davis', along with one of John Spain's, on the 18-page diary. Spain is the prisoner who was charged with trying to escape with George Jackson, and is one of the San Quentin Six. He'd also found one of Angela's thumbprints in one of her books. Vasos said he inspected the yellow van inside and out for prints, and could only come up with one of Jonathan's, on the right outside mirror.

A handwriting expert, Sherwood Morril, also of the CII, testified that signatures on checks bearing Angela's name were indeed in her handwriting, and also, that it was she who had signed receipts for the guns bought in her name. Morril said that he could not identify a two sentence postcript signed Jon, that was on the bottom of Angela's June 22 letter as having been written by Jonathan. He could say that the signature, Diane Robinson, which appeared in a San Quentin visitors log on August 5 and 6, 1970, immediately below Jonathan Jackson's, had not been made by Angela Davis but was in Jonathan's handwriting.

There was an additional item to argue about. Harris proposed putting Lt. W. P. Sellmer, a San Quentin guard who had witnessed the July 8 meeting between Angela and George Jackson, on the stand. Sellmer had apparently been scandalized because the two, when they met, greeted each other with considerably more than handshakes, and remained in physical contact throughout the meeting. Considering the fact that there were eight or nine other people in the room at the time, George and Angela were limited in the extent to which they could be openly affectionate toward each other. Nevertheless, Harris felt that a description of this passionate interlude in a county jail would make good testimony.

Branton argued that Harris was using the Sellmer testimony as a foundation to the prosecutor's case, which he described as a bootstrap operation. "Sellmer would testify that he saw a meeting between Angela Davis and counsel and George Jackson with counsel." Branton said he expected that as a result of Sellmer's peeking, he would testify that he saw "great warmth and affection shown." He characterized the proposed testimony as completely inadmissible. "This testimony may be critical. The prosecution intends to call Sellmer to testify to what he saw rather than what he heard . . . if he saw them kiss and embrace and anything else, it was a violation of the confidentiality of communication which should be unseen as well as unheard. The guard deliberately eavesdropped on the confidentiality of two clients."

Harris said that everyone was aware of Sellmer outside, and in fact they told him to leave, a fact quickly verified by defense attorneys. Harris continued: "It was his job to watch Jackson. He wasn't about to let a prisoner accused of murder get out of his sight." Besides, Sellmer did not violate the attorney-client privilege in talking about the conduct of two people who were clients. "The embraces had nothing to do with confidential material."

Most of Branton's argument dealt with the 18-page letter, which he said was properly called a diary, since it was addressed to no one and signed by no one and had several entry dates beginning with July 8 and ending July 23. He said there "is an unbridgeable evidence gap" between the events of August 7, 1970, and the writings of the diary almost a year later. "Will the court allow the jury to read the most private thoughts" on the single theory that Angela's state of mind a year later is probative of her state of mind prior to August 7? He said that the letter contained a lot of revolutionary rhetoric which would prejudice the jury. "What is in these letters that constitute an admission? . . . These letters express a love and admiration for George Jackson . . . This is the first time in my life that I've heard love as a motivation for a crime."

These letters express her state of mind, countered Harris, saying that all of the writings had to be considered. "I might agree that there are parts of these letters which might properly be excluded . . . ," but he wanted the juicy parts left in. "Nonviolence as a philosophy is a philosophy of suicide," he quoted from the letter of June 10, as an example of Angela's state of mind.

"The letters show that Angela was willing to undergo very serious risks for George Jackson," he continued. "Jonathan's postscript to one of Angela's letters tends to show the close relationship of Angela to the younger Jackson, and their mutual devotion to George Jackson. They contradict Angela's opening statement that affection and emotion grew with time. They were strong then. We see nothing in these letters that are prejudicial." Referring specifically to the 18-page document, Harris said, "this letter is totally different in dimension . . . this document shows in many places that this defendant considered herself George Jackson's wife . . . If the people are not allowed to present this letter to the jury, then the truth will never come out in this courtroom."

That argument "demonstrates the sin and the evil Mr. Harris wants to generate through these letters." Branton was back on his feet, shaking a sheaf of papers. "The first and last page have messages of love and in between is a myriad of irrelevant data," he said of the diary.

Branton began to read from some of the letters, utilizing all of the dramatic training and courtroom experience of his past. He read a section dealing with the rape of black women, then looked up, "what's wrong with that? She dreams they were fighting and killing pigs. What's wrong with that?" And as for nonviolence as a philosophy of suicide, Harris read it out of context. Branton proceeded to put it back into context.

"Concerning nonviolence: The spectre of Sharpville, South Africa—thousands machine-gunned, kneeling in the streets, protesting Apartheid, nonviolently. Nonviolence as a philosophy is a philosophy of suicide."

Branton said he was not about to stipulate to the excising of irrelevant material from the letters. The only stipulation he wanted was that all the documents should be suppressed.

Actually, the defense would not have been too bothered if the letters seized in 1970 were admitted into evidence. There was nothing in them they considered damaging. But the 18-page diary was something else again. There was nothing resembling a confession in the diary, and no reference to August 7. It was a deeply personal document, rambling over Angela's life, revealing pieces of her innermost thoughts, fantasizing about she and George Jackson, dealing with revolutionary ideas with a sensuousness that was part of her person rather than her politics, and generally revelatory of Angela Davis as a woman. The defense felt that the diary might create the problem of individual jurors being deeply affected by the tremendous emotional charge in the letters, and that their decision would be filtered through that, rather than be guided by what factual inferences about Angela's state of mind could be made from the diary.

The objection to Sellmer's proposed testimony was on similar grounds. The defense did not want to grapple with the moral attitudes of any of the jurors. They had no way of knowing whether Sellmer's description of the embraces of Angela and George would offend the contemporary standards of a Santa Clara County jury and they had no intention of finding out.

Doris Walker suggested that Leo had been so brilliant in arguing against the admission of the letters before the judge that Arnason would rule against the defense so as to give Leo an opportunity to repeat his performance before a jury. Arnason ruled that the letters taken from Angela's apartment, along with the one intercepted at Soledad were, "relevant, probative and competent" as evidence.

Sellmer's testimony was out. "A Defendant's constitutional right to counsel would be seriously and unlawfully proscribed, if testimony of this type would be permissible."

As to the 18-page diary: "It contains much that is totally irrelevant to the issues before this Court and jury. It would appear to be a herculean task to excise the inadmissible and irrelevant material so as to leave only legally relevant and admissible evidence . . . The court is equally satisfied that, if the entire document were allowed to be received in evidence, it would entail undue consumption of time and create substantial danger of undue prejudice and tend to confuse the issues and possibly mislead the jury."

Arnason upheld the defense, "without prejudice to the People again proffering the document properly edited so as to exclude all legally inadmissible material." The jury was brought back in.

Harris stood up and began reading the letters which had been admitted into evidence. He could not approach the style with which Branton read, but then, few people can. Harris read haltingly, almost as if he were finding meaning in the letters, implications that he had not recognized before. The prosecutor began to perspire, but doggedly kept on reading.

At one point, he reached a Che Guevara quote which Angela had included as part of remarks she was making about a black who had been found on a deserted road with two bullets in his head. She had written that he was a revolutionary, and that his last thoughts must have been similar to what Che said about death: "Whenever death may surprise us, it will be welcome, provided that this, our battle cry, reaches some receptive ear, that another hand reach out to take up weapons and that other men [Angela had added "and women"] come forward to intone our funeral dirge with the staccato of machine guns and new cries of battle and victory."

Harris gave the impression, as he stumbled through this quote, that for the first time he realized he was quoting someone other than Angela Davis. His reading of the letters which Arnason allowed into evidence seemed to strengthen his resolve to force the 18-page diary back into evidence.

Immediately after the reading of the letters to the jury, the

prosecutor demanded a chambers session in order to force reconsideration of Judge Arnason's banning of the 18-page diary. He reminded the judge of references to the document he had made in
his opening statement: "We consider this an extremely important
part of our case. So, very frankly, I think our case is somewhat
in jeopardy right at the moment . . . The key thing, I think about
this document, is that it's a totally private and sincere document,
meant for nobody's eyes except George Jackson . . . That's why
it's so important to me, in that it shows her true feelings . . ."

"This letter changed our whole theory of the case . . . We
didn't view the case as we headed into trial after discovering this
letter and reading it and thinking about it as a political effort at all,
a political coloration as to what we think the Defendant did . . .
This is the reason why I asked to strike the Overt Act No. 1. I
didn't feel that it was material anymore. It didn't add anything to
the case. It would misinterpret the reasons why the Defendant did
what she did . . .

"There is not one word in here, in which she even suggests
that she is innocent, that there is a frameup, that she's being railroaded. There is not one suggestion of what the cornerstone is of
the defense in this case.

"This is the real critical significance of this letter. Here was
the chance to tell George: 'They know I'm not guilty. Why do they
keep doing this? Why are they imagining these things? You know
I'm not guilty. You know I didn't help Jon.' There's not one word
in this whole thing.

"We feel that this is of critical importance in the trial of
this case because the defense has been claiming for a year and a
half that this is a railroad, it's a frameup and so forth. Well, if
there was one sentence in this document, because it is a personal
and private and sincere document, if there were any place in here
where there was a statement that, you know, 'I didn't want Jon to
do what he did' or 'I had nothing to do with that' or 'this is a
terrible frameup,' I think this case would never have gone this far.

"Now I don't think we can try this case before the jury and
bring out the truth about the relationship between the Defendant
and George Jackson without this letter . . .

"I don't think the full truth about this case will ever be

known unless this letter or, at least, significant parts of it are admitted—is admitted into evidence and is heard in open court and so that the public and the world knows about this event. It's of an importance that I just can't overemphasize . . .

"This case is important not only to us and to the Defendant; it's important to the nation. I think it's important to the world."

Harris suggested that the defense should edit the letter and remove those sections offensive to them. "We are prepared to take it up and to do it an any way the defense wants to do it, page by page, line by line, whatever it might be until the relevant evidence that's in this document is culled out and admitted in Court because we don't think the case can be tried without it . . ."

Branton was incensed. "The prosecutor has admitted . . . that he kept a defendant in jail on a serious charge . . . for a period of almost a year and had no case against her and did not discover the evidence which was going to make his case against her until August of 1971 . . . more than one year after the crime was committed and more than ten months after she was in custody . . .

"For him to say here that he can't proceed with this case and his whole case is in jeopardy because he cannot get into evidence a letter . . . is a shocking kind of condemnation of misconduct on the part of the Attorney General's office.

"He should have dismissed this case months ago if he had to rely upon something which he had not yet found and was desperately searching for and didn't find it until he happened to run across that document . . .

"Mr. Harris chose to change the theory of his case because he didn't like the first one. He didn't want to say that it was a political killing. Now, he wants to say that it was a killing out of passion because he found that letter. He didn't have any right to bring this case in the first place if he was constantly searching for a theory upon which he could get a conviction . . .

"If he hasn't got any more evidence that he can proceed with in this case . . . I suggest that the only honorable thing for him to do is move for a dismissal in this case. I want to remind Mr. Harris that it is not the responsibility or the duty of a prosecutor to get a conviction at all costs. But when he is convinced that his case is not such that can prove the guilt of a defendant beyond a reasonable doubt, it is his responsibility to move for a dismissal and not wait for the defendant to do it. I suggest that that is his only remedy at this point if he feels that he cannot proceed without that letter . . .

"I really think that the people of the world and of the nation and of the Attorney General's office and everybody else would be much further ahead if Mr. Harris would do the honorable thing and dismiss this proceeding because it's obvious now by his own admission that that is the only thing left to him . . .

"Based upon the record, as it now stands, we will take no part in attempting to aid Mr. Harris in excising or editing any part of that letter so that it can get in evidence because we believe that the entire letter is inadmissible as has been ruled by the Court at this time."

Howard Moore, Jr. moved into the argument, pointing out the absurdity of Harris' argument saying that the writing of the 18-page document provided Angela with an opportunity to disclaim responsibility for August 7.

"You are going to advance a very strange notion. Because she didn't say this or she didn't say that, then, this is a reflection that she must be guilty."

Judge Arnason pointed out to Harris that had the letter contained the disclaimer he was referring to, that it could not be used as evidence at all. "There are cases galore in California indicating that statements made by a defendant afterwards in private writings and so forth cannot be used if they are self-serving."

Harris continued to press for reconsideration. He insisted that the letter, "did change my thinking about the motive. It didn't change my thinking at all about the fact of guilt."

He said that he would edit the letter, and, "if as edited, it is excluded, then we will re-edit it and re-edit it, and we will continue to re-edit it until we get down to what the Court feels can be admitted in evidence." The prosecutor asked for a continuation to give him time to edit the letter and place it into evidence, saying that the sequence in which evidence is presented to a jury is of importance.

Branton agreed with him about sequence, but in agreeing, impugned the prosecutor's motive for wanting that diary, or parts of it, read to the jury in a particular time period. Branton said the defense would oppose a continuance for that purpose because there was nothing in the diary which had any relationship to the witnesses Harris was going to call. Yet to be heard were people testifying to Angela's association with Jonathan Jackson and witnesses to Angela's flight.

"What Mr. Harris really means is he wants the time to be able to get something before that jury in that letter which will so prejudice that jury and make them so receptive to thinking a certain thing about Miss Davis' character, that, therefore, they will be in a better receptive mood to accept other evidence that he knows, standing by itself, does not mean a thing. So we would certainly object to any period of time being given to Mr. Harris for purposes of doing something which can only have the effect of giving him time in which he can put something before the jury which can only prejudice them as far as the evidence is concerned."

Arnason, who had done much more listening than talking, temporarily resolved the issue. He proposed that Harris continue with his witnesses for the rest of that day and the next, and that the following day, Thursday, he would recess court allowing the prosecution a long weekend in which to come up with a version of the diary that might be acceptable. After some discussion they arranged to meet in chambers again Thursday and go over the document in order to determine what might reasonably be left in.

Harris' detailed case continued for a day and a half. He brought in Mercedes Hornsby, who worked for the Savings and Loan Association which rented Angela an apartment. He was apparently beginning to produce for the jury one of the things he had talked about in his opening statement, evidence that Angela had moved from 45th Street to 35th Street in Los Angeles, during July 1970, in connection with the conspiracy. His bringing Mrs. Hornsby from Los Angeles to San Jose seemed a waste of time as the defense was willing to stipulate to everything she had to say, namely that Angela rented an apartment and gave a $75 check as a deposit.

Next came Otelia Young, a black lady between 55 and 60, whose dark hair was both thinning and becoming mixed with grey. She seemed to stride forward to the witness stand, a short lady bent over at the waist as though bothered by back pain, and was determined to be strong through it all.

Angela Davis? Moved in July, but I don't remember the date. Miss Young had lived downstairs in the four unit apartment building that Angela moved into.

Young man? I seen him. He was real tall and bright, with bright hair and very muscular.

"Do you recall the last time you saw Miss Davis in person?"

"It must have been on Monday . . . I work from 7 o'clock in the morning until 8:30 at night the rest of the week."

"Did you observe anybody moving Angela into the apartment from a white station wagon?" Harris was moving on his assertion that Jonathan shared the apartment with Angela.

"No. All I seen was books . . . Angela carried most of the books."

She'd seen Jonathan, but not helping Angela to move. Although he had been around, Miss Young did not have the impression that he spent a great deal of time there. Harris stopped questioning and the defense had no need to. Miss Young came off the stand, walking with determined steps away from the witness stand and toward the rail that separates the spectators from the court. After passing Angela she turned around, waving "hi" toward her, breaking out into a large smile. Angela smiled and returned the gesture. Just folks—a once upon a time neighbor greeting another as though it were a chance meeting on a street, rather than in a courtroom where the words of one were being solicited so as to help forge a conviction for the other.

The prosecutor didn't get over the idea that Jonathan had been living with Angela, but he had more to get across. His timing on the letters became clear. He had wanted to read all of them before plunging into the complex testimony dealing with gun and ammunition purchases. Harris had the guns programmed. Two of them, the carbine with the collapsible stock and the 380 Browning automatic, had been testified to. At the same time the jury found out that Jonathan had displayed those weapons in the courtroom, they were told that Angela bought them.

The second time weapons were mentioned it was to establish

that Angela had bought large quantities of ammunition, had given a Stephen Mitchell money to buy a carbine which she subsequently exchanged for another carbine because the first was defective, and that one of the salespersons who waited on her noticed Angela smoking a small cigar.

Then, with the final struggle over the 18-page diary pending, the prosecution and the defense got into another prolonged discussion over the possible testimony of John Thorne.

Thorne, as George Jackson's attorney, had frequent contact with Angela in 1970. After her arrest in October, Thorne interrupted a European trip to fly from London to New York to speak with her. If there was anything that angered the defense more than the fact that a letter written a year after August 7 became the center of the prosecution case, it was John Ebson Thorne. Their anger came from the fact that Thorne, on September 29, 1970, had gone to the Attorney General's office and given a statement which helped to form part of the prosecution theory.

Thorne, a large, full-bearded deep-voiced man, seems eternally challenged to avoid countering an utterance with silence. Therefore, when he appeared at the Attorney General's office he made a statement, just because he could not resist. He apparently gave them what he thought was irrelevant or inaccurate information. Defense attorneys say that his statement was totally without truth. But Harris was so pleased with what Thorne said, that he wanted the attorney to get up and say it again before the jury that was trying Angela Davis.

Imagine the irony. George Jackson's lawyer, who was a conduit of information between George and Angela, who had been involved with Angela in the affairs of the Soledad Brothers Defense Committee, getting up on the stand and giving evidence that would contribute to Angela's conviction.

Thorne had told Harris of remembering a phone call from Angela in which she was supposed to have said that she and Jonathan were in San Jose and on their way to Santa Cruz. Something about that statement made Harris believe that Thorne said the call came in on August 5. That was the day the shotgun was bought, and that evening, according to rumor that never reached the height of testimony, Angela and Jonathan went somewhere in the Santa Cruz mountains and cut the shotgun down.

Thorne, who somehow had failed to realize, in September 1970, that Harris was trying to use anyone he could to help indict, and ultimately convict, Angela, finally caught on when he was subpoenaed to come to court as a witness. He immediately obtained the service of Charles Garry, and resisted testifying.

The defense objected to Thorne's testifying, and when his name was called as a witness there was a huddle at the bench which did not include the court reporter. As Harris and Branton were returning to their seats, the judge was dismissing the jury again for another voir dire.

Thorne took the stand as Garry told Arnason that he had advised his client that, "for him to testify would be to lay himself wide open to legal prosecution for malpractice and might subject him to disciplinary action by the state bar and possible disbarment." Garry explained that Harris, in questioning Thorne, was attempting to breach the sacred attorney-client relationship, and that he had advised his client not to answer any questions.

Harris asked: "Did you represent George Jackson?"

"I'm going to advise Mr. Thorne not to answer that question. The very fact of answering that question bares the seed of the attorney-client relationship."

Harris reminded Garry that Thorne's representation of Jackson was a matter of public record.

"All right, I will stipulate that Mr. Thorne represented George Jackson," offered Garry.

Harris did not want to hear from Garry, he wanted answers from Thorne. Arnason advised Garry that if he were not claiming any constitutional basis other than the attorney-client relationship, that his client might be in trouble. Garry confidently replied that the law was clear and that his client did not have to respond, "I've researched estate, malpractice, disciplinary action."

Arnason told Harris to proceed.

"Did you have occasion to be in Salinas in April 1970?"

Garry said the question was analogous to the prior question, but that he would stipulate that "Thorne made all necessary appearances on behalf of his client." Harris expressed his total disinterest in stipulations from a witness' lawyer, saying that Garry had no standing in the case and that he wanted to hear Thorne. "If there is any place in the evidence code that keeps an attorney from testifying as a witness I'd like to see it."

"You know what's happening," said Garry. He reminded Harris that Thorne had sent him an express letter saying that he would not testify so as to avoid violating the attorney-client privilege. Garry spoke of precedent, and said he would not open the door to violating that privilege by having his client answer questions which might constitute a waiver of his right to remain silent.

What Harris wanted from Thorne was the testimony that he was in his San Jose office on August 5, and received a call from Angela Davis who said that she was in San Jose with Jonathan Jackson enroute to Santa Cruz to pick up some things. Supposedly, Angela had said that Jonathan had been living in Santa Cruz and was moving to San Francisco, an assertion which defense attorneys said was completely false. The reason Angela was supposed to have called was to inquire about a writ of mandate seeking to set aside Judge Drewe's denial of Angela's appointment as an investigator for George Jackson.

Branton was maintaining that an attorney-client relationship existed between Thorne and Angela in July, 1970, in addition to the relationship between Thorne and George Jackson. Thus, Thorne could not be compelled to testify. But even if he were, asserted Branton, the telephone call was made prior to July 21, the day that the writ of mandate was filed.

"We do not intend to testify to any of that," said Garry.

Arnason decided to continue to allow Harris to ask questions, cautioning Thorne, who had been interjecting remarks all along, that as he was represented by counsel, he should speak only after advice.

"I've heard that rule a long time ago about representing one's self and having an idiot for an attorney and a fool for a client," Thorne remarked. And Garry, who was sitting in a chair immediately in front of the barrier which divided the spectators from the court, waved his hand saying, "and that goes for right now."

"On July 15, 1970 were you in the city and county of San Francisco?"

Garry waved with a downward motion of his hand as if he were Frank Sinatra cutting off Neil Hefti's band. "I claim the attorney-client privilege."

Harris by now was boiling. He had been questioning for at least 15 minutes, and had not succeeded in having one answer on the record. Branton and Garry had been double-teaming him, effectively blocking the prosecutor from developing any consistent line of questioning.

"I request the court order the witness to answer," Harris said, almost in desperation.

Garry persisted. "Once opened as a waiver, the entire attorney-client relationship is jeopardized." He asked the judge to make a ruling that answering that particular question would not open the door to queries that intrude on that relationship. Arnason did so, and Garry leaned back and told Thorne that it was all right to answer.

Then Thorne balked, questioning the advice of his attorney. "Suppose I get cited and lose on appeal, what then?" Garry went to the witness stand and whispered something in Thorne's ear, after which the witness answered, "assuming I was in court that day."

"Were you in San Francisco?"

"I assume I was."

Harris then tried to introduce a letter which Thorne had written to the Superior Court in San Francisco, causing another squabble that was settled by both Branton and Garry stipulating that Thorne wrote the letter.

By now, Harris was livid. He repeated, emphatically, that he was not interested in a stipulation from a witness' attorney. He turned back to Thorne. "Now, did you file that declaration?"

Garry advised his client not to answer, and Thorne complied.

For over a half hour, Harris, constantly being harassed by a combination of Branton and Garry, failed to get one answer from Thorne into the record. His task was complicated by the fact that at the beginning of the session, Angela Davis had taken the stand

and testified to the relationship between her and Thorne. She explained that Thorne had acted as her attorney in filing an appeal to have her appointed as an investigator for George Jackson. She had also asked the attorney to represent her in the publication of a book she planned to write. Judge Arnason had ruled that there had been a clear attorney-client relationship between her and the witness, that extended up to August 7, 1970. Harris could ask questions about a phone call, but could not go into the subject matter of communication between Thorne and Angela Davis. But finally, Harris succeeded in getting a response of sorts.

"Now on August 5, where were you, Mr. Thorne?"

"I have no memory at all."

"Were you in the US?"

"I don't remember."

"Were you in your office in San Jose?"

"I don't remember."

"Were you in the Attorney General's office September 29, 1970?"

Garry objected, but Arnason overruled and Thorne did not remember. Garry insisted that Harris was creeping up on the attorney-client relationship. Arnason said no, he's not trying to get into that relationship. Branton chimed in, "I know where he's going."

Harris took a new tack. He gave Thorne a copy of the September 29 transcript, recalling for the witness that he had been represented at that time by two attorneys and had been under oath. The prosecutor was obviously tired of the whole examination. He reviewed the hearing, pointing out that every word in that transcript had been recorded only after Thorne had consulted with his attorneys. Further, that no claim of an attorney-client relationship with Angela Davis appeared in the transcript. He accused Thorne of fabricating that relationship subsequently to September 29.

"Is the prosecuting attorney accusing my client of perjury?" Garry was indignant. "This kind of innuendo means that Mr. Thorne will not answer any questions."

Arnason, obviously having decided that some other approach was needed in order to satisfy Harris' need for answers from Thorne, which would skirt the defense objections regarding the attorney-client relationship, decided to end the questioning of Thorne. The judge ordered him to return the following Monday and to be prepared to testify, hoping that by then something could be worked out to accommodate the needs of both sides.

The jury came back to hear that Angela paid for a repair to Lester Jackson's car by check and other details of her banking history which included cashing checks when accompanied by someone who answered Jonathan's description. There was also testimony about Angela and Jonathan being stopped at the Mexican border July 30, 1970, and that Jonathan had been stopped the following night in Los Angeles while driving Angela's car. Then, Harris made a request for a continuance until May 1, because of a matter of critical importance regarding the 18-page document, which Arnason granted reluctantly. The judge's reluctance was understandable, as Harris was formally asking him to preside over another session in which the 18-page diary would be in contention.

The next morning, opposing attorneys, including Angela, were in the judge's chambers, with Harris presenting an eight and one-half page version of the diary that he had prepared.

Branton responded angrily: "I realize that . . . all lawyers are supposed to cooperate with the court and other counsel in determining whether or not evidence is properly admissible. But, speaking for myself, I must say that I cannot participate in this session. I consider this entire session an obscenity. I feel almost like a man who has been forced, at gun point, to watch the rape of his mother. That is how sickening I think this whole procedure is here in which we are attempting to pry into the most intimate, the most personal expressions of another human being, because the Prosecution in this case feels that, without doing that, he cannot get a conviction."

Branton was not acting. He was genuinely offended, and wanted everyone to know how he felt. "Mr. Harris has talked about all of the things he has eliminated, and I say that he has also eliminated all honor, all sense of conscience and all integrity.

"There will be other lawyers, your Honor, who may very well argue from a legal standpoint, the inadmissibility of certain parts of this letter, all of it, but I feel myself incapable of doing so because I now know, for the first time, what Martin Luther King meant when he said, 'you can't cooperate with evil.' This is evil, and I can't do it." And Branton left, he walked out, he turned his back on the whole thing.

Moore called the session, "the functional equivalent of what is going on in the prison system today—the introduction of psychosurgery. That is what . . . Mr. Harris would have this court do, participate in what turns out to be a literary lobotomy. You take out the part of the brain you think that is not helpful to your point of view. In the prison system you take out the part of the brain you feel is detrimental to totalitarianism in the prison system, and you leave in that part of the brain which you feel is compliant or helpful to your cause."

As it turned out, Branton was outside. He had nowhere to go. The attorneys had come in one car and would leave that way. Moore left the session, caught up with Branton, and persuaded him to come back—an unaccustomed role for Moore. He was used to pleading, that was his profession, but it was Branton who usually bridged the gap between Moore and Harris, and now it was turnabout time. By the time the session ended, however, things were back to normal. It was Branton who was presenting legal arguments and Moore who was battling with Harris.

Mrs. Walker came to argue the law, and did so at some length, using a textbook, *Wigmore on Evidence,* some notes from two law professors at UCLA, a number of legal citations, and, of course, the prosecutor-edited diary. She pointed out that Harris eliminated a portion of the letter which referred to political differences between George Jackson and Angela, and that the editing generally excised those items which would allow the jury to grasp some of the meaning of passages which would remain. The defense position was that the document should go into evidence as a whole, or not at all, recognizing that Judge Arnason had previously determined that the entire diary could not be used.

"What he would be doing and what he would have the Court permit is simply a recital of expressions, intimate expressions of love and emotion, totally out of the context in which the expressions originally appeared so that the prejudicial effect and the inflammatory effect is . . . of course, and must be so intended, of course, emphasized and intensified by this kind of approach . . .

I want to call your Honor's attention in connection with, whether we call it relevance or whether we call it remoteness, whether we are talking about materiality and admissibility . . . the fact that part of what the Prosecutor would excise from this document is this statement on page 15, about the middle of the page, 'but then, some of this may be projection, a desire to rediscover Jon, who I love so deeply in you.'

"Now, in his opening statement, the prosecutor said that he would prove that Miss Davis had sacrificed young Jonathan Jackson to her love for George, yet, yet perhaps because this statement of her love for Jonathan does not fit into his theory, he would excise it. This statement made on . . . July 12, 1971, is not relevant to his purpose, so he would excise it."

Harris, who had walked out during part of Mrs. Walker's presentation, had no patience with the defense arguments. He had started out wanting the entire document admitted, and his position had not changed. He'd gone through the diary day by day, line by line, and eliminated what he considered to be irrelevant. He crossed out all references to music, books, past associations and political matters. He was willing to let the defense put back anything they wanted, but meanwhile he maintained that everything in his edited version was relevant and probative.

Harris argued: "Now, the charge in this case is the Defendant conspired with other people in essence to bring about the freedom of George Jackson through violent means. That is the charge. Here is the statement. We think this is relevant . . . It is not prejudicial. It is of high probative value which I would agree may convince the jury that Miss Davis had a state of mind by which she would undertake a conspiracy, and she would undertake violent means to bring about the freedom of George Jackson . . .

"Now, if we are not allowed to prove that . . . if we are not allowed to prove that, then we might as well all pack up and go home. That is what this case is all about. This is not an academic discussion or a debate. This is a lawsuit. It is a criminal trial, and I want to see justice brought about. This is an admission. It is relevant. We think it should go into evidence."

"It is disgusting." Howard Moore, Jr.'s voice reflected all of the loathing he felt.

"Thank you, Mr. Moore. I appreciate that."

The two threw a barrage of words at each other, causing Judge Arnason to ask that they speak one at a time.

"Your point of view is disgusting," Moore repeated. "You are a distorted bigotist. It is disgusting, absolutely."

There in chambers, the real meaning of adversary proceedings was being acted out. Harris and Moore represented different sides of a legal issue, and they did so from stances that were based on entirely opposing philosophies about what the law was about, how society should be organized, and what the words "the people" really meant. The gap was wider than that described by referring to the prosecutor and the defense attorney. Those terms only refer to the role which an attorney takes on in court. Harris and Moore would oppose each other on the street, in a tavern, at a party—be on opposite sides of any public controversy, and ultimately, if both were admitted to practice before a heavenly bar, one would seek to appeal to a higher celestial court, the presence of the other.

They were suited to their loyalties. Moore is an advocate of a future public authority in which the people determine the nature of their judicial system. He had to be emotional, there was no other recourse. He had gone to the US Supreme Court 19 times and come back with 15 victories for people who had been battling official decisions, and he had grown to express himself in terms of the aspiration of people he represented, people who found existing state authority frustratingly repressive.

Harris, on the other hand, was the embodiment of a concept which he had repeated in court over and over again. He was dutiful. His loyalty, expressed in terms which described him as an advocate of "the people," was to a system which his sense of duty told him was supreme. Harris was every bit as combative as Moore. He also had emotions. This was not a callous, heartless person intent on destroying the innocent. No, this was a man who did his duty, and his duty was to prosecute in the name of the people. For Harris there was always some higher authority. But that authority was delegated, was enshrined in law and custom, and was recognizable in tradition, and in the orderly workings of whatever administration claimed to be in command of that tradition. He expressed satisfaction that Moore, in his anger, had referred to his bigotry, and made it a part of an official record, because he expected the system, rather than his own sensibilities, to vindicate him. Harris did what was necessary, what his position as Assistant Attorney General demanded, and knew he was right.

The two were engaged in conflict so basic, so elemental, so completely symbolic of the schism in our society between those who cleave to the system and those who vigorously question the injustices it perpetrates in the name of justice, that Judge Arnason, who normally inserts his authority between combatting attorneys, allowed that contest to continue, until both Moore and Harris reached the point where they recognized that each of them had to take care of the business at hand, and afterwards work toward the day that they could totally engage and defeat the forces with which the other identified. Neither was dealing with revolution, only a revolutionary, and the battle to have her declared innocent was here and now.

"We have cut out all references to family members," Harris explained, "we have tried to eliminate all references except to those matters that involve the author of the letter and the recipient of the letter and to matters involving the state of mind of the Defendant which we think are relevant to the case. I am sorry if these thing are found obscene."

"It is not the things in the letter that are obscene, it is your pawing over it that is obscene. That is what I mean," Moore replied.

"I don't care what you mean."

"I don't care what you care."

Arnason had to step in. "Mr. Moore—"

"I wanted the record to be clear as to what I think is obscene . . . I just find it incredible that anyone could, with a straight face, while urging on you this section . . . as being reflective of Miss Davis' state of mind sometime prior to August 7th, and perhaps on August 7th, and being indicative of what her motive, if she had any motive toward criminal disposition might have been." Then Moore went back to the passage which Harris called "an honest, sincere statement of her feelings . . . which . . . may convince the jury that Miss Davis had a state of mind by which she would undertake a conspiracy, and she would undertake violent means to bring about the freedom of George Jackson."

Moore read from page eight: "A scene frozen in my mind: I am standing in the little glass cubicle downstairs, standing waiting, loving, desiring, and then hot cold rage when the chains begin to rattle as you slowly descend the stairs surrounded by that small army of mindless but armed automatons. I, your wife, your comrade who is supposed to love you, fight with you, fight for you. I'm supposed to rip off the chains. I'm supposed to fight your enemies with my body, but I am helpless, powerless, I contain the rage inside, I do nothing. I stand there watching, forced to assume the posture of a disinterested spectator—the whole scene perceived through glass, laboratory-like—mad at them for thrusting this thing upon me. Mad at myself at doing nothing. Mad at myself too because I could not fail to see how much counter force you were exerting upon yourself. Each step—long, hard, unwilling to be restrained by chains and pigs—your entire body with each foot movement in a hard sway and the muscles of your face tensing with each sway. As I re-experience this now, my pulse beats faster, I begin to breathe harder, and I see myself tearing down this steel door, fighting my way to you, ripping down your cell door and letting you go free. I feel as you do, so terrible is this love."

"What are these thoughts," asked Moore. "These thoughts are her reaction, her experiences to an event that happened on July the 8th. But yet Mr. Harris wants to stand before the jury and say that these were her thoughts almost a year earlier. It is very clear from this letter that what she is responding to is her own predicament, to being locked in, and then seeing a man whom she admires greatly, loves greatly, for all of his attributes . . . as a brilliant thinker, a brilliant writer, a beautiful revolutionary. And she is describing her own feeling of helplessness being locked in herself, and she is as a spectator helpless . . . she can't do anything, and then she talks about what she is supposed, what she should do, she is imagining, and this is, Judge, you are being asked to put this before a jury as indicative of her state of mind a year earlier meaning if that isn't obscene, what is obscene—to completely distort the manifest character of this particular writing . . .

"Mr. Harris is inviting the Court to put before the jury in expurgated form and edited form her thoughts—to narrow down the complexity of her thoughts, to distort the character of the thoughts, to do anything to give him a chance to put something before the jury that he feels is more sensational than that which he has already put before the jury. I think that the Court should be mindful of the fact that Mr. Harris didn't stop the proceedings when you made your ruling, but he proceeded to read the three letters and apparently the vibration that he got or didn't get from the jury must have upset him or troubled him, and then he became frantic to get this particular letter in."

Arnason, with that informality of understatement commanded by those who know they are in charge, and are secure in that knowledge, spoke softly to the opposing counsel, whose sounds of battle had shaken the chamber.

"I know the pressures build up during trials, and we all sometimes show reactions to pressures in different ways, and there are days in which I am sure that all of us perhaps are not quite what we want to be . . . It is a measure, I think to some extent of a man's character . . . to be able to engage in discourse and present matters in a calm and understanding and rational viewpoint and not be subject at any time to allow feelings to get you into a different spirit. Because when we do that, we have just taken ourselves down a little bit, and I don't want that to happen to counsel in this case. You are all too competent and too qualified and too well trained to allow that to happen to you."

Arnason took the matter under submission, and directed Harris to get on with the case, which Harris did. The following Monday the prosecutor began his careful chronicling of Angela Davis' movements between August 3 and August 7.

He brought the Supervisor of Passenger Service for United Airlines up to San Jose, to testify that Angela took a 5:36 p.m. flight from Los Angeles on August 3, and paid for her ticket with a check, an item which the defense was willing to stipulate.

A kind of a mystery woman, Mabel "Mickey" Magers, came in from Kansas City to testify, accompanied by her attorney, Sidney L. Willins. Leo Branton, Jr. specifically asked the court to advise her of her fifth ammendment rights. The judge referred both Branton and the witness to her attorney.

Mickey Magers had a room in Joan Hammer's home in San

Jose in 1970, and had met both Jonathan and Angela while living there. She drove Joan Hammer and Jonathan Jackson to San Quentin on July 28, where she waited four hours for them to complete their visit with George, drove Jonathan to the airport and Joan Hammer and herself home to San Jose.

The prosecution had a guard testify about that visit also, how he saw Jonathan and George with their heads together, while Mrs. Hammer sat through most of the visit saying nothing. The guard couldn't figure out which side of the table George Jackson was sitting at, even though the prison waiting room is designed so that prisoners always sit on the same side of the table.

Harris brought Magers in to testify that she loaned her beige Volkswagen to Jonathan Jackson on August 4, 1970, and did not see it again until the latter part of August or first part of September. Georgia Jackson came to Mrs. Magers' room late one night and told her about the car. Joan Hammer drove Mickey Magers to the airport garage, where the Volkswagen was found, with a $43 parking bill attached.

Mickey Magers told Harris that she met Jonathan in mid July 1970, and that she saw him on August 2, at the opening of Soledad House, and August 4, when she loaned him her car. She remembered seeing Angela at Joan Hammer's house, but did not remember speaking with her. Harris prompted her to remember and testify that an empty coke cup and an empty box of small cigars had been on the floor of her car when she recovered it.

No, she never observed Jonathan carrying an attaché case such as he brought into the Civic Center. Branton's sustained objection prevented Harris from asking about information which Georgia Jackson might have given Mickey Magers.

Howard Moore cross examined. "Have you ever used the name Mickey Jackson?"

"Not verbally, I have written it."

"Was it because of your close relationship with Jonathan Jackson?"

"Yes, it had something to do with my relationship with Jonathan Jackson. I was returning a compliment to someone."

"The relationship was warm and affectionate, is that right?"

"Yes."

"I don't want to embarrass you or your family, but didn't you spend the evening of August 6, 1970, with Jonathan Jackson in the Holland Motel in San Francisco?"

The only thing that moved in that courtroom was Attorney Willins, who streaked up to the bench and arranged for an immediate recess. After an hour, Mickey Magers, a pleasant looking lady in her mid-twenties, with extremely long blond hair, retook the stand.

"No," she answered.

"Did Mr. Harris promise that nothing you said would be used against you?"

"I signed an affidavit of immunity if that's what you mean."

It turned out that both Moore and Harris had received pre-trial statements from Mickey Magers. Why the prosecution had to offer immunity to the witness was never apparent from anything produced in court. What also was not produced in court was a birth certificate showing that Mickey Magers had delivered a baby boy in a San Jose hospital in April 1971, named after the father, Jonathan P. Jackson.

It required a week for the prosecution to complete its version of Angela's and Jonathan's whereabouts during the week of August 3. He next entered into a series of stipulations relating to the route Angela took from California to New York, after disappearing August 7. Harris then announced that the people had no more witnesses until certain legal matters were resolved. Those matters were John Thorne and the edited letter.

Thorne appeared as a witness, and although there was much of the extended legal byplay of the week before, he was a more compliant witness. Thorne denied receiving a phone call from Angela on August 5, while acknowledging that he had made a statement to that effect on September 29, 1970. Harris read from the transcript of that statement. "Did you give those answers?"

"Yes," but, explained Thorne, "I have now learned that the conversation was prior to filing the petition for the District Court of Appeals on July 21, 1970. So the August 5 date was clearly erroneous." Harris couldn't shake that testimony.

The following Monday, after a long and complicated explanation of how the Attorney General's investigators had traced the $43 ticket on Mickey Mager's car, and a series of stipulations between prosecution and defense, Judge Arnason announced his decision on the diary.

Arnason, knowing that the defense would not participate, had edited Harris' version himself, and had come up with a two-and-one-half-page version of the prosecutor's eight and one-half pages. The judge said that his criterion in editing was to remove everything that was immaterial, irrelevant or prejudicial. Howard Moore, Jr. after looking over the judge's work remarked, "you're a hell of an editor judge."

Harris had said that if the document were reduced to one sentence, he would read that sentence into the record. He read the pages, seeming somewhat incongruous, as he labored through fragments of letters, reading words of love in a flat voice, and giving those words no more coloration, no more inflection or purposeful nuance, than he had given the reading of the lists of exhibits which he had placed into evidence. After the prosecutor read the lines: "I'm glad we saw each other when we did—it makes me realize that I have not always been as alone as I feel at this moment," he announced that the prosecution had rested its case.

10 : Justice in the Round II

The jury was excused for two days after Harris closed his case, so that the defense would have the opportunity of entering and arguing motions.

Leo Branton, Jr. argued that the case should be dismissed. "May it please the court," he began, "when the Prosecution ended its phase of the case by saying 'The Prosecution rests,' it was my immediate reaction to say: 'You what? You mean that you have kept this Defendant in jail for over 16 months, and you have subjected her to agony and the terror of having to go through a criminal trial with charges of such magnitude, and that's the only kind of evidence that you have!

"And I felt like turning to the Prosecutor and saying, 'Are you ready, sir, to make your motion for dismissal?' That's the way I felt from behind this table."

Branton moved quickly, covering the space between the defense and prosecution tables to stand behind Albert Harris. "On the other hand, if I had been behind this table, your Honor, I would have immediately stood up and I would have said to this court, 'It is not the responsibility of the Prosecution to see to it that there is a verdict of guilty at all costs, but it is the responsibility of the Prosecutor to see to it that justice is done, and in my opinion, the only way that justice can be done in this case is for this court to dismiss this Prosecution on my motion at this time.'

"But the Prosecutor didn't do that. If he had, I do believe that he would have restored some of the respect, some of the dignity to the Prosecutor's office that I feel has been so severely tarnished by reason of subjecting the People of the State of California to such millions of dollars in costs and this Defendant and everybody else to all of the worry and aggravation of a useless prosecution. Mr. Harris didn't do that, I suppose, because to quote some words I have heard before: 'Hope springs eternal.'

"On the other hand, your Honor," Branton was moving again, this time to the jury box, to sprawl in the front row seat of Juror 12, Stephanie Ryon. "If I had been sitting over here in this jury box, perhaps even in the seat of the most pro-prosecution minded juror, my reaction would have been to turn to the prosecutor and say: 'Sir, you mean that's all you have, that after seven weeks of trial, 100 witnesses, 200 exhibits, and that's all you have? You've proven a hell of a case against Jonathan Jackson. But against Angela Davis, the only thing you have proven is that she is a warm, articulate being, who has love and compassion, yes, for George Jackson, but for humanity and, especially, the black people whom she represents so well.'

"And I would have felt like getting up and saying to this Court: 'Your Honor, we hear no more. We are ready to vote at this time.' "

Branton was up on his feet once more, striding toward the defense table. "But I wasn't sitting in this seat," pointing to Ryon's chair, and then momentarily pausing behind Harris again, "and I wasn't behind this table." He reached his chair, grasped it, looked down at the papers before him, and then back at the judge: "I was behind this table. Since the jury didn't act and the prosecutor didn't act, the only thing left to do is for the defense to act."

Branton asked Judge Arnason to direct a verdict of acquittal, saying that there was not enough proof of Angela's guilt in the record to sustain a conviction on appeal.

He didn't have much hope that Judge Arnason would direct an acquittal, but the argument had to be made. There was the record. It had to reflect the fact that a reasoned argument for dismissal was made. Branton was also arguing to his colleagues, trying to convince them that the defense had done all it needed to do, save present a closing argument to the jury. "Here is his case, look at it yourself," he seemed to be saying to his fellow lawyers, including Angela. "This judge will do what he has to do with my argument, but Harris has got to answer it. Listen to him, and determine for yourself whether we have to do anything more than we have done."

Harris did respond. "Essentially, the Court had the same question before it many months ago . . . when the Motion for Bail on the charges here was presented . . . and I think your Honor cited ex-parte Troia . . . in ruling that there was sufficient evidence presented to the Grand Jury to sustain the conviction on appeal.

"The charges were exactly the same at that time as they are today—kidnapping, murder, and conspiracy. Your Honor's ruling (denying bail) was taken to the District Court of Appeal, and the District Court of Appeal denied relief to the Defendant, in effect, affirming your Honor's determination.

"An application for relief was made to the California Supreme Court, and that Court denied relief . . .

"As we look back over what has transpired over the last 26 days in this court, the People have produced 84 witnesses who have testified from the witness stand. The testimony of nine other witnesses was stipulated to so that we have a total of 93 witnesses . . .

"Now, if the conclusion of the Court was based on the Grand Jury record, that there was sufficient evidence to sustain a conviction on appeal then I think it would be no service to the Court for me to make an extensive argument that the evidence today is much stronger than it was before the Grand Jury . . . the case, as it stands . . . is not only sufficient to sustain a conviction, but the evidence compels a conviction.

"I'm not unmindful of the fact that we have no witness who testifies that he observed the Defendant and Jonathan Jackson agree to do the criminal acts that are charged in the indictment. If it were the law in the State of California or in the United States that, absent such proof—that is, absent direct evidence of the discussion of the plan and the execution of the plan, that there could be no conviction, no bringing to justice of those people who are involved in a conspiracy, then I think our whole system would be in great jeopardy."

"The fact is of course," said Harris, "that conspiracy by its very nature is concealed, it is hidden. It is not discussed in public meetings. It is not made a matter of written agreement. You can't subpoena into court contracts and documentation of that kind. But we can prove it, and we think we have proven it."

Leo Branton, Jr. did not feel that Harris had proven anything. He took the position that the best defense was no defense. Howard

Moore, Jr. disagreed. "My position," explained Moore, "was we had to put on a defense. I felt that psychologically the jury wanted to hear something from our side, and that we couldn't safely conclude the trial without putting in some defense.

"I felt legally that Leo was correct. That as a pure question of law he was right. But I didn't feel the jury was going to consider it as a pure question of law . . . I felt that the jury wanted to hear evidence in three areas: first, they wanted an accounting of Miss Davis' whereabouts during the week of August 3rd through the 7th, second, they wanted an explanation for the purchase of the shotgun on August 5th, and finally they wanted some explanation as to why she fled, and I felt that our defense could be limited to those three essentials." [1]

Potentially, the most damaging testimony was that of eyewitnesses, who placed Angela at San Quentin on the 4th and 5th of August, and in the vicinity of the Civic Center and riding with Jonathan in the yellow van on the 6th. The testimony was somewhat contradictory, and had been weakened considerably through cross examination. In itself it proved nothing, as there was no claim that Angela had either directly conspired with George Jackson, or been in the Civic Center on August 7. Nevertheless it was dangerous.

The charges of murder and kidnap depended totally on the jury's ability to find Angela guilty of conspiracy.

Madeline Lucas, a stern, hostile, broad beamed woman in her mid-50's, who seemed obviously unhappy to be on the stand, said that she saw Angela on the afternoon of August 4 at San Quentin. Mrs. Lucas said that she was walking to her car after visiting her son, and saw "A young Negro couple . . . It was Angela Davis . . . I had seen her on TV many times."

Next, Lt. Robert C. West, identified by partisans of the Soledad Brothers as the head of San Quentin's goon squad, said that he saw a woman matching Angela's description in the prison waiting room on August 5 and 6.

On cross examination, Howard Moore, Jr. forced Lt. West to admit that he had refused to cooperate with an investigator for the

[1] Howard Moore, Jr., in post trial interview with the author.

defense who wanted a statement from him prior to the trial. "I kind of look at Mr. Harris as my lawyer," the prison guard explained. Lt. West denied he was a member of the American Independent Party, which had George Wallace as a candidate in 1968. It developed that he changed his registration from the American Independent Party just two weeks before he came to testify.

West denied that he was drawn to the AIP because of racial feelings. "The only issue that I was interested in was the question of the working poor." West could not be shook on cross examination. He insisted that he had seen Angela Davis in San Quentin on both the 4 and 5, both times in the company of Jonathan Jackson.

Another San Quentin guard, Robert Ayers, also said that he had seen Angela with Jonathan. He recalled that Jonathan had come to the prison at 2:30 p.m. on the 4th, and was too late for a visit. He returned the following day, accompanied by a "tall, rather slender, light complected Negro woman (with an) afro light brown natural."

"Which one is Angela Davis?" asked Leo Branton, Jr. Ayers hesitated, "I don't see her in the courtroom." Angela was there. She was seated against the rail separating the spectators from the participants. Next to her was Kendra Alexander. Angela's head was lowered, and she slowly raised it. Then Ayers said he saw her and pointed her out. "I just remember her face," he told the lawyer.

"Do you remember every face you see?"

"No."

"Then why do you remember this face . . . what about it do you remember?"

"Her sharp facial features . . . She has a distinctive face."

"Look at the lady at her left! In what way is her face more distinctive?"

"Well, Miss Davis has a gap in her teeth."

"Did you see this lady at the prison with her mouth open?"

"No sir."

Ayers said that he did not realize that the woman with Jonathan was Angela until about August 12, when he was at a summer camp for army reservists. He saw Angela's picture in a newspaper given him by a friend. The friend turned out to be Stephen Cook, the reporter covering the case for *The San Francisco Examiner,* who by coincidence had been in the Marin Civic Center on August 7.

Cook was startled to hear his name come up in testimony, and said in conversation with other reporters, that he had no memory of giving Ayers the newspaper.

Ayers testified that he saw Angela's picture and immediately called Lt. West to tell him that the woman he had seen in the waiting room was Angela Davis.

West did not acknowledge this phone call in his testimony. He too had been unable to identify the mystery woman until after seeing her photograph in the media. West had testified that he saw Angela's picture on television on August 14, two days after Ayers' reported call, and then he called Captain Weber at San Quentin and notified him.

William Twells, one of the San Quentin guards who accompanied McClain to Marin on August 7, said that he also saw Jonathan and Angela at San Quentin on August 5. Twells, who was in the hall with William Christmas on August 7, and who testified that at one point both Magee and Jonathan held guns on him, said that he saw Angela waving at George Jackson on August 5. "She was about 5'8", not quite a short afro hairdo." Twells said that he was on lunch relief on the 5th, for Ayers, who left before he could see Angela or Jonathan.

Thus far, Harris had placed Angela at San Quentin the afternoon of August 4 and between 12 noon and 2 p.m. on August 5. Employees at the Eagle Loan Company in San Francisco had testified that Angela, accompanied by Jonathan, had purchased a shotgun at about 5 p.m. the afternoon of August 5.

Harris' prior questioning of Attorney John Thorne was designed to show that Angela and Jonathan were in the San Jose area the evening of August 5.

Harris had promised testimony from one of the prisoners at San Quentin, and there was some fear that he might produce an inmate who would have claimed to have heard McClain or George Jackson discussing or plotting the events of August 7.

Louis F. May, the ex-convict brought in to testify against Angela, had nothing to say about a prison plot. He was placed on the stand to back up the testimony of the other San Quentin eyewitnesses. May was a large, blonde fellow who looked and acted like the

stereotyped hardbitten convict in class B prison films. He said that
he had seen Angela four or five times at the prison, always accompanied by Jonathan Jackson. He particularly remembered Angela
with Jonathan on August 5, saying that he saw her sitting beside
Jonathan in a yellow van. He didn't notice whether Hertz was written on the side.

Howard Moore, Jr. determined that May was a convicted sex
offender, serving two one to life sentences. He had made a statement to the Attorney General's office in September 1970, was
paroled December 1, with a tentative discharge date of December
1975, but was actually discharged early in 1972. May denied that
he had been offered his discharge in exchange for testifying against
Angela. His testimony was somewhat suspect anyway, as the van
in which he said Angela was riding on August 5, was not rented
by Jonathan until August 6.

Harris did produce four witnesses who linked Angela with Jonathan and the yellow van on August 6. They were Alden Fleming,
his son Peter, Dennis Bosch, an employee of Fleming's, and
Michael Vonada, a fireman. Fleming is the owner of a service
station located close to the Civic Center. He is also a full-time
fireman for Marin County. Fleming and the County have a convenient arrangement, insofar as his service station is also the
county fire sub-station where he has been assigned, for 24 years.

Fleming said that he saw a couple whom he identified as Jonathan and Angela walking toward the station. Jonathan came into
the office, while the person he identified as Angela stayed outside.
"The woman was tall, afro hair style, fair complected."

"Have you had very much experience in distinguishing the
features of those you refer to as colored women?", asked Branton.

"Yes," Fleming answered. He estimated that about 20% of
the people who came into his station were black, and 15% of
those wore naturals.

"Mr. Fleming, don't you think all colored people look alike?"

"Not in Miss Davis' case. After you've been around them
awhile you begin to notice individual differences . . . I won't
say she has as heavy a face as colored people have . . . I would
say the women I deal with, their faces are flatter . . ."

Fleming had identified Angela in court by getting down from

the stand, moving his ponderous body toward the back of the court, near the rail where Angela and Kendra Alexander were sitting, and pointing an index finger at Angela, saying, "she's the one."

Branton asked him to explain how Angela differed in looks from Kendra, sitting next to her.

"I would say the fairness of the complexion and the Afro . . . she [Angela] has fair features, she's different than most . . . more good looking than most black people . . ."

"Have you ever seen Miss Davis in person other than on August 6?"

"No."

"Have you ever seen Kendra Alexander?"

"I think in the paper, long ago."

"On Friday, April 21, do you remember Howard Moore in your station?"

"Yes."

"There was a lady in the car?"

"Yes, but I didn't notice her."

"Describe her."

"I didn't see—can't remember."

"You don't remember a lady getting out of the car and walking around?"

"No."

"Can you explain to me sir how you can see Kendra Alexander three weeks ago and not remember and yet you can remember a 15 second meeting with Angela Davis?"

Fleming had seen Angela only through a glass in the rather small office of the service station. Branton directly attacked Fleming's identification of Angela, which had come about through a packet of photographs shown him by investigators for the Attorney General's office. He gave Fleming the group of nine photos, and asked him to pick out Angela's. Fleming selected four of the nine. "That would leave five that are not photographs of Miss Angela Davis." Leo was standing immediately next to the witness. He looked lean, on the attack, snapping descriptions and phrases at Alden Fleming. Branton dealt first with the photos Fleming had rejected.

"Now this one, she doesn't have a natural. And besides it's a mug shot with the name F. A. Trotter written across her chest. You know that's not Angela Davis." Next was another mug shot with a name written across the picture. "Now look at this one, how old would you say she was?"

"About 55."

"Well that's obviously not Miss Davis . . . Now that leaves four photos that you say are Miss Davis." Leo checks him out again to make sure that the witness does not want to change his mind. Fleming says no, the four were of Angela.

"All right. Now three of these look like the same scene taken at the same place. They're different angles, but each of them have a microphone in front of her face . . . Only one is different."

The witness agreed.

"And this one," said Branton, walking away from the witness stand, past the jury box, and to his seat as he concluded his cross examination, "is of Fania Davis Jordan."

Fleming's story was that Jonathan had asked for help in starting a disabled rental van. He described Jonathan as inept, saying that he practically had to take him by the hand, show him a phone book, and help him place a call to Hertz in San Francisco. Fleming's fireman friend, Michael Vonada, was in the office at the time and later testified that he helped Jonathan place the call to Hertz. While Jonathan was on the phone Vonada stepped out and noticed a, "Young black woman, afro hairdo, about five feet six or five feet seven I guess, light complected, good looking."

"You notice anything about her mouth," asked Harris.

"Yes, her teeth were spaced, there were spaces between her teeth."

"Was she doing anything?"

"Yes she was smoking a little black cigar."

When Branton questioned Vonada he asked sarcastically, "What were you doing, waiting for her mouth to open so you could see the gap between her teeth?"

Alden Fleming's son, Peter, was a carbon copy of his father at maybe six feet two inches and 300 pounds.

Peter, following his father's orders, put the woman and Jonathan in a pickup truck, drove to the van, and then, with the woman behind the wheel of the van, started it with a push. He described the woman who for a time rode in his truck, "She was tall, slender, pretty good build on her. She had an afro too, glasses. As far as I can remember she had a minidress on." Peter Fleming was closer to the woman described as Angela, and for a longer period of time, than the other three witnesses, but he could not make a positive identification. Dennis Bosch, Fleming's mechanic, was working on a car at the time, and testified to having seen Angela, but his description was excessively vague.

The Communist Party contributed to the shaping of the response to the prosecution case. National Chairman Henry Winston, along with Mickey Lema, Northern California Chairman of the Communist Party, met with the attorneys and members of Angela's Legal Defense Committee on May 11, 1972, to decide on the nature of the defense, and the extent to which it would be political.

"The position of the Party, as I understood it, and as it was told to us by Henry Winston, was that the politics of the case was victory," stated Howard Moore, Jr. in his interview with the author. The Party recommended that there be no testimony from Angela and no defense. Branton and Moore agreed that Angela should not take the stand.

They felt that she could take the prosecutorial badgering that would inevitably result, but were unsure about Angela's reaction to questions Harris might ask about George Jackson. The relationship was not only personal, but painful, and in practice sessions where either Branton or Moore played prosecutor they hammered away at every facet of the prosecutor's case with a fair amount of ease. When the questions came about Jackson, Angela would hesitate, loose the cool candor that was her usual style and begin to stammer, search for words and generally tighten up.

They had no illusions about Harris, he was tough. Moreover, they suspected that the surprises they had been looking for in the prosecutor's part of the case might turn up on cross examination. The defense was still shocked at the thought that the piece of evidence which Harris thought was most devastating was literally handed to him by Angela Davis over a year after the August 7 incident. For all of their disdain of Harris' crime of passion theory, they respected his ability to draw out every possible link, every possible nuance in Angela's response, and from that make implications which might make it harder to get an acquittal.

Harris, they reasoned, had laid a theoretical background for conspiracy. It was based on circumstantial evidence, but it could possibly be made to sound more plausible if he could get Angela, or anyone close to her, to make an unconvincing appearance on the stand.

Moore felt confident that the manner in which the case had been conducted thus far had minimized the risk of Angela being convicted of a reduced charge.

"Under no circumstances did I want to suffer a conviction for kidnap with bodily harm. That would have meant imprisonment for life without possibility of parole. One of the things we worked with was the whole idea that no kidnap had actually occurred. There had been no proof of extortion. Also, there had been no proof of movement of persons which exposed the hostages to a greater risk of harm than that inherent in an escape."

The basic strategy was formed, there would be a defense. But the attorneys needed time to fashion their response to the prosecution case.

Judge Arnason had adjourned court after taking the motion to dismiss under submission, and told the defense to be prepared to have their first witness on the stand two days later, Thursday, May 18. But, the defense was not ready. They had compromised between Branton's position of no defense, and the prior plans to have a full and elaborate presentation of Angela's case. "It has been the position of the defense," Howard Moore, Jr. told Judge Arnason, "that the case will reach the jury at the earliest possible moment. We have prepared an extensive and exhaustive list of witnesses . . . We're going to ask you in the interest of saving time if you will recess until Monday . . . We will present a very brief and abbreviated case . . . It is in that spirit that the request is being made."

The defense was "brief and abbreviated," in the sense that a hurricane is a strong wind. The defense took three days to produce 11 witnesses, only one of whom was on the stand for any appreciable length of time. Moreover, one of the 11 was not scheduled to testify, and was called to the stand on an impulse by Leo Branton, Jr.

The first witness was Susan Castro, the director of a nursery school and a long time political activist. Miss Castro was a member of the Communist Party, a fact that Harris was unable to exploit. In chamber sessions Harris had insisted that the nature of this supposedly nonpolitical case was such that determining whether or not a defense witness was a member of the Communist Party would be material, at least to the extent that it would give the jury a measure of the witness' credibility. Arnason rejected that approach. He did agree that questions about the extent of a witness' association with a principal in the case could be explored, but drew the line at the "are you now or have you ever been a member of the Communist Party" kind of question, which has in the past been both a question and a condemnation.

Leo led Miss Castro through her involvement with the Soledad Brothers. It developed that she had been the person directly responsible for interesting Angela Davis in the case. Attorney Fay Stender had asked Miss Castro, who is a walking compendium of political activists in California, to attend a hearing of the Soledad Brothers trial, and then, if she felt strongly about it, to try and interest people in Southern California to help strengthen the movement to defend the three.

She went, saw the three men brought into the courtroom wrapped in chains, and became involved in the work of the Soledad Committee. Angela, she explained, had been involved in the Soledad Brothers case, but only peripherally, as an adjunct to the political work she had been doing in Los Angeles around the problem of political prisoners. Subsequently, explained the witness, she met Angela through Franklin and Kendra Alexander, who were old friends of hers, and she also met members of the families of the three defendants.

Branton directed this first witness to the week preceding August 7, beginning Sunday, August 2, when Soledad House was officially opened. She had attended the opening and remembered that Jonathan Jackson, as well as his mother Georgia, had attended, but that Angela was not there. She was aware that Angela was coming north, and in fact received a call from Angela August 4, inviting her to lunch the following day.

Miss Castro testified that she met Angela at about 12:00 noon, and discussed problems related to the functioning of the Soledad Brothers Defense Committee for about two and a half hours, and then went to Soledad House, where they stayed for about 45 minutes. She said that Jonathan Jackson arrived at Soledad House at about that time and offered to take Angela home. Miss Castro's testimony accounted for Angela's whereabouts between 11:30 a.m. and 2:30 p.m., when Jonathan Jackson and Diane Robinson were reported to have been at San Quentin.

Branton asked about the activities of the Soledad Brothers Defense Committee in relation to Soledad House, and Jonathan's contribution to the discussions around security for the house.

Yes, she said, they did discuss how to carry on the work of the committee and physically protect the names and lists that were located in the house. Jonathan participated in some of these meetings and one of the subjects discussed was the possibility of buying firearms to be used for protection of the house.

Harris moved in to cross examine, establishing that Miss Castro had absented herself from her job as director of a children's nursery school in order to keep the luncheon date. "How did you meet Franklin Alexander," he asked, seeking to establish mutual membership in the Communist Party by indirection. "Was it club activities that brought you together?"

"We share many activities."

Branton objected, "Franklin Alexander is not on trial."

A few more questions about the workings of the Soledad Brothers Defense Committee, and then Harris launched into a visit two FBI men made to Miss Castro's San Francisco apartment in September 1970, "when Miss Davis was a fugitive."

"Objection," corrected Branton.

"When she was unavailable?" Harris substituted. "How many men?"

"Two."

"Describe them."

"Well, they were gray. They had gray suits on."

"Did they come into your house?"

"No. I talked to them through the glass."

Harris wanted to know whether Miss Castro had reported her meeting with Angela Davis to "any law enforcement agents in the United States."

"No. I didn't see any reason to," she replied.

"Did you attend an Oakland rally to free Angela Davis October 24, 1971?" Harris was working at establishing the bias of the witness.

"Yes."

"Have you attended any hearings?"

"No."

"Have you seen Angela Davis since her release."

"Yes . . . I think it was a birthday party."

"Did you discuss the testimony you were going to give?"

"Yes."

"When?"

"In San Jose, yesterday."

"Have you been active in the Angela Davis Defense Committee?"

"Yes."

"Is there any person you can identify other than Jonathan Jackson, now deceased, who was present when you saw Angela Davis on the date mentioned."

The witness had answered that question previously. She had, at Harris' insistence, named a few people who were at Soledad House regularly, saying that they might have been there that day, but that she was not in a position to state with certainty that they actually had been at the house.

Harris determined that Miss Castro had not made any memos, notes or calendar entries regarding her date with Angela, nor did she tell anyone, including her secretary, of the meeting. He went back to the visit from the FBI.

"When they asked you about the whereabouts of Miss Davis, you told them you didn't know and if you did know you wouldn't tell them."

"No, I told them I would meet with them at an attorney's office if they wanted. I couldn't think of which attorney, and said Charles Garry."

Next came Juanita Wheeler, a short, stocky black woman who had been employed by the *People's World,* San Francisco's Communist Party weekly, for 21 years. She told Branton that Angela had stayed in her house four or five days beginning the evening of August 3, and on August 7, Carl Bloice, the editor of *People's World,* drove Angela to the airport in the witness' car.

"Did she spend each night at your apartment?"

"Yes."

"How do you recall?"

"We had breakfast together every morning."

That took care of the inference that Angela had spent the night of August 6 with Jonathan, as well as throwing doubt on the prosecution implication that Angela, in company with Jonathan, was in the San Jose area the night of August 5.

Marvin Stender, an attorney, and the husband of attorney Fay Stender who "was more or less the unofficial legal advisor for the Soledad Brothers Defense Committee," was the next witness.

"Were you aware of discussions involving security at Soledad House?"

"Yes."

"Any involve the advisability of firearms?"

"Yes."

"Was Jonathan Jackson involved?"

"Yes."

Stender reported receiving a phone call at "roughly 9:30, sometime between 9 and 10 in the morning" of August 6. He made a date to meet with Angela at a parking lot roughly midway between the *People's World* office from where Angela was calling, and his own office, which is also located in downtown San Francisco. They met at noon, drove to Berkeley, sat outside Angela's destination and talked for about five minutes and then Angela left his car. This testimony accounted for the time that the four witnesses at the service station, and two at San Quentin, had said they saw Angela in company with Jonathan.

Harris questioned Stender closely about the meeting, and asked whether he had reported his August 6 conversation with Angela to "anyone in the United States."

"After her return to California I told her attorneys about it."

Harris wanted to know why Stender did not notify the Attorney General's office of his meeting with Angela.

"I did not particularly feel that your office was interested in finding out the truth in this case."

Branton led Stender into explaining his reluctance to give any information to the Attorney General's office by having him testify about the raid made on Friday, August 14, at Soledad House. He said the police had caused disarray at Soledad House in a search for which no warrant had been issued. Stender recalled that he went to police headquarters and demanded the release of Fania Jordan, who had been taken into custody during the raid.

Harris' examination of Marvin Stender was close, tough, and acrimonious. The implication that Stender was a liar rode heavily on almost every question he asked. Stender gave an appearance that was not dissimilar from that of Gary Thomas. Both men are large, with deep voices that are used with authority. Both had short clipped dark hair, both came to court with versions of events that were not vulnerable to contradiction inducing cross examination. Neither the defense or prosecution cross examination of the two witnesses resulted in any advantage, or created any doubt about the consistency of their memories. And both Thomas and Stender were examined very closely, with the slashing skills of expert examiners, trying to wear down by strength of personality, another lawyer, another advocate, a person who knows how to defend himself in court.

These were not witnesses who an attorney could believe would break, or even fold slightly, under cross examination. But attorneys must joust, must always test their weapons of advocacy against each other, whether there's any point to it or not. Nowhere is there more precisely worded questions and answers, as when one attorney is cross examining another. Yet, in the very midst of that precision, the examining attorney knows exactly how much information he will actually extract, and goes right on to challenge the witness long after that information has been submitted.

Harris brought a sharpness to the questioning of Stender which went beyond the usual sharp clash between examiner and witness when both are attorneys. He would challenge Stender as a lawyer, implying somehow that fidelity to the rules governing lawyerlike behavior was lacking in Stender. This was no honorable man before the prosecutor. He was a left wing attorney, a participant in the organizational structure that supported both the Soledad Brothers and Angela Davis, and therefore, suspect. This prosecutorial harshness, the not at all veiled attitude of contempt for the witness on the stand, carried over to Carl Bloice, who followed Stender.

Bloice was a member of the Communist Party, a question that Harris asked, and had answered. Harris wanted to make that clear, just in case the jury couldn't figure out that a man who had worked 12 years for the *People's World,* and had been its editor for three years, was very likely a member of the Communist Party. Bloice said that he had arranged for Angela to stay at Miss Wheeler's house, and that he had seen Angela several times that week. He met with her the morning of the 4th, for about two and a half hours, accounting for most of Angela's morning. Bloice testified that he was with Angela on Wednesday evening, August 5, at a dinner party in San Francisco. This accounted for the time that Harris was trying to place Angela in San Jose, talking to John Thorne. He said Angela was also at the *People's World* office the morning of August 7, from 8:30 a.m. until about 1 p.m., when he drove her to the airport to catch a three o'clock flight. Angela was informed that if she rushed she could catch a two o'clock Los Angeles flight. He bade her goodbye and went back to the office.

Harris worked on Bloice, revealing possible discrepancies. Bloice said Angela bought her ticket at the main ticket counter, and it had already been established that the transaction was completed at a hurry up desk adjacent to the loading gate. Harris had Bloice name others who had been at dinner with Angela and him. He explored his background as a reporter, hospital worker, and Communist Party member who once worked on a newspaper in Washington state. He had Bloice recall a three-year-old phone number that had long been changed.

"I've since moved three times," pointed out Bloice.

"362-6739"

"Sounds familiar."

"Did you receive a phone call from Angela Davis on August 15?"

What was he asking? Harris had read into the record testimony which placed Angela in Chicago on August 15. Was he trying to demonstrate that Carl Bloice knew of Angela's whereabouts after the arrest warrant was issued and did not notify authorities about her long distance call from Chicago?

"I did speak to Angela once, I recall."

Harris pounced, "When was it that she called?"

"I don't remember."

"About 9 in the morning on August 15, did you receive a phone call from someone from the home of Franklin and Kendra Alexander? Did you receive a phone call from someone named Miss Jamala? . . . Did Angela Davis ever use the name Miss Jamala?"

"Not in my presence."

"Was it the practice of the Che-Lumumba Club to use these kinds of names . . ."

"I don't know."

"Isn't it unusual for you to get a call from Kendra Alexander?"

"No, it's not unusual."

Harris was leaving the phone call question up in the air. He seemed somehow to convert a witness into a co-conspirator, by implying that Angela Davis, using the name Jamala, called Bloice from Los Angeles on August 15, and then dropped the entire subject.

"Did you visit Angela Davis at Marin County?"

"Once."

"What did you hear about the events that occured in Marin County that day?"

"I was told that people had heard it on the radio."

"And after that date, did you hear that Miss Davis was wanted for questioning?"

"Yes, in the newspapers."

"Isn't today the first time you have ever made any kind of disclosure to any law enforcement agency in this country?"

"That's right."

There had been whispering at the defense table, and as Harris turned away from questioning Bloice, Branton stood up. He had

Bloice correct his testimony, changing the arrival time at the San Francisco airport from 12:40 to 1:45. Then he asked:

"Do you know someone named Miss Jamala."

"Yes."

"Is she present in the courtroom?"

"I think so."

"Could you point her out?"

A light skinned woman sitting in the section of the courtroom where the Davis family generally sat, stood up and was identified by Carl Bloice. Branton established that it was this Jamala who had called Bloice on August 15, "You would only wonder what the Attorney General would be doing with your private phone call?" asked Branton, and the witness assented.

Harris came back and questioned Bloice with the ferocity of a man caught cheating at liars dice. He insisted that Bloice received a call from Angela Davis after August 7, and "before she left for Chicago." Bloice said, no, and Harris called him a liar. On what knowledge he didn't say. Some of the questions he asked, based on the knowledge of phone calls, suggested to observers that the Attorney General was privy to more about the telephone calls of some of the witnesses than could logically be provided by telephone records of transactions.

What Harris had heard to lead him to the conclusion that Angela Davis had called Carl Bloice was never revealed, nor is there any way to figure out why he thought that Jamala was a code name for Angela. As far as the code name, he wasn't the only person to have applied a name to Angela that she never used. The "wanted" poster put out by J. Edgar Hoover listed the name Tamu as Angela's alias.

The witness following Carl Bloice was the actual Tamu, who had lived with Angela on 45th Street in Los Angeles until July, 1970. Angela moved out, she explained, because the apartment had become too active for Angela, who needed a quiet place to work and study. Their apartment had become a center for Soledad Brothers Defense Committee activity, as well as the meeting place of the Che-Lumumba Club. Tamu was there to tell of the Che-Lumumba Club, and the fact that it considered the weapons bought by members of the club as collectively owned. The guns, she explained, were kept in a rack that had been introduced into evidence by the defense. She remembered that in July and August of 1970 the rack included three of the guns shown her in court, along with a Mauser rifle. She explained that Angela did not take any of the guns with her when she moved. Leo led Tamu into describing target practice sessions in nearby mountains at a place called Jack Rabbit Pass, sessions in which she and Angela, along with other club members, practiced with their weapons.

Tamu said that Jonathan Jackson had been in the apartment many times, and was given the freedom of the apartment because of his involvement in Soledad Brothers work. The last time she saw Jonathan in the apartment was Saturday, August 1. Jonathan was running a mimeograph machine when Tamu left her apartment in order to drive north to San Francisco, to attend the opening of Soledad House. She was back on Monday, early in the morning.

"Did you see Angela Davis August 8?"

"Yes, with Franklin. They came to my house. They seemed to be pretty upset and concerned. They asked me if the weapons were still on the gun rack in the closet. We opened the closet door and the two carbines were gone. We immediately checked in the drawer and the Browning was missing also."

"When Miss Davis and Mr. Alexander saw the guns were not there, what did they say?"

Tamu seemed hesitant, almost shy. "Do you want me to say it all?"

"Yes, everything they said," Branton assured her.

"Franklin said 'oh shit,' " and she delivered that quote with all of the emotional fervor of a man responding to the world dropping out from under him.

"What did Miss Davis say?"

"She said 'oh no.' Franklin asked me what happened to the weapons. I told him I didn't know, I didn't open up the closet. And he showed me the newspaper that Angela had in her hand. I saw Jonathan Jackson with a carbine in his hand."

Harris moved in to what was the most difficult cross examination for him. Tamu had explained that hers was a Swahili name, meaning sweetness, and she exuded that quality on the stand. She was a strikingly beautiful, dark brown skinned woman, with gold rimmed granny glasses setting off her high round cheeks. She sat there in her long skirt and blue turtle neck shirt, looking every bit like the young mother of a two and a half year old daughter, which she was, and not at all the image Harris would have chosen for a revolutionary woman who shot at targets in the mountains.

He couldn't possibly pound questions into this witness as he had the two men who preceded her. The jury was intrigued with Tamu. She had accounted for three of the weapons, had given the jury an explanation of how guns registered to Angela could show up in Jonathan's possession, without Angela having anything to do with the transfer. She seemed believable, and he had to shake her story. He knew how to be persistent, but now he had to be gentle, a more difficult task.

Harris seemed overwhelmed by most of the women who testified, and completely lost with Tamu. He questioned her closely about the closet where the gun rack was kept, and found out that much of the ammunition he placed into evidence had been stored near the rack, along with old clothing and books which Angela had not moved. He had Tamu identify weapons, give a history of their purchase, and account for a check which she received from Angela Davis that was given her by Franklin Alexander. He also extracted from her the fact that she had been questioned about her movements between May 8, 1970, and August 7, 1970, by members of the Attorney General's office, and that she refused to answer on 5th Amendment grounds.

Branton angrily pointed out that Tamu had claimed her constitutional privilege under the advice of counsel, and that the laws governing the conduct of prosecutors forbids them to even hint about the taking of a constitutional privilege to a jury. "It was impropriety on the part of the prosecutor that borders on misconduct," he insisted, and then gallantly dismissed Tamu from the stand.

He then turned around, announced that here was a witness he had not intended to call, and summoned Mrs. Carol Broadnax. She was Jamala, who explained that, "because I'm black, I thought I should adopt an African name." Branton then had Jamala explain that she had made a call on August 15 to Carl Bloice. The call, she said, had been placed from a phone booth in the Los Angeles airport and charged to the Alexander's phone number. The purpose was to inform Carl Bloice that she and other members of the Che-Lumumba Club were coming up to attend Jonathan Jackson's funeral that day, and needed transportation from the airport to the church.

The day's testimony had ended. The defense had sketched in Angela's movements in the week preceding August 7 sufficiently to contradict prosecution eye witnesses. An explanation had been given about how Jonathan had come into possession of the weapons. In addition, in a move that usually was witnessed only by Perry Mason watchers, the defense had dramatically produced a witness from the courtroom who not only refuted the Prosecutor's implications that Angela Davis had made a phone call, but left the jury open to the suggestion that wire-tapping, or some similar surveillance technique, had been used in certain phases of the investigation.

The second day was slower paced. Ellen Broms, a social worker in Los Angeles, and an old friend of Franklin and Kendra Alexander, said that Angela and Franklin were her dinner guests on the night of August 7. Under questioning from Branton she described a quiet evening at home, eating, listening to records and playing scrabble, that was interrupted by a phone call from Kendra to Franklin. He relayed the news to Angela and she in turn "became very upset, she began to cry 'he was so young.'" They turned on the television and the radio, and with media verification Angela became even more upset. Both she and Franklin spent the night at the Broms home, and in the morning they picked up the daily papers. Mrs. Broms reported Angela saying, "My God, there's something about a shotgun in here, and I just bought a shotgun for the defense of the Soledad House. I gave it to Jonathan."

Harris' cross examination seemed designed more to discredit Mrs. Broms as a witness than to reveal contradictions or inconsistencies in her testimony. He established that the witness had known Franklin Alexander for about 13 years, and his wife for a lesser time.

"What was it that caused this contact between Franklin Alexander and yourself?"

"We are friends."

He wanted to know about organizations, obviously seeking for Communist Party membership. Mrs. Broms gave him CORE. Any organization in common in the late 60's? No. Ever to Miss Davis' apartment? No. Had not seen Angela for about a month preceding August 7. Yes, she was active in the Echo Park Committee to Free Angela Davis, to the extent of having attended a few meetings. No, she did not report her August 7 dinner engagement to authorities, not when the fugitive warrant was publicized in the papers, and not when Angela was arrested. She was excused.

Howard Moore, Jr. then questioned Robert Buckhout, a psychologist with a long list of publications, membership in a number of prestigious professional associations and an expert in "social and perceptual factors in eye witness identification."

"Eye witness reports range from the ridiculous to the near accurate," he reported to the court, and proceeded to dissect the fabled accuracy of eye witness observations. Buckhout's position was that unless a person was totally prepared to be a witness to an event, that his accuracy in remembering details of that event varied considerably. The defense, at this point, was simply questioning Buckhout in order to have him certified as an expert witness. Harris asked for a delay until the following morning so that he could clear up what he called a serious legal question.

Court was adjourned early, after the brief testimony of two subpoenaed witnesses. The first was Robert Beren, a special agent and investigator for the Attorney General's office, who testified that he investigated the telephone number found in Jonathan's wallet only in the 415 area code, covering San Francisco and surrounding territory. Next came James Finnigan who had previously testified for the prosecution, who said that telephone company records showed that in July 1970, 588-9073 was an operating number in the 213 area code of Los Angeles, where Jonathan lived. The subscriber was a Rome Kasinikowski, and no one knew whether he actually knew Jonathan Jackson. The defense had made a point and didn't push it.

On Wednesday word flashed around that Fleeta Drumgo and

John Cluchette would testify. Cluchette, it turned out, had been released from prison the previous day. Cluchette had a release date in April, 1970, promised him at the time that he was accused of participating in guard John Mills' murder. After his acquittal in February, 1972, the Adult Authority still acted as though they wanted to hang on to him. They decided to let him go after being threatened with a lawsuit.

First, however, Harris had to deal with Robert Buckhout. The prosecutor actually tried to discredit him. He inferred that Buckhout was not actually teaching at Hayward State University. Harris pointed out that the witness was not licensed as a psychologist in California. Not necessary, said the witness, I'm teaching, not practicing, and besides I'm licensed in Missouri. Are you paid to testify? Yes, $100 a day. Harris picked at publications of Buckhout's, selecting titles that implied that Buckhout had a radical set of politics, and commenting on others which indicated that perhaps Buckhout's credentials as an expert in perception were without foundation. Judge Arnason did not agree with the prosecutor, and certified Buckhout as an expert witness.

The thrust of Buckhout's testimony was that a person witnessing an event files it in a very complex system, and does not at all act like a biological tape recorder. The eye witness, he explained, is subject to inaccuracy for a variety of reasons including insignificance, short observation time, and physical conditions such as color blindness. Also the observer is subject to conditioning, and may follow a leader and live up to expectations. Buckhout talked about a story which reputedly was planted by someone in the Associated Press, about a baby sitter stuck to a newly painted toilet seat. They sent out reporters to follow up this fictional story and came up, not only with eye witnesses, but with a fireman who pulled the victim off the seat. Buckhout also cited a standard experiment in which a group is shown a photograph of a white with a knife attacking a black, but afterwards, with the picture removed, whites reported the knife in the hand of the black.

Buckhout found it fairly common for witnesses to identify someone in a photograph as a person he has talked to, in a search for approval, because they thought it was expected of them.

Can a person who is red-green color blind be affected in his ability to see a brown face? Oh yes. Brown has a lot of red in it. A person who can't see red, can't see brown. "Mr. Fleming is color blind, yet he reports he saw a color red in her hair. It is obvious from his condition, in his own testimony, that he could not see the color red. Besides, the set of photographs shown Fleming were arranged to give three out of five correct answers, if a person simply guessed."

Harris' cross examination could not shake Buckhout. The prosecutor challenged his professional competency to make judgments about color blindness. Buckhout informed him that color blind testing is a common tool of psychologists. Harris asked about stress influencing an eye witness account, having apparently spent part of the previous night reading Buckhout's testimony in another case. Harris was trying to prove that the absence of stress and fear tended to make identification more reliable, but Buckhout insisted he was not indicating that the human race was unreliable, but that people in all situations tend not to recognize as much as they have been given credit for. "If we tried to remember everything, it would be very inefficient. But that very process in some cases may interfere with accurate recall."

Do these factors apply to a doctor as well as anyone else? Harris asked—especially passing on a theory and desiring to be a part of history? Buckhout had sat in the witness chair, open, somewhat pedantic, but obviously in the grasp of his field. He wouldn't take the bait, and declined the opportunity to assure the prosecutor that he, in his testimony, was being objective—an opportunity which undoubtedly would have led to questions about Buckhout's bias as a witness.

"Mr. Harris," he replied softly, "if I started examining the motives of anyone, I could redirect that question." Harris ended his cross examination.

Later, Howard Moore, Jr. said, "I felt that Buckhout's testimony would be very helpful in attacking the eye witness identification by showing it as unreliable. It gave the jury a way of deciding with us, without saying that Harris' witnesses were lying. When Buckhout testified I saw something come over that jury. I told everybody, 'We've got it all, we've just won this case, this jury is completely turned around.' "

After a short recess, the jury returned to the courtroom to see Fleeta Drumgo seated in the witness box.

Defense attorneys had argued that Fleeta should not be brought into the courtroom in chains, because the sight might possibly influence the jury. Harris was in favor of bringing a prisoner in in chains, and pointed out the security problems that might exist. A compromise was reached. Fleeta was brought in in waist chains, and seated in the box with the chains out of sight. His right hand was unchained, so that he could raise it to swear to the truth of his testimony, and also, in the course of his appearance, direct a power sign to his mother and supporters who were in the audience.

Drumgo's testimony was short and to the point. He had been in the San Quentin Adjustment Center on August 7, 1970, and McClain was in the next cell. He said he had no knowledge from McClain, or anyone else, that there was going to be an attempt to free the Soledad Brothers. Another recess, and Drumgo, still in chains, was removed from the courtroom.

Then came Charlotte Gluck, who had been principal clerk at UCLA in 1969 and 1970 in the Philosophy Department. Miss Gluck told the court about the impossibility of conducting regular business because of harassing calls coming into the department. One person was assigned to do nothing but handle Angela's mail, most of which was hate mail. The prosecution attempted, through cross examination, to limit the time of this overwhelming, popular vilification of Angela Davis to those times when her name and face were in the paper. Miss Gluck insisted that the overwhelming mail and phone business began in August, 1969, and continued unabated until July of 1970.

Having given the court an opportunity to recognize that Angela Davis' fellow citizens bombarded her office with phone calls and hate mail, on no more information than the fact that she was a member of the Communist Party, the defense rested.

It should have been all over but the decision, and it almost was. Harris produced a couple of rebuttal witnesses. The first was an ophthalmologist, Bruce E. Spivey, who taught a course in color deficiencies at a medical center in San Francisco. Spivey said that he had examined Fleming, who could not visually deal with green and red. "Color deficiency of dichromatic type, green defective" was the way he put it. Fleming can determine light and darkness of skin without relating to color, Spivey testified, and besides, "visual defectives are taught from birth to describe a color." The most a visual defective, incapable of seeing red, can be taught, is that portions of the spectrum which he sees as a variant of gray are in the area in which brown tones lie. Not only does he not see brown, but he sees other similar shades of gray, which are not brown.

Another rebuttal witness was Keith Craig, the Marin County coroner's investigator who was in the van moments after the shooting, and who testified earlier that officers stopped him from examining McClain to discover whether he was alive. Craig's only function was to buttress the testimony given by those eye witnesses who saw Jonathan wearing beads. Craig identified a set of beads which he said was taken from Jonathan Jackson's body, and which were then entered as the 201st piece of evidence.

Then came Lester Jackson, subpoenaed by Harris to testify for a prosecution which considered both of his sons criminals, and was in fact the advocate for those people who had killed his sons. Lester Jackson was the prosecution's last rebuttal witness.

Albert Harris, Jr., Assistant California Attorney General, head of special investigations for the criminal division of the Attorney General, and prosecutor of Angela Davis and Ruchell Magee, knew, before he ever issued his subpoena, that Lester Jackson would be of no value to his case.

Mr. Jackson was interviewed days after the August 7 incident and was asked about Angela Davis. "Everybody knows Angela," he said. "She may be a communist or whatever, but she's fighting for black rights."

Lester Jackson was bitter. At that point he had lost only one son. "No one will ever know," he answered to the query of whether or not Jonathan had been Angela's bodyguard, "But it seems that if Miss Davis were going to choose a bodyguard, she could do better than a 17-year-old boy. All I know is that my son is dead." He talked about Judge Gordon Campbell, the Monterey County Judge who presided over both Soledad Brothers trials, and whose decisions in those matters could have been dictated by prison officials: "Judge Campbell is as much to blame as the guards who shot Jonathan."

He remembered that Jonathan, everytime the family went north for a hearing in the case, was "clapping with his hands and his feet to show that he believed his brother was being unjustly tried for murder."

The family could not afford an attorney when George Jackson was accused of murder. A conviction, in which prosecution evidence would be produced from the prison, would have resulted in an automatic verdict of death. They could not afford an attorney when George was sentenced originally and got one to life for doing no more than driving a getaway car in a robbery that netted $70.00, and in which no one was hurt. They did not have available to them attorneys, or advocates, who could successfuly argue that George Jackson, who had served ten years on what Lester Jackson called "a silent record," was entitled to be freed after the average time of two and a half years in California [higher by six months than the average sentence served in the United States for robbery.]

When the family went out to find attorneys who would attempt to defend George Jackson on a murder charge they found out that the price would be $50,000. Lester Jackson rejected the radical politics of those who supported George Jackson, yet he knew that it was the radicals, rather than political moderates, who came to the aid of his son.

He described Jonathan as, "strong—he listened to nobody . . . He had his own car and his freedom. He had never been arrested. Didn't smoke, drink or use barbituates . . . was well behaved . . . I never had to lay a hand on him . . . He had many friends . . . black, white, brown . . . But as for guns, I can get you any kind of gun you want if you give me a few days. If Jon didn't have enough money for the guns, I have a lot of relatives. He could have borrowed from a lot of people." Despite his estrangement, his response was almost the same as his wife's: "Jonathan was a good person, and nobody can say he wasn't as long as I am alive . . . It is ridiculous to think Angela Davis would give a 17-year-old a gun . . . I have no idea where he got the guns . . . Plenty of good people have weapons in their hands."

Lester Jackson, a black man who has no illusions about the condition of black people in this country, and who lost two sons as a direct consequence of that condition, in being called before a court to testify for the prosecution was being placed in the position of the good nigger. Lester Jackson might have had information which the prosecution could use in its case against Angela Davis. But the case against Angela was a case against Jonathan. Albert Harris, Jr. brought that man into court, essentially to testify against his own son. What is so chilling about this is that the testimony he was attempting to extract was not part of his original case, but was thought of as a means of rebutting testimony which possibly detracted from Harris' case.

Lester Robert Jackson could have nothing to offer a prosecution which was condemning his son. But, he could be punished for being the father of George Lester and Jonathan Peter Jackson. He could be broken on the stand . . . , and thus reveal whatever innocent information he might have about his son's movements—or be paraded as Lester Jackson, father of Jonathan and George.

Harris asked Jackson one question: "On Saturday, August 1, 1970, at about 9 a.m., did you drive your wife and son Jonathan Jackson to the Los Angeles International Airport?"

Undoubtedly Harris had more questions. He was willing to ask Lester Jackson anything that would invoke a response that would help hang Angela Davis. It seems perfectly logical that Mr. Jackson would have driven his wife and son to the airport. The opening of Soledad House was Sunday, August 2. Both Georgia and Jonathan were part of the Soledad Brothers Defense Committee and involved in the affairs of Soledad House. Both of them were going to the opening, and both of them lived at that time in Pasadena. Harris' entire case revolved around the week beginning August 2. He had already involved Lester Jackson in the record of the case by making reference to a night when Mr. and Mrs. Jackson, accompanied by Jonathan and Angela, stayed in a Berkeley motel. That trip was related to a hearing for the Soledad Brothers.

Lester Jackson, brown skinned, clean shaven, soft spoken, and obviously fighting for control, paused after the question was asked. "Well sir. I lost two sons. I just don't want to take part in these proceedings for the preservation of my mental health."

Jackson was represented by Jack Tenner, a Los Angeles attorney, who leapt to his feet and objected to the proceedings, calling them "morally outrageous."

Judge Arnason turned to Mr. Jackson and asked if he understood the question.

"Yes," he replied.

"If you refuse to answer that question I can hold you in contempt," the judge explained, pointing out that a contempt citation could involve a jail term until he had purged his contempt by answering the question.

"I can't reply to it sir. As a matter of fact I refuse." His tone of voice made it clear that he would have refused to answer any question put to him by the prosecutor, even perhaps a query as to whether he was the father of two sons.

Leo Branton, recognizing that Judge Arnason would find Jackson in contempt, asked the Attorney General to join in asking Judge Arnason to suspend any judgment in this matter as the least the court could do. Harris refused. He explained that he had Jackson subpoenaed because he felt Jackson "could offer relevant and useful evidence. I am concerned only with this case. I am at the end of my road. I leave it to the court."

Tenner suggested a compromise; that Judge Arnason find Jackson in contempt, and confine him for three hours, roughly the rest of the court day. "I am not recommending to the court any confinement, I am not recommending anything," was Harris' response. He had set Mr. Jackson up. Arnason had to find him in contempt. The bereaved father turned to the judge, "Because of the death of my sons I hope you will understand my position. You are a family man."

"Our system requires that we must have compliance by all citizens in our society," responded Arnason, who decided to impose a $100 fine with a ten day stay of execution. It was all over. Jackson left with his attorney and went back south. The $100 was paid immediately, primarily through a collection that was taken up by the newsmen in attendance. Court was dismissed, the trial had ended. All that remained were the final arguments, and of course, the verdict.

11 : The Finale

Both Howard Moore, Jr. and Leo Branton, Jr. delivered closing arguments for the defense. Moore began by pointing out that there were no blacks on the jury: "The absence of members of Miss Davis' race on the jury could very well handicap and impede the search and the quest for justice in this case.

"However, we think that you, men and women—women and men—are capable of deciding this case on the evidence and on the facts and applying your own common sense.

"So we will submit the fate of Miss Davis, her freedom, her life to you."

Moore restricted his argument to the eyewitness portion of the prosecution case. "In this case you will have to determine the credibility of witnesses . . . We don't claim that the witnesses who testified on behalf of the Prosecution perjured themselves. What we do claim, however, is that they are mistaken in their testimony where they seek to identify Miss Davis.

"We brought before you an expert . . . Dr. Buckhout listed some 14 factors which make eyewitness identifications unreliable. He testified as an expert. His expert opinion was not challenged or undermined in any way. He testified that eyewitness identifications are unreliable."

Moore listed for the jury some of the items Dr. Buckhout enumerated in explanation of the unreliability of eyewitness testimony.

"Personal bias, racial prejudice, need for social approval, desire not to appear a fool, desire to be a part of history, lack of independent recollection . . . I'm not holding up the one on color blindness, because I think it's very clear and very convincingly shown by the prosecution and the defense in this case that Alden Fleming was color blind and that his color blindness has handicapped him in making identification."

Moore recapitulated the testimony of prosecution eye witnesses, beginning with the prison guards who testified to seeing Angela at San Quentin. He called them "people watchers . . . Mr. Ayers, he watched people in the waiting room and in the visiting room. Mr. Twells also was a people watcher. Mr. West was a people watcher. How extensive was their description of the person or the woman that they say they saw? Mr. West, a people watcher, a professional people watcher of ten years' experience, described a fair skinned lady, natural hairdo, tweed-like dress. That was on the 4th of August.

"On the 5th of August—natural hairdo, fatigue or military type jacket. What kind of description is that for a trained people watcher?"

Moore pointed out that West testified that he saw Angela's picture on television Friday, August 14, and called his superior at San Quentin to inform him that the Angela whom he had just seen, and the person who had been in the waiting room with Jonathan on August 4 and 5, were one and the same person. He made a report to this effect on August 17. Nevertheless, another guard, Ayers, had testified that he called Lt. West on the 11th or 12th of August to tell him about a picture of Angela Davis he had seen in a newspaper.

"Now that is an important circumstance, an important discrepancy, that Lt. West would have that information, but yet tell you . . . he recognized Miss Davis on the 14th when he had already received information from Mr. Ayers. Wouldn't the information from Mr. Ayers stimulate his recollection as to what he had seen much more so than waiting for a television program? Can you believe either one of those witnesses? Whether you do is left entirely up to you, but the Defense would submit that both of those witnesses are unbelieveable and that their testimony can be denied or ignored."

He moved to Mrs. Lucas, who also placed Angela in San Quentin on August 4. "Now listen carefully at the description (of Angela given by Mrs. Lucas): 'Well, she was a Negro. She was, I think you would say, tall, slender.'

"Now there is some uncertainty about the tall, slender because if she were positive she probably would have said tall and slender because there would have been nothing for her to add . . . But then Mr. Harris goes on. I think Mr. Branton didn't object or I didn't object. We didn't object to everything. And the question was, 'And about her hair, was that worn in any—' and she interrupted then because she knew what she was to fill in . . .

" 'She had an Afro hairdo.' Does that sound like a witness who is making a strong and positive identification? . . . She was walking on the stage of history. She had a duty. We don't have a letter from Mrs. Lucas like we have from Mrs. Leidig who talked about our national courts need a victory, but I submit to you, that the way this lady behaved on the stand in your presence can lead you to draw that conclusion.

" 'Question.' This is Mr. Harris questioning Mrs. Lucas. 'And where was it that you said you lived?' That was the question. 'Answer. In San Diego.' I submit that that is a sufficient answer to that question. That is directly responsive to the question . . . The witness went ahead and said, 'she got quite a lot of coverage down there.' Why did she say that? Why does she have to volunteer that? She had already answered the question."

Moore read portions of Mrs. Lucas' testimony. The point where she hesitated to identify Angela in court, because Angela was not smiling as she had been at San Quentin. At one point Mrs. Lucas had estimated that Angela had been in her vision a full 30 seconds. But Branton in his cross examination had asked Mrs. Lucas to indicate by pointing, the distance involved, and it turned out to be about 12 feet, a distance that was corroborated in court by Albert Harris. Moore argued that at that distance "If she saw these people, she saw them for not more than two or three seconds on August 4 of 1970. But yet on the basis of that kind of observation time, she would testify in this court 'I had no doubt then, and I have no doubt now.'

"She wants you to believe that. She wants to stake her life— her life as a witness on that. But it's not her life that is at stake. It's Angela Davis' life that is at stake."

Next came Louis May, the ex-convict. "I'm not going to dwell too long on Mr. May because I think it's very obvious to all the members of this jury the motivation for Mr. May's testimony.

". . . he was serving two sentences of one year to life. No

one knows how long you serve when it's from one year to life. He had two sentences. . . .

"He gave a statement on August 15 of 1970, after he had seen newspaper coverage of Angela Davis linking Angela Davis with the August 7 incident.

"In September of 1970, he went before the Pardon Parole Board or the Adult Authority, as they call it in this state. On December 1 of 1970, he got out. He got what he wanted. He wanted to be free. He wanted to get out of jail, and he helped them out.

"Look how confused he is, or appears to be confused. He said that the yellow van was there on two days, and about that he had no doubt . . . He also testified that he saw Jonathan Jackson come to San Quentin in a black Jaguar . . . He also testified that he saw Angela Davis on August the 3rd. He was positive about that. You know that she wasn't here on August 3rd that she didn't come up here until that night . . . I think it stands out that the witness' testimony is mistaken. There is a reason for it being mistaken. He has a motive to give a statement, the testimony. And he benefited from giving mistaken testimony."

Moore pointed out that Alden Fleming, at the service station, in addition to being color blind, was actually a part of the law enforcement apparatus of the county, and that Fleming had received a call on August 7 to "be on the watchout for the escapees."

Fleming's son, Peter, who "was the best situated witness of all, testified that he was unable to recognize Miss Davis. Remember, Peter Fleming got into the vehicle. Miss Davis is supposed to have gotten into the vehicle. Jonathan Jackson is supposed to have gotten into the vehicle."

He pointed out that Michael Vonada, the fireman friend of Alden Fleming, had answered the question, "How would you describe the facial characteristics of the person you saw in the station on August 6th" [a question that could have been answered simply by looking across the courtroom at Angela and describing what he saw] with 'light complected, black woman.' Do you think that is a fair answer? Mr. Branton asked for the facial characteristics of the person that he saw, and he gave them what may be a racial description, light complected black woman."

Moore's main criticism of Vonada's testimony was the fireman's statement, "I know one thing. She has spaces between her teeth, and, if she is smiling, you can notice that."

"Now I haven't found any indication that she smiled for Mr. Vonada," said Moore. As a matter of fact, Vonada had said that the woman he saw was lighting up a cigar. "I don't see how you light up a cigar and show your teeth. Maybe some people do, but I doubt it very seriously."

The attorney closed his remarks by quoting from a United States Supreme Court decision: "A major factor contributing to the high incidence of miscarriage of justice from mistaken identification has been the degree of suggestion inherent in the manner in which the Prosecution presents the suspect to witnesses for pre-trial identification."

Moore had concentrated on that portion of the Prosecution case the defense felt would contribute the most to the jury's verdict. The idea that neither a murder nor a kidnap occurred had been inserted earlier in the trial, as part of the constant chipping away at the prosecutor's case engaged in by the defense. The closing arguments were actually geared more to the prosecution close, refuting what he had to say, while at the same time, stressing those parts of the prosecution case which were contradictory or weak.

But there were really two parts to Harris' case. There was first a series of facts, or alleged facts. Then, there was the theory tying these facts together. The defense had challenged a number of factual statements other than the eyewitness testimony during the trial, but their basic contention was that if all of the testimony presened by Harris was true, that it did not add up to conspiracy. Howard Moore, Jr.'s task was to take one section of this testimony, that which would tend more than any of the other testimony to indicate conspiracy and demolish it. But that left the theory, which had been formidable enough to keep Angela in jail for 16 months, despite closely reasoned arguments with a number of courts and individual judges. The presumption of innocence was never so great as to allow her out on bail. A number of judges had said, in effect, that they would sustain a conviction if the case constituted no more than what had been presented to the Grand Jury, and there had been no defense.

The dynamite eyewitness evidence which identified Angela for the Grand Jury was given by Peter Fleming.

Q. What kind of hair style did she have?

A. Afro.

Q. And what kind of hair style did he have?

A. Gee, I don't know; I guess you'd have to call it an Afro. Their hair styles were comparable.

Q. I will . . . ask you to . . . see if you can identify the picture of the head in that photograph.

A. It looks like—a lot like her, again, but I can't remember about the teeth. That's the only thing. That's the only distinctive thing about her, you know, in the face, with the teeth, I can't.

Q. Does the hair seem to be the same?

A. Yes, her hair is the same.

Q. Does her features—do her facial features appear to be the same?

A. Far as the face goes, far as the teeth go, I couldn't give a positive—

Q. You didn't see her teeth?

A. Well I can't remember that.

Q. All right. But does that appear to be the girl that was in your store that morning?

A. It looks like her.

If that evidence could be sustained on appeal, then there had to be something compelling about Harris' theory that would transform such supposed facts into a conviction that judges would accept. For all the shouting of frameup, the defense took Harris' theory very seriously. The fact that they were in no way persuaded by it, made them take it even more seriously, because their arguments based on this lack of persuasion had netted them very few victories in their quest for judicial relief.

Howard Moore Jr.'s precise banging away at a series of eye witnesses was crucial to the defense insofar as it was designed to convince the jury that they, in the face of conflicting eye witness testimony, had to have a reasonable doubt concerning Angela's guilt, and acquit her.

Now the items implying conspiracy had to be refuted. This was Branton's job. Leo Branton, Jr., actor, superb defense advocate, commander of a range of emotional, psychological and legal appeals, had to put Harris' case to rest.

Harris had stressed no one part of his case in his summation. He very carefully defined murder and kidnapping within the context of the case to such a fine degree, that he could say "we think the evidence shows clearly that Jonathan Jackson did commit a burglary in entering the Marin County Civic Center . . . with the intent to commit the crime of kidnapping." Why burglary? Possibly part of Harris' constant attempt to impress the jury with the thoroughness with which he had investigated this case—to overwhelm them with detail, forcing them to step back and get the larger picture, and in the process perhaps not notice that some of the details are muddy.

"I want to turn my attention just for a few moments to this question of the nature of the murder . . ." Harris had said.

"Now we submit . . . that any plan that has as its object the use of prisoners, state prisoners who were on trial in a court and were a part of that plan, and probably the most significant part is to take the Judge from the bench in his robes and hold him as hostage with a threat to take his life—we submit that a plan such as that is almost certain to result in premeditated killing and, in fact, that's precisely what happened on August 7th of 1970 up in Marin County."

But Harris then discussed August 7 in a way that described Jonathan, Magee and Christmas, and at one point McClain, as wanting to kill people. His murder and conspiracy charges were not quite in harmony. Murder, explained Harris, was "the natural and probable consequence of the conspiracy." But the conspiracy, on the other hand, was supposedly geared to the exchanging of the hostages for the release of the Soledad Brothers. Under this formulation we should not have expected anyone to have been murdered until some point after negotiations for the release of the Soledad Brothers had begun.

"It is clear that the killing of Judge Haley was a premeditated killing by Ruchell Magee, and that it was precisely what one would expect from conspiracy of this nature," argued Harris. But he had only charged Magee with joining the conspiracy on August 7, meaning that Ruchell, if he had murdered the judge, had no more than 30 minutes to premeditate. Further, if Ruchell did the premeditating, then there was no logical connection between his motives and that of the conspiracy which existed before he joined it.

McClain was the one who knew about the conspiracy said the prosecutor. McClain picked witnesses to testify for him whom he knew would join his conspiracy without hesitation. Harris reminded the jury that Mrs. Norene Morris, one of the jurors who had not been taken as hostage, testified that McClain asked Jonathan for the tape with which to attach the shotgun to the judge's neck. McClain was not surprised when Jonathan came in. McClain took charge of the operation. "He knew what was going to happen. He knew what was available. He knew the means that were available. He knew how to use them. He wasn't a 17 year old from high school. He wasn't from high school in Pasadena. James McClain was from San Quentin, and James McClain was a mature man, and he took charge of that kidnapping."

George Jackson was the contact between McClain and Jonathan. Harris had brought a witness from San Quentin who testified that McClain's cell was four numbers away from George Jackson's. Fleeta Drumgo had testified that his cell was next to McClain's. The fact of life in the adjustment center is that the men are in their cells 23½ hours a day, except for visits, and in McClain's case, court appearances. Despite this, it is necessary for Harris' theory that George Jackson be the means of transmitting precise information about the upcoming conspiracy to McClain. Drumgo said he knew of no conspiracy. When trial time came George Jackson was dead, and couldn't deny that he had knowledge of a plan predating August 7.

Harris knew that a plan existed because he knew that Jonathan Jackson was devoted to his brother. "I don't think there is any question in your mind . . . based on what you've heard, that one of the most important things in Jonathan Jackson's life was the state of his brother George. Think about this, that when he entered that Marin County courtroom and he stood up and he pulled that gun, with that movement, he gave up every other opportunity that he would ever have to help his brother.

"Now it's just that simple. Once he participated in this kidnapping, once he started it, that was the—that had to be whether he survived or not, the end of any efforts he could make for his brother unless that very effort—unless what he did in that court-room up in Marin County was for the purpose of helping his brother and seeing that his brother was released.

". . . He was, in effect, by what he did in that courthouse abandoning his brother unless it was the purpose—unless that was the purpose of what he was doing . . . Do you think for a moment that Jonathan Jackson did that so that a man named James Mc-Clain could get out of San Quentin State Prison, a man that he never visited?

". . . That is really, I think, the basic reason we submit to you that the purpose of this conspiracy was to free George Jackson because we think it's incredible. It's beyond belief. It's beyond what you could interpret from what happened to believe that Jonathan Jackson undertook this enterprise in order to see a man named James McClain got out of prison. We think it beyond be-lief."

The problem with this construction is that Jonathan went into a courtroom with guns and took out James McClain at a time when George Jackson was also appearing in court, and was thus just as vulnerable to an escape attempt.

"We have evidence of this," said Harris, and reminded the jury that James Kean heard, "Tell them we want the Soledad Brothers released by 12:00 o'clock." Captain Twells' "You have until 12:00 noon to free the Soledad Brothers and all political prisoners," was quoted. Harris cited Niederer as remembering "someone at the elevator say in a loud voice 'they wish the Soledad Three released by this afternoon.' "

That was a misquote which may or may not have been caught by the jury. Niederer actually testified that he heard someone say something "to the effect that he represented a new revolutionary movement." Chief Dan Terzich had heard, "Free the Soledad Brothers by 12:30 or they all die."

The plan was frustrated, explained Harris, by the shooting at the South Arch. But that was the evidence with which he hoped the jury would conclude "that the purpose of that conspiracy was to free the Soledad Brothers." If the jury needed further evidence that the plan involved an exchange of the hostages for the Soledad

Brothers, Harris referred them to a revolutionary text which was one of the pamphlets brought into the courtroom by Jonathan. "But, if you look into what is called the *Mini-Manual of the Urban Guerrilla*,[1] a book published or pamphlet I guess, published in 1970, Jonathan Jackson had with him along with his ammunition and the guns and the other things he brought to the courthouse.

"Kidnapping as a technique of urban guerilla tactics is discussed over at page 30, and the statement is made, 'Kidnapping is used to exchange or liberate imprisoned revolutionary comrades or to force suspension of torture in the jail cells of the military dictatorship' and there is more discussion about kidnapping as a technique for the urban guerilla."

That was true, but the discussion says, "The kidnapping of personalities who are known artists, sports figures, or are outstanding in some other field, but who have evidenced no political interest, can be a useful form of propaganda for the revolutionary and patriotic principles of the urban guerilla provided it occurs under special circumstances, and the kidnapping is handled so that the public sympathizes with it and accepts it." [2] Actually, Marighella, whose Mini-Manual Harris was using in an attempt to prove that Jonathan was motivated by the thought of freeing his brother by exchanging hostages, gave a justification for what Jonathan had done on the very page from which Harris quoted.

"The urban guerilla who is free views the penal establishments of the enemy as the inevitable site of guerilla action designed to liberate his ideological brothers from prison.

"It is this combination of *the urban guerilla in freedom and the urban guerilla in jail,* that results in the armed operations we refer to as the liberation of prisoners."

He then lists five possible guerilla actions geared to liberating prisoners. The second is: "assaults on urban or rural penitentiaries, houses of detention, commissaries, prisoner depots, or any other permanent, occasional or temporary place where prisoners are held."

Marighella, had Harris cited him properly, would have actually supported the theory that Jonathan Jackson went into the Civic

---

[1] Carlos Marighella, *Mini-Manual of the Urban Guerrilla,* Tricontinental.
[2] Carlos Marighella, op. cit., 44 & 45.

Center, a "temporary place where prisoners are held" in order to free McClain, Christmas and Magee.

Having proven to his satisfaction the existence and the dimensions of the conspiracy regarding Jonathan, Harris turned to Angela. "The conspiracy contemplates an agreement between the parties. In this instance it would be the Defendant, Angela Davis, and Jonathan Jackson.

"For all practical purposes, the evidence is interrelated and interconnected. And what it boils down to is this: Did she know about it? Did she know what was going to happen on August the 7th? And did she render assistance? . . .

"Now we have focused—presented evidence which, we thought, tended to show a pattern of association between Angela Davis and George Jackson's younger brother, Jonathan. We did that, not because we think that mere association, merely being with someone proves a conspiracy. It doesn't. Obviously, it doesn't.

"But it's not immaterial either. You have to start someplace. If people don't know each other, it's unlikely—it's not impossible that they can conspire, legally. But, as a factual and a practical matter, it's not so likely."

Harris said that in May, 1970, Angela became "involved in the cause to which Jonathan Jackson was so devoted . . . By June the 2nd, 1970, there's a letter. She's come to the point in her relationship with Jonathan that she writes to George. The point is . . . the connection between the two of them as early as June the 2nd."

Angela gave money to Stephen Mitchell, to buy a gun which she traded in a month later for a carbine that was found in the van but never used. On July 14, Angela, Jonathan and his father register in a Berkeley motel the night before attending a hearing of the Soledad Brothers. The subject of the hearing was John Thorne's petition that would have permitted her to be an investigator and therefore visit George Jackson. Of course, Angela never received permission, and therefore did not have an opportunity to make conspiratorial visits to Jackson, but Harris ignored that fact.

July 17 Angela moved to a new apartment, "the place at which Jonathan Jackson is seen occasionally thereafter." July 25 Angela and Jonathan are at Western Surplus in Los Angeles where she buys the carbine and some ammunition which he carried into the courtroom.

July 29, Angela cashes a check, and a man answering Jonathan's description is with her. July 30, Angela and Jonathan return from Mexico. The night of July 31, Jonathan is picked up in Angela's car. She comes to the police station and says he had her car with her permission. Another day of conspiratorial association. August 3, to San Francisco. Tuesday the 4th, she cashed a check for 100 dollars. Also on the 4th, Jonathan signed in at San Quentin at 2:15, and also signed the name of Diane Robinson. Mrs. Lucas who signed out of the prison at 2:10, saw and identified Angela Davis. And then, there are the San Quentin personnel.

Harris had anticipated that the defense would concentrate heavily on his eye witness testimony: "I doubt if there is a witness who testified here, I doubt if there has been a witness who has testified since we have had courts as to whom you couldn't find some element of unreliability, if you thought about it long and hard enough." He made specific mention of guard William Twells, and the inadequacy of Twells' testimony.

Twells, Harris explained, had "only seen Diane Robinson briefly on Wednesday. He hadn't seen her at all Tuesday.

"As he came down the steps, he saw a lady standing by the steps. He described her for you. He did not purport to make any identification. You heard the description. She was black, she had a short Afro, in her 20's, light skinned . . . Separate and apart from how good his memory was and how many times he saw her, she did something in his presence. How long he saw her, how long it was he saw her do something—and what was that?

" . . . he saw her wave. At who? George Jackson. How does he know that? As I recall, he saw him wave back."

Harris, in this instance, was doing the same thing to the jury that he had done by citing the *Mini-Manual of the Urban Guerrilla*. He was using a show of authority to corral the specific ignorance of the jurors into his corner. Men in prison wave at everybody who wave at them, and often initiate the gesture. Outside of prison, people tend to return such a gesture, a move usually motivated by a desire to avoid offending the friendly overtures of someone they cannot recognize, but do not wish to slight. Within prison, a response is mandated by the need for human contact with people whose lives are lived outside those walls—contact with free men and women.

But even had that wave signified recognition, the woman that George Jackson was waving at did not necessarily have to be Angela Davis. Twells recognized a short Afro, a description which does not match Angela Davis' hair style. Nevertheless, the fact of a wave from George Jackson to a woman said to have accompanied Jonathan, was offered by the prosecutor as proof of the fact that Diane Robinson was actually Angela Davis.

"Whatever you do, you know one thing," the prosecutor emphasized, "that if Madeline Lucas saw Angela Davis on Tuesday, August the 4th, then Angela Davis was there on August the 5th, because Madeline Lucas saw the woman who was represented by Jonathan Jackson as Diane Robinson, and Diane Robinson was there both days."

Why? If there was a Diane Robinson who was there both days, and who was thought to be Angela Davis, why is her presence at San Quentin on two successive days indicative of her being Angela Davis? Suppose Jonathan, for reasons of his own, brought two separate women into the prison, but signed the register with the same false name?

Harris said that Angela had ample reason to use the name Diane Robinson because she had been denied visiting privileges, and therefore had to use another stratagem to see George Jackson. He reminded the jury that attorney John Thorne, whom he had called as a prosecution witness, declined to testify, as he had in September of 1970, that Angela had called him the night of August 5. Thorne, he pointed out, was the attorney who had tried to have Angela appointed as an investigator so that she could visit George Jackson.

Thorne also was the assumed conduit of letters between George and Angela, at least one of which was intercepted by prison authorities. Essentially, he said that Thorne lied on the stand, but did tell the truth on September 29, 1970, when he made a statement that Angela Davis had called him from San Jose. Susan Castro, the defense witness who testified she had been with Angela for two and a half hours, beginning at noon, was identified as someone who had been active in the Angela Davis defense fund, and partisan, if not a personal friend of the defendant. "I have three witnesses who said they saw her, and she has one."

Harris' approach to defense witnesses was interesting. He is a master of the uncertainty. "I think, I believe, maybe, I can't remember exactly," or some equivalent, surrounds a certain number of the facts he lays out. When he got around to defense witnesses, Harris became even more uncertain.

"Now there was some Defense evidence bearing on August the 5th, and my recollection of it is that this was by Mr. Bloice, I think the editor of the *People's World,* and he testified that he had had dinner with Miss Davis on that very night, Wednesday night, and he said he went out to, I think, Laura Holland's apartment (it was Laura Holms), I guess. I don't recall Mrs. Wheeler having mentioned that event in her testimony earlier." (She hadn't).

The 6th of August is important, Harris says. For now there are four witnesses who saw Angela and Jonathan at the Marin service station. We know Jonathan was there, not just because of eyewitness identification, but because of a record of a telephone call placed by Jonathan at 10:44. Again Harris eases in a nonexistent fact. He refers to the notation of the call as recorded by the operator.

No one was arguing that Jonathan was not at the station as claimed or that a call was not made. So, Harris vaguely filled in a few details beyond the testimony that the ticket gave nothing but Jonathan's name, the two telephone numbers involved, and the duration of the call.

Four people saw the two. "Each of them had a different vantage point, each of them saw the person involved from a different vantage point physically, if you please, different periods of time, different periods of a difference or variety of attentiveness, varieties of recollection, varieties of ability to—to draw upon recollection and to describe or to identify, and these persons are as varied as anybody else, as we would be."

Mike Vonada, the fireman, had seen Angela smoking a small cigar, and so had Josephine Valle, a clerk, some months before, and both times Angela was described as wearing leather clothing. Besides, Vonada said he saw Jonathan wearing red and white beads and the last item of evidence introduced was a set of beads taken from Jonathan, "some red and white. There are some that are green. You can look at them and see if that casts any light in terms of reliability of Mike Vonada's identification of Angela Davis as the woman who was at the service station with Jonathan Jackson." Again, the same note. If a witness correctly identified Jonathan, then it follows that he could correctly identify the woman with Jonathan as Angela.

The same goes for Louis May, the ex-convict, who, according to Harris, had been attacked by the Defense. They had to attack May he explained, because "whatever Louis May's faults may be, if he saw Angela Davis in a yellow van with Jonathan Jackson, then he saw Angela Davis at the prison on August the 6th, 1970, because that is the day that Jonathan Jackson had the van. He rented the van that morning." But May had also testified that Jonathan and Angela had been there the day before in a yellow van, an impossibility. And Harris handled this contradiction with his bumbling finesse, with as fine an obscurist sentence as could be composed by an attorney. "He (May, in his testimony) had the yellow van there a day before it was in fact rented. Jonathan Jackson didn't have it on August the 5th. He couldn't have been there for any other thing or not very likely at least, but nevertheless, that was his testimony."

Marvin Stender had testified that he met Angela at 11:30 that day. Marvin Stender, he pointed out, had been John Thorne's attorney in September 1970, and that fact should help the jury resolve the obvious contradictions between prosecution and defense witnesses relative to Angela's whereabouts on August 6.

"We think, from the evidence, that there is only one reasonable inference. If you accept the fact that Angela Davis was with Jonathan Jackson, that she was Diane Robinson, on the 4th and the 5th and, if you accept the fact that she was in the service station on the 6th . . . then we don't think it is a matter of choosing between reasonable inferences because what is the other reasonable inference other than she knew what was going to transpire the next day?"

He put in more detail for the jury, reminding them that testimony placed Jonathan in the Civic Center three times that day, testimony which implied to him that Jonathan actually wanted to act on August 6. San Quentin guard Gordon Farrell testified he saw Jonathan with a trenchcoat and briefcase on the morning of August 6. Lois Leidig said she saw him in the afternoon, dressed in an open necked shirt, with a sweater or jacket wrapped around him. Layne saw him later on, again dressed in a trenchcoat and carrying a briefcase.

"Now I don't want you to speculate," Harris told the jury. "I want you to look at these facts, if you think they are facts, and draw the inferences you think are reasonable."

Jonathan had the coat on in the morning (the temperature was 84) when he went into the courtroom "and he had the briefcase, and we know what the purpose of the briefcase was . . . and then he came back to the van, he did not have the coat on, so we would understand he put a coat on to go into the building, and he took it off when he came out . . . the second time [he went into the courtroom] he didn't have the coat on, and he didn't have the bag [briefcase]. He had a paper sack, according to Mrs. Leidig." Jonathan then left, he said, and returned later, again wearing the coat, and carrying the briefcase.

"I think it is reasonable to believe he had the shotgun by that time. Whether that was the time—we will never know, and I don't ask any speculation. But you do know this, that Angela Davis was with him. I think you know that based on the evidence on the 4th and the 5th, and on the 6th and under such circumstances, that there is no way she could not have known what Jonathan Jackson was going to do.

"If she knew it was going to happen, then the final question was whether she knowingly rendered assistance. If you are satisfied that there was guilty knowledge on her part from all of those events on the 4th, 5th, on the 6th, then I think the question of whether she furnished assistance is a relatively simple one. These were her guns."

Right down to the very end, every time Harris mentioned the guns, he walked over and waved a few of them around. "These were her books," he just pointed and then moved back behind the lectern. "It was her ammunition. Then, if Jonathan Jackson had those things and if she knew about the conspiracy that was going to occur, then we think you can reasonably infer that these were furnished by Angela Davis." He mentioned the testimony of Ellen Broms, who told of Angela's recognition that the shotgun mentioned in news stories might be the same as that she bought for the defense of the Soledad House and gave to Jonathan. Harris scoffed at the idea that the gun was meant to protect a house.

"You fire it once, and then you have to reload it. I suppose it's some sort of self-defense—scarcely the equivalent of this with 30 shots one after the other, scarcely the equivalent of the other carbine, scarcely the equivalent of an automatic pistol. These were the weapons in Los Angeles."

But then Angela's concern for self defense had lessened enough so that when she moved she didn't bother to take her guns with her.

The shotgun was bought to be taped to the head of a judge, and what if Jonathan did take the guns. He took them with Angela Davis' knowledge and consent, along with the books that showed up. Angela said it herself, in her opening statement. "The only real questions in the case are knowledge and intent." And Harris found he had to agree with her. She committed acts, overt acts, beginning the 3rd of August, and she manifested guilt by leaving California on August 7.

"We think she fled. She fled California, and she fled because she was guilty. Remember the Mager Volkswagen and its $43.00 ticket. We computed that and it worked out that the VW came in at 8:19, August 7.[3] She bought a wig, went to Miami and was arrested in New York by the FBI. She was disguised. Angela told you she feared as I think she put it in her opening statement, 'police violence.' I do call your attention to one fact, and that is that her experience with the California courts over the most important question . . . she had had so far in her life, . . . we have the Summary Judgment here . . . from the Superior Court in her favor and against the Regents of the University of California . . . she had been in the trial courts on that rather explosive subject, and she had prevailed."

[3] This would mean that Harris' theory required that Angela Davis sit around the San Francisco airport for six hours.

He never spelt out what that explosive subject was, implying somehow that a decision saying that a person cannot be fired simply because of membership in the Communist Party, was a victory.

Finally Harris said he wanted to talk about motive. "In fact, the motive, if you please, we think, distinguishes or separates George Jackson from the other Soledad Brothers—because in connection with George Jackson, we have evidence of the deep commitment of Angela Davis prior to August the 7th. Two letters were taken from her apartment, and another was intercepted at Soledad."

Over a year after the conspiracy manifested itself and resulted in the death of Judge Haley, this series of letters was found in George Jackson's cell in the adjustment center at San Quentin.

Harris started the jury with the letter dated June 2: "My love, your love reinforces my fighting instincts and tells me to go to war." He said that Angela was hooked on George, described herself as his cousin, and did whatever she could do to be in communication with him. "I never said Jon was too young for anything . . ." And then there was the dream where "we were together fighting pigs. Winning. We were learning to know each other."

"John will cooperate . . . I trust him" said another letter, this one seemingly referring to John Thorne's willingness to smuggle letters in. "I'm completely free, fired, grades in. There are beautiful plans ahead," Harris read from her letter. "No doubt there were plans ahead," was his comment. He read another extract: "The solution is not to become less aggressive, not to lay down the gun, but to learn how to set the sights correctly, aim accurately, squeeze rather than jerk, and not be overcome by the damage. We have to learn how to rejoice when pigs' blood is spilled." Harris read from the letters found August 21, 1971, following George Jackson's killing.

Harris finished with what he termed a poignant scene. "Diane Robinson was in the waiting room, and she went over to the steps that go up into the visiting room, and she waved to George Jackson. Now I think, you know she couldn't visit him. Her letters had been intercepted. She had been turned down in terms of getting in to see him, but she could wave to him. We think that, if that was Angela Davis who waved to him, and it was Angela Davis who was there the day before, and it was Angela Davis who was at the Civic Center and at the service station, and when she bought the gun, the shotgun and when she was with Jonathan Jackson in the yellow van at the scene of the crime, and that she knew about the crime, that she is responsible under the law.

"Angela was motivated in relevant ways, and the relevant way is simply this: The freedom of George Jackson from prison . . . she was motivated by passion that knew no bounds . . ."

The entire focus of the courtroom was on the jury during closing arguments, and the 15 people in the box transmitted absolutely no indication of their responses to the statements that were delivered from behind a lectern that faced the jury box. Stephanie Ryon, who had taken notes throughout the trial, stopped, when defense arguments began. Most people assumed that this juror wasn't particularly interested in the details of the defense argument, having made up her mind for the prosecution.

Ralph DeLange, who drove a motorcycle, sometimes distributed ecology literature outside the courtroom, and often, had breakfast with a black hobo who hung around the Civic Center, was counted as a vote for the defense. Mary Timothy, who was to become foreperson, and whose son was a conscientious objector, was considered a sure vote for acquittal.

It was the retired librarian, Mrs. Winona Walker, the totally immaculate James Messer, Annapolis graduate, and Nicholas Gaetani, who were of concern to the defense.

It was really a show where the defense outdrew the prosecution. The judge's son, the prosecutor's wife and staff, and Bruce Bales, Marin County District Attorney, turned out to hear the closing statement by the defense.

"May it please the court, gentlemen of the prosecution, my colleagues and Angela Davis, ladies and gentlemen of the jury, I rise to speak to you today on one of the most important days of my life, one of the most important days of the life of my client," Leo Branton, Jr. began.

"I rise to address you as an officer of this Court, a member of a very noble profession. But more importantly, I rise to address you as a black man, a black man to defend my black sister, Angela . . .

"My colleague has called attention to the fact that there is not one black face sitting in that jury box.

"You are a cross-section of Santa Clara County. You are the young and you are the old. You are the Jew and you are the Gentile. You are the worker, you are the executive. And to that extent, you are a cross-section, but not only do I see no black face, but I don't think that I would be mistaken if I said that not many of you in the totality of your lives have been close enough to black people to know what it means, and the reason I want to talk about that first is because it deals with a very important aspect of this case, as the Prosecution has indicated . . . and that is the use of flight, and how flight, according to the Prosecution, is supposed to indicate some consciousness of guilt.

"In order to understand this, I think you have to understand what it is about the history of this country which has made an Angela Davis. I am going to ask you, if you will, for the next few minutes to think black with me, to be black." He looked up from the lectern smiling, "Don't worry, when the case is over, I am going to let you revert back to the safety of being what you are. You only have to be black and think black for the moment or minutes that it will take me to express to you what I am talking about.

"If you are black, you know that 300 years ago your fore-bears were brought to this country in chains on slave ships, and you know that only the strongest of them survived. You know that the weak died in the holds of those ships because of the fact that they died of their own vomit and their own stink and their own stench."

He moved away from the lectern to stand closer to the jury box. "Every time you look at the color of your skin, you realize that it is the result of some white man having raped your grandparents."

That could be taken as nothing other than a personal reference. Leo Branton, Jr. who in the midst of jury selection had jolted the entire jury by revealing that he was black, was finishing the job. Stephanie Ryon, from whom Doris Walker had extracted the observation that she could see where black could be beautiful, was now being asked to view this evidence through the eyes of a man who had a complete black heritage, but an ancestry that had robbed him of the ability to be instantly recognized as beautiful black.

"You come to this country, and they pass a law. They call it the Fugitive Slave Law. It means that they can chase a slave across every border, bring him back, bring him back in chains, no trial, no jury, just sign an affidavit, that this slave is mine . . .

"In the beginning, we weren't even a whole man—three fifths of a man."

"Here we are in the 20th Century. As a black person, you realize that the chains of slavery, visible or invisible, are still there in your everyday life. You realize that you can't buy a home where you want to because somebody is going to complain about it."

He told them of Frederick Douglass' fleeing, of the Dred Scott Decision, saying that the black man has no rights which a white man is bound to respect. Branton went into the case of the Scottsboro Boys, and the assassinations of Medgar Evers, Martin Luther King, and Malcolm X. The four girls killed in a bombing in Birmingham, Alabama.

"Well you might say that that is the South, that that is not the North, that is not the West. But if you are black, you also know that in Los Angeles, in December of 1969, three hundred and fifty Los Angeles policemen, armed with bulletproof vests and automatic rifles, synchronized their watches at 5:00 a.m. and made simultaneous raids on Black Panther headquarters in Los Angeles . . . You know that two days before, the police in the City of Chicago moved into a Black Panther residence and murdered two people in bed . . ."

He pointed out that in Los Angeles the Panthers held the police off in a five hour gun battle and surrendered only after there were a large number of people and press observing "so that, when they came out and they surrendered they wouldn't be shot down like dogs . . . and you know that all of those people were put on trial for conspiracy to commit murder against the police officers for defending their homes, and you know that many of those people spent many many months in jail fighting those charges until they were finally acquitted of the charges of conspiracy to commit murder against a police officer.

"Yes I tell you, ladies and gentlemen, if you are black, you remember these things.

"On August 7th, an Angela Davis also remembered what happened to other black militants: That a Huey Newton had to go through three trials before he was finally let free; that a Bobby Seale was kept in jail for months and months in Connecticut on a phony charge before he was let free; that an Ericka Huggins spent many months in jail before she was let free; that 21 people in New York stayed in jail for over two years before they were let free."

Angela is not only black and militant, she is a member of the Communist Party, Branton explained, and that was part of her thinking on August 7. He mentioned the "anti-Communism which is rampant in this country," along with the many court battles involving communists deprived of rights because of that fact. "Do you remember Miss Elsie Gluck?" Branton asked, the Office Manager in the Philosophy Department at UCLA who had testified about the threatening phone calls and hate mail that flooded the office during the year that Angela was at UCLA. He read some of the mail:

"Hey you with the Fiji hairstyle. Communism is for whites only. When we take over, there won't be a nigger left in North America." Another, "The Klu Klux didn't fool around with Courts and judges. They acted then asked questions. Thank God there are still some left in America who love the US enough to stop this type . . . Where can this Commie go? She has had her day in front of the camera of TV. She is marked for life," signed, a true American.

"I want you to remember how you know that many Americans, many Californians feel about you as a black woman and a black woman communist, and then, on August the 7th or August the 8th of 1970, you know that you have been very active in constitutional measures to free the Soledad Brothers. You know that you've had a close association with Jonathan Jackson, the young brother of George Jackson, and you find out that, without your knowledge, that young Jonathan has taken three guns that you bought and which are registered in your name, and you discover that a shotgun which you bought for the legitimate purpose of defending a place that was subject to attack may have also been

used in the crime because you read about it in the newspaper, what
do you do? Do you go forward to the police, and you try to explain
to them, oh, those were my guns, they were all registered to me, and
I bought that shotgun, yes, I did, and, sure I was a close friend
of Jonathan Jackson and, sure, I worked in the Soledad Defense
Committee, and I did all these things, but I know you are going to
be fair with me, you are going to treat me equal, you are going to
let me go because you know I had nothing to do with it. Do you
think you would have done that? . . .

"It is not really important whether you believe that she was
right or wrong. Maybe, in retrospect, as she looks back, maybe she
might say to herself, gee, maybe I made a mistake, maybe I should
have gone forward and spoken to them, but that is not the point.
The point is: Do you believe that there is evidence before you
from which you can determine that it was a reasonable thing for
her to do, even though you might not have done the same thing?
In other words, has the Prosecution proved to you beyond a reasonable doubt that her reason for leaving this state was because she
was guilty?

"I say to you, when you look at the situation through the eyes
of a black person, you must realize that no black person in this
world would have wondered why she fled. They would only wonder
why she allowed herself to be caught. And that is the way you must
look at this case, through the eyes of Angela Davis.

". . . No matter what you say about Angela Davis, no matter what the Prosecution might say or what you might think about
Angela Davis, I think there is one thing we can agree on. She is
no fool. This woman is a college professor. You have heard her
articulate writings enunciated here by the Prosecution. You heard
her make the opening statement to the jury. Can you believe she
is a fool? Well, in order to find her guilty of these offenses that the
Prosecution has thrown against her, you have got to believe that
she is a fool."

Branton talked of his cross examination of one of the witnesses
who had sold a gun to Angela, who testified that they accept whatever identification is given without checking. But Angela, he pointed
out, not only gave the right identification, but provided an auto-
graph at the time she bought the shotgun, two days before Haley's

death. He picked up two carbines, pointing out that they were exactly the same gun, but that Harris' description had made it seem that the beast carbine, with the collapsible stock and its 30 round clip, was somehow more dangerous than its mate. It was bought, he pointed out, long before Angela Davis knew of the Soledad Brothers, as were the other weapons, with the exception of the shotgun.

He kept reiterating that the jury had to think Angela Davis a fool in order to convict her. Branton, in talking of the Diane Robinson jail visit said: "This brilliant college professor, who has worked out a plan to free her lover, as the prosecution says, is so passion stricken, is so stupid, is so idiotic that she rides out to San Quentin . . . sits around and allows herself to be seen and waits in the waiting room two hours while Jonathan visits his brother. And the only way that she attempts to disguise herself is by the name Diane Robinson . . .

"Do you believe that outrageous story? Do you believe that Angela Davis is that much of an idiot . . . Here she was planning the next day to take people out of a courtroom and, if it became necessary to do so, kill everybody in that courtroom . . . She didn't have sense enough to get rid of her Afro or to disguise herself in any way."

Branton's voice ranges over the entire scale, and this question ended on a high querulous note, almost pleading that if the jury is going to find his client guilty, that they do so through a route that begins with respecting Angela's intelligence.

Look at the witnesses, he said, for it's just not a matter of weighing one set of witnesses against the other. "There's no question about where Angela Davis was according to our witnesses. These are not people who said: 'I think I had lunch with Angela Davis. I had lunch with a light-complected Negro woman with an Afro, and I think it might have been Angela Davis. All of these people know Angela Davis. In order to believe the prosecution's case, you've got to believe that we called a group of witnesses up here who, when they raised their right hand to God and swore that they were telling the truth, that they lied, they perjured themselves.

"The Prosecution says that I am a party to perjury, and he

says for you to believe it. That's what he's saying, in his nice, soft, quiet, gentle way. He doesn't use those words. But that's what it gets down to."

Branton ridiculed the State's case, and the theory on which it was based. "This plan that he's talking about called for a situation where people were going to go into a courtroom with guns, take hostages, and after taking hostages, attempt to exchange those hostages for the defense of the Soledad Brothers . . . he admitted that he didn't know what the plan was after that . . . And what does Diane Robinson, alias Angela Davis according to the Prosecution, do? Now, this is less than 24 hours before the big caper. And they have battery trouble.

"And they go to a service station, and they don't know what to do. They don't know how to fix a battery and somebody suggests, well, maybe you ought to call Hertz and see how much they will authorize to fix the battery. Now here is this gigantic plan coming off the next day, and they are concerned about who is going to pay for charging the battery. They find out that Hertz will authorize up to $6.00 for the battery, and the man says to Jonathan, 'I can send my boy over to bring the truck over,' but Jonathan does not know what to do, and he goes out and talks to this lady, and they have a hard time deciding.

" 'Gee, shall we spend $6.00? Does the budget allow spending $6.00 more to free the Soledad Brothers?' Finally they decide, well, $6.00 is too much, that is above the budget, I think maybe we shouldn't go that far,' so they don't get the battery charged. That is over the budget for this big caper the next day. That is what you have got to believe if you believe this idiotic plan that has been concocted by the Prosecution out of his fertile imagination, because that is all it is, imagination. There is no proof of it, no evidence of it."

He pointed out that the prosecution had Angela waiting for a phone call, presumably from Jonathan. "What was he going to call for? Was he going to call and say 'Angela, the jig is up. We didn't make it. You better take off.' Or did someone else call Angela and say that the jig is up. And then, what Angela Davis said, according to the Prosecution, after she got that phone call at the American Airlines terminal even though right next door to her was an airplane that left at two o'clock for Los Angeles, she rushes out of that air terminal all the way down to a different air terminal in order to catch a PSA flight that left at 2:30."

The defense attorney kept hammering home the number and kind of assumptions inherent in the prosecution approach to the case. The assumption that Angela conspired with Jonathan, gave the guns to Jonathan, bought the shotgun to use on the judge, and that Angela was the person who stayed with Jonathan at the Holland Motel in San Francisco. "Mr. Harris tells you that Angela Davis drove that VW to the airport, but not one word of evidence to support it. He wants you to guess. He tells you that Angela Davis was waiting by that phone booth for a phone call, but not one word of evidence to support it. He wants you to guess."

Branton unveiled a drawing of a young woman with an afro, bound in chains. "In order to demonstrate to you, what we mean when we talk about the chain of circumstantial evidence." The links were marked Motive, Object, Agreement, Knowledge, Intent, and Flight. If any link in this chain is broken, he said, "the prosecution has no case."

And, he added "there is no single link in that chain which can stand the scrutiny of truth." He started with the link Object, explained that dealt with the assumed objective of August 7, to free the Soledad Brothers, and then recapped the prosecution testimony concerning the demand. Gary Thomas, the trained observer had not heard one word about the Soledad Brothers. Also, a juror, Norene Morris, had never heard it. He accused the prosecutor of programming Maria Graham, who had made several statements over a two year period in which there was no mention of the Soledad Brothers, and suddenly remembered hearing "Free the Soledad Brothers at 12:00" the day she was on the stand, the day after she had discussed her testimony with the prosecutor. And then, Mrs. Graham said she heard the words spoken over the phone, an event unrecorded by the other prosecution witness who had been in the courtroom.

"You and I know that that statement is not true. How do we know it? Because the telephone call was made to Sheriff Mountanos. If Sheriff Mountanos had been called on that phone and told, 'Free the Soledad Brothers by twelve o'clock,' the prosecution would have called the receiver of that phone call in here, the Sheriff himself of Marin County, who would have said: 'I received the phone call from the courtroom of Judge Haley, and he told me that if I didn't let them out and free the Soledad Brothers, the judge would be killed.'

"But he never came in. The reason that he never came in is Sheriff Mountanos would not take the witness stand and lie about something that Mrs. Graham has given testimony about, not even to corroborate a very important part of the prosecution's case."

Leo had hit one of the weakest spots in Harris' presentation of the case against Angela. Mountanos had not only received the phone call from the judge, but had been at various points in and around the Civic Center at critical phases of the activity.

The Sheriff, according to other witnesses, had been in the corridor outside courtroom 3 moments before the group exited. He had been in the area near the elevator, where one of the men was supposed to have shouted "free the Soledad Brothers." He had given the orders not to fire, and was aware of the ways in which that order was either countermanded or ignored. He had at one point given a press conference, clearly charging San Quentin guards with the deaths of everyone including Judge Haley. Despite this critical awareness of the details of August 7, Sheriff Louis Mountanos was not called for the Grand Jury, and was not asked to testify at the trial.

Branton named the 12 witnesses who could have heard something about the Soledad Brothers, noting that each of them heard something different or did not hear anything at all, and that some of them changed their stories after their initial statements.

"Of all the criminal cases in the history of the world, I have never heard of a more outlandish theory than the one that has been advanced by the prosecution in this case as to say that what this means is that the object of this conspiracy was to free the Soledad Brothers. Here is a plan to take hostages, a judge, a district attorney, three women jurors, take guns from everybody in the court. And they don't even have enough organization about them to make their demand known."

Branton's most vigorous attack was on Harris' use of Angela's letters. He quoted from the letter written June 2, "My feelings dictate neither illusionary hopes nor intolerable despair." Are those the expressions of "a woman who has lost all hope, who feels that the only way that she can free George Jackson is by some bizarre plan?" The lawyer reads those passages from the letters which involved planning for the future, getting together a defense, the writing of essays, the need for increased communication between herself and George Jackson, so as to advance efforts in his behalf. "Is she talking about blowing a judge's head off? . . . it would seem to me that, within the very letters that this man would make criminal, is the proof of the fact that she was doing things in a legal, above-ground manner.

"Now!" Branton braced himself, became even more stern. His questioning expression turned to one of disgust. "It is one thing for Mr. Harris to take out of context portions of those letters which were found before August, which were written before August 7th. It is another for him to take out of context and to attempt to brand as criminal those warm and tender expressions of love and affection which were written almost a year after Miss Davis was in prison herself.

". . . I think it is an obscenity to delve into the most personal, touching aspects of a person's life, and that is what he did without it serving any purpose. He has attempted to apologize for it by saying he didn't want to do it. Well, if he didn't want to do it, why did he do it? Because it proves nothing in this case. He has taken those words out of context and attempted to make something criminal out of them."

"Well," he went on, "I did the same thing. I took some words out of context, and with the help of Dalton Trumbo put in poetic form words extracted from the letter, and the reason for that is to say to you we do not know how deeply Angela Davis felt for George Jackson. We only know how deeply she was able to express a feeling . . . I want to read to you now and ask you if anyone who writes words like these about love between two human beings can be said to be of a vicious, criminal mind where life of other human beings mean nothing. She wrote:

'Do you know how elated I was
When I first discovered you loved me? . . .
. . . I see you

We are one
They'll never wrest away from us
Those feelings—
Feelings accumulating over centuries,
Today infinitely magnified,
Undiminished in their intensity.
That so much love could exist
Anywhere
In any two people
Even between us
I never realized. . . .
Goodbye—goodnight
I'm going early to
That other cell
To rejoin you.
I love you
I love you with love
Unbounded
Unconquerable.'

"There is a woman by the name of Elizabeth Barrett Browning who also had the ability to write a letter. She is revered and she is respected, and I don't think that anybody ever would say that because she had the ability to recite her love and her affection for another human being, that that was some evidence of some criminal intent, or plan, or conspiracy, or motive.

"The life of my people, ladies and gentlemen, has been one of tragedy, oppression, and hatred, and injustice.

"The life of Angela Davis for the last two years has been one of terror and agony.

"This case, in my opinion has been a sorry stain—a sorry chapter on the history of justice in this country.

"Ladies and gentlemen, before I came here, my friends told me that I could not get a fair trial for Angela Davis in this country; I could not find 12 white people who would be willing to be fair to a black woman charged with the serious crimes with which she is charged in this case."

Branton was standing in front of the center of the jury box, speaking softly—in that stage whisper which carried throughout the courtroom. He walked to his right, and started to address each juror individually, beginning with the back row. "But I tell you, Mr. Delange, and you, Mr. Gaetani, Mrs. Charlton, Mr. Seidel, Mr. Messer, Mr. Franco," and then again to the right, calling off jurors 7 through 12, "Mrs. Timothy, Miss Savage, Mrs. Frederick, Miss Walker, Mrs. Wade, Mrs. Ryon, and any of the three alternates who might eventually sit on this case, you have an opportunity to be a part of history . . . Whether you want to or not, you are going to be a part of history. We on the Defense are a part of history. We have labored hard and long to try to get over to you the gigantic hoax that has been committed, not only against this defendant but against the name of American justice in this country.

"With these last few words of mine, we are now going to transfer that responsibility from our shoulders to yours. We hope that in so doing, that when you 12 people, tried and true, write the final chapter in the case of the People vs. Angela Davis, you will say that you were chosen, you served, you considered, and you brought back the only verdict that could comport with justice in this case, and that is a verdict of not guilty. I'm sure you will."

The arguments were in. On Friday, June 2, Judge Arnason gave instructions to the jury. There were a total of 11 possible verdicts. Not guilty on each of the three counts, guilty on each, and the possibility of lesser guilty findings on the kidnapping and murder charges. The jury, which was sequestered during deliberations were turned over to a group of Sheriff's Deputies. The defense team went back to their offices and began to pack. A vigil of Angela Davis supporters began outside the courtroom, and everyone waited.

12 : Political Epilogue

A verdict in a case such as Angela Davis' is a method of keeping score, a determination that one side or the other has been declared the winner. But more goes on in a political trial than the verdict, and there are many people, other than a jury, who become influenced by information relating to a political trial, independent of its outcome.

Albert Harris had been successful in reducing the scope of Auguust 7, from a revolutionary act, to an episode of homicidal terror. He had reduced, nay, dismissed Jonathan Jackson as a serious contender for a place in history. Jonathan did not come out of the trial a freedom fighter, or a revolutionary, or even an extremely dedicated person. No, his image was murky, lying somewhere between a dupe for Angela Davis, and an instrument of convicts, namely McClain, who took over Jonathan's operation.

Georgia Jackson summed up the treatment of her youngest son, "the prosecution called him a murderer and the defense made him a thief."

Likewise, Angela became something other than what she had been as a result of both the prosecution and the reportage surrounding that prosecution. One of the constancies of the trial was the repeated linking of Angela Davis with acts of violence. Not all of this was the fault of the prosecution, but it is undeniable that the line which Albert Harris promulgated from the very beginning, that Angela Davis was a student of, and activist for, violence, received repeated emphasis in the press. Even if it did not directly affect the trial, it had to help shape public attitudes toward Angela in subtle and unmeasured ways.

In February, 1972, Leo Branton Jr., in arguing for a change of venue, noted that security provisions around the Santa Clara Courthouse, "lends an air of an armed camp" to the proceedings, creating an atmosphere of fear.

Harris defended the security measures, citing court cases which have upheld such armed precautions and have sustained appeal. One case which Harris did not cite involved an entire wall of the San Diego Federal Courthouse, which has hidden microphones and loudspeakers capable of picking up any conversation held near the wall. The installation occurred in the aftermath of the August 7 incident and was held to be legal by a Federal Judge.

The San Jose site of the trial was across the street from both a National Guard headquarters and an Army Reserve post. Entrance to the courtroom, and the area surrounding it, was through a ten-foot-high barbed wire cyclone fence, which was monitored by closed circuit television. Everyone entering the courtroom passed through a metal detector and had to be searched. Mug shots were taken of all spectators before they were allowed to enter. Anyone with an outstanding traffic warrant anywhere in the state was arrested. Anyone who seemed suspicious was skin searched. Each and every pill carried by anyone entering the trial was subject to inspection, and was compared to a picture in order to determine that the pill was not contraband.

"We know this," Harris stated, "that wherever this trial goes there will be security measures. They seem to be inevitable. . . . The same people who complain, bring on conditions that require security.

"I think there is an aura of fear. When you go up by a group waving their signs, chanting their slogans, raising their fists . . . there is an aura of fear."

Harris submitted newspaper clippings to the court, which included the story of a hijacker "who was shot for his trouble" who demanded money and the release of Angela Davis. He was apparently referring to Garret B. Trapnell, a 34-year-old man from Miami who was wanted there for a probation violation and in Dallas for armed robbery. Trapnell hijacked a 707 bound for New York from Los Angeles on January 29, 1972. He demanded freedom for a friend held on robbery charges, a personal chat with President Nixon and the release of Angela Davis. He maintained a telephone conversation with Dr. David G. Hubbard, a Dallas psychiatrist who had treated Trapnell two years before, and who since has written a book about what motivates hijackers. Trapnell allowed 93 passengers to leave the plane at Kennedy Airport, and took off with a crew to circle the airport for a time. The plane landed for refueling and an FBI agent shot him. This story was one of the prosecutor's justifications for security.

"There are unknown people in this world," said Harris, who might want to come into the courtroom with a gun. What he wanted, he said, was for Angela Davis supporters to be disabused "very quickly and disabused very firmly" of the idea that they could participate in the trial, even to the extent of mounting a picket line outside the court.

There were other incidents that were somehow linked to the Angela Davis trial. In November, 1970, Minneapolis-St. Paul police arrested a man who they said had plans to kidnap the governor of the state, hijack a plane, leave the country, and trade the hostages for the freedom of three jailed friends of his and Angela Davis. Two months later, former South Carolina State representative Jamie Lindsay and a black man, Charles Scales, shot it out with each other. Lindsay claimed that two blacks, Scales and Grover Bennet, had kidnapped eight people in Bennetsville, 100 miles northeast of Columbia, the State capital, preparatory to hijacking a plane. The plane was to take the group to Cuba, and from there they would demand ransom, and also trade their hostages for Angela.

There was, in addition, the jailbreak attempt which delayed Angela's opening statement, and the killing of James Carr which occurred the following week. Both were linked in some way to the trial.

The jury was instructed June 2, court was dismissed and a vigil began to form outside the courtroom on a stretch of lawn which fronts the Superior Court building. Newsmen, some of whom mingled with those at the vigil, had arranged for the Sheriff's Department to inform them of every move the jury made, so as to fill out the non-stories filed during jury deliberation. The waiting for a verdict is rough and it is necessary to file something, even though nothing is going on to which newspeople are privy. That means stories related to how the defense and prosecution are holding up under the strain of waiting.

Earl Caldwell and myself decided to chase down Angela Davis for an interview, on the assumption that the trial was over and the gag rule inoperative. We left the fenced in compound just minutes after a bulletin had come over the radio that a hijack was in progress. Outside the next building we ran into Howard Moore, Jr. and we were talking to him when Lt. Don Tamm, the head of the Sheriff's Community Relation's effort, popped up and asked Moore to stay available to the Sheriff's office.

Moore said that he would, and then as the three of us began to walk toward his office we saw Leo Branton, Jr. and Doris Walker approaching. A car appeared, screeched up beside the two attorneys, and seemingly sucked them inside. Seconds later the car shuddered to a stop next to Moore, and Lt. Tamm asked him in. Caldwell, ever a reporter, jumped in to sit beside a baseball capped FBI man. The car then raced to a restaurant and bar, Plateau 7, two blocks away from the courthouse. Angela Davis and the inner circle of her defense committee were preparing for lunch, to celebrate the formal end of the trial and to plan the details of their public posture during and after jury deliberations.

I found my way to the meeting place a few minutes after the group of policemen and lawyers arrived. Angela and her companions had been forewarned. Judge Arnason, who apparently had his own intelligence sources, had called Angela at the restaurant and had asked her not to leave without checking with him.

The combination of Sheriff's deputies and FBI men who came into the restaurant did not come as a total surprise to her. Nevertheless, Angela was jolted to discover that the hijackers of a plane then in Seattle had demanded $500,000, a plane with a longer range capability than the Boeing 727 they had captured (along with 98 passengers) and the release of Angela Davis. Angela, reportedly, was supposed to be delivered in a white dress, to the San Francisco airport, ready to take a plane.

I catch on quick, and when Angela, her attorneys, and the police jumped into what was becoming a caravan, I jumped in too. They caromed around a few blocks and ended up in the compound which Caldwell and I had left 20 minutes before. We left the car to realize that Angela had been busted. They called it protective custody. Angela was confined in the judge's chambers, waiting for the hijackers to find out that she was not coming.

The plane landed in San Francisco, the hijackers exchanged it for a half million dollars and a long distance plane, and flew to Algeria. It turned out that the hijackers had never demanded that Angela be delivered.

NUCFAD had already issued a statement: "We don't know anything about this hijacking. We don't agree with it as a method of freeing Angela Davis. We have built a strong mass movement and are sure she will be acquitted."

By 6:30 p.m., newscasters had reported that the hijacker did not want Angela, and had never mentioned her. Lt. Tamm, before pulling into his "no comment" mode, insisted that he had been informed by Seattle police of the demand. The story had gone out on the wires, however, and was transmitted to enough police agencies so that the FBI contributed to the apprehension of Angela Davis. She was released about 7:30 p.m.

The image of revolutionaries is being built by law enforcement, is being broadcast by the press, and is replete with flaws, misinformation, and calumny dangerous to the development of a realistic awareness of what militance, and revolution, black, white and otherwise, is all about.

Although seemingly relaxed, security provisions were very much in evidence Sunday, June 4. By 10:00 in the morning there was a minimum of 100 people on the lawn in front of the courthouse. Across the street, no more than 200 yards away in the parking lot, were a group of uniformed National Guardsmen who were just hanging around with an air of innocence, as though one could expect to see 50 or so National Guardsmen loafing in a parking lot early of a Sunday morning. At about 11 a.m. a rumor swept through the crowd that a verdict had been reached. It was verified almost immediately by the appearance of Angela and her attorneys. By 12 o'clock, everyone was processed through the search and security area, and were standing in the corridor immediately outside of the courtroom.

"Woke up this morning with my mind set on Freedom."

Singing voices could be heard and heard clearly. They weren't loud, nor were they insistent. If ever a modern slavemaster wanted to look upon a compliant group, there they were. Angela's entire family. Franklin and Kendra Alexander. Haywood Burns, who had come from New York when the final argument was in progress. A group of people from Glide Methodist Church. The regular trial goers, including the thirty newsmen who were allowed inside. The fight had been fought, there was nothing left to do but sing and wait for the decision.

Caldwell was up there singing with the rest. Normally, he would not have been in the group of people in front of the courtroom door. Caldwell, in fact most of the blacks who attended that trial regularly, was constitutionally incapable of making the line up on police time. The tardiness was not so much a protest as the beginnings of resistance, a quiet ideological tensing up in rejection of absolute police authority. In the early days of the trial, Sheriff's deputies rounded up the press like so many child care charges and walked them to the search area. There was almost never a black face in the group. We were late to the lineup, having sauntered over after a second cup of machine made coffee, or a careful reading of the day's editorial in three newspapers.

But on June 4, we were up front. The deputies were making an announcement about something which required newspeople to stand behind a white line and wait for something else. Fifty feet in front of them, standing next to the gates, waiting to be searched, were Caldwell and Major. And Caldwell was right in the middle of the singing group in front of the courtroom doors looking directly at the deputy who opened the door and told everyone that if the singing continued, there would be no spectators allowed in the courtroom that day.

I stood there thinking of Albert Harris, and an interview we had in January which touched upon his almost hysterical reaction to very normal, reasonable and quite orderly activity in support of Angela Davis at the beginning of the trial in Marin.

There was a point when Harris, who automatically opposed everything proposed by the defense, very seriously objected to the suggestion that the trial be moved to larger quarters, or otherwise be made available to a larger audience. Harris wrote briefs and argued against the defense motion, and one of the grounds he used dealt with avoiding a circus atmosphere at the trial. He cited the same incident in several memoranda. Ruchell Magee says "right on" and members of the audience respond, "right on." Nothing else happened, there was no movement, no shouts, no emotional outburst, just a recognition between blacks on one side of the bar and blacks on the other.

I asked him why he was so shook up about that, pointing out that the black church, which is probably held in greater esteem than the courts by black people, conducts solemn and meaningful business in an expeditious fashion, and can tolerate "amens," "preach," "tell it brother," and other interruptions without difficulty. I was trying to get him to react to the possibility that what he heard in court was not revolution, but black folk, most of whom were raised relating to institutions which did not interpret an interruption, a remark, a noise, as some sort of profanation to be immediately stamped out.

"An 'amen' in church," I suggested, "could be an equivalent to a 'right on' in court, and is a perfectly natural and reasonable kind of reaction."

"Yes, I suppose I hadn't even thought about that analogy," said Harris. "I think it works." But then he paused a second. "I really don't think you can have cheering sections in a courtroom, even though it's spontaneous reaction on the part of the people. And I think it would be just as bad if we were out in someplace where people were very hostile to Angela Davis and they had people who boo'd her or cheered the prosecution." [1]

But we weren't talking about booing or cheering. The subject was his citing a spontaneous reaction as an example of disruptive conduct in court. He was talking about disapproval, the difficulty of witnesses "or even professionals to face disapproval, you know, that's overt."

Harris once had faced that disapproval with both spontaneity and seeming good humor. He was the villain to most of the courtroom audience, from the first arraignment to the last not guilty. In the beginning, when he walked into court, some of the audi-

[1] Albert Harris, Jr. in interview with author 13 Jan. 1972.

ence would start a low keyed but very audible hissing sound. Once, Harris walked in to this chorus of hisses, smiled, and put his fist in the air—a move which completely disarmed the audience and coincidentally stopped the hissing. It was Harris, and not a court order, which earned for him the right to enter a courtroom without catcalls.

"I'm not so sure this is a spontaneous reaction," Harris continued, in talking about the "right ons" in court. "I didn't get that impression at all. I had the impression it was a sort of calculated effort to show their support for whoever it was, Angela Davis or Ruchell Magee and that's just not the forum in which they are entitled to do that." [2]

The man who prosecutes in the name of the people had spoken. Those who attend trials are not supposed to show support for anyone, in any form, and if they do it might be evidence of a conspiracy. Therefore, it was no surprise when the bailiff opened the door to an empty courtroom, located in a corner of a building that had been sealed off by brick from the rest of a structure that was closed down because it was Sunday, and told Angela's supporters to shut up or stay out.

The group shut up. A few minutes later, at 12:32 p.m., everyone was in the courtroom waiting. Captain Johnson, the head of security, was personally in charge. A deputy named Partch, who wears a flag next to his nameplate, and who for a time read the daily admonition to the audience to not sit on the edge of their seats, stand up, or do anything untoward upon penalty of ejection from the courtroom, wasn't there. He'd broken an arm a few weeks before quelling an anti-war demonstration at Stanford. It was the same demonstration which had produced for the *Stanford Daily,* an almost full page picture of Captain Johnson, ex-marine, completely garbed in battlegear, and flat out on his ass, having been pelted with something, or having tripped and hit his head.

Bowling wasn't there either. He was the black deputy, fairly popular with the newspeople, who searched the men as they came into the court area. At one point he had become angry with a couple of the black reporters who were comparing Santa Clara

[2] Albert Harris, Jr. in interview cited above.

with San Francisco County, and reared back with a pride that seemed a combination of Chamber of Commerce and rural certitude to announce, "we've got a good county here and we intend to keep it that way." It was Bowling who had been chosen over all the rest to push Gary Thomas' wheelchair into the courtroom, who had been the first at Captain Johnson's side when he was felled, and who, when hair trigger alarms went off signifying that some unwary person had leaned against a door with a red NO EXIT sign, was the first to leap over barriers and rush to the offending door, ready to repulse raiders, or turn the alarm off and make a proper report over his walkie-talkie. Bowling didn't make the finish, but Captain Johnson had eight other deputies in the courtroom with him who did.

The jury came in, walked down the middle aisle, all looking grim. Their faces weren't blank, they looked sad, although in truth, there were no frowns. Everyone was convinced that there could not have been a guilty verdict. Certainly Mrs. Timothy or Ralph Delange, would have held out against a guilty longer than one day. But that conviction was not upheld by the demeanor of the jury. They walked back into that courtroom as though they had a heavier burden on their shoulders than when they had walked out.

"Mrs. Timothy," said the judge, "I assume from certain communications I have received that you have been selected as forelady or foreperson or however you wish to be designated." Arnason leaned forward, waiting, the last person in the courtroom to do so. "Madam foreman, has the jury reached a decision?"

"We have your Honor."

"On each of the three counts?"

"On each of the three counts your Honor."

"Will you please hand the verdicts to the clerk." She did so.

"Mr. Clerk, will you please read the verdicts."

Long sentences, words having to do with the charge of murder and way at the bottom the verdict—"not guilty."

Franklin Alexander was in the back row, one seat removed from the aisle. With the not guilty pronouncement he began to sob. Two bailiffs moved over to him immediately and didn't know what to do. Franklin was the most disliked regular who came down there.

He was big, brash, and had a perfect sense of when to stop asserting himself, so that his adversary, usually one of the bailiffs, had to pause in midstroke, knowing full well that Franklin had not done anything to warrant either a beating or arrest. Franklin Alexander had once circumvented the law against demonstrations around the court, while forcing the entire Santa Clara County Sheriff's Department to regroup, by leading a thousand previously demonstrating people on a "tour" to the gates of the courtroom area which he called a $700,000 persecution complex. Both Franklin Alexander and Fania Davis Jordan lectured the group filing by the cyclone fence about the purposes, costs and functions of the various security devices.

Now, Franklin was crying, sobbing, releasing what was in him much as Job had to have wept when relieved of his boils and Lot released the terror that he dared not reveal to himself before becoming aware that he could leave Sodom and that his wife could follow.

The bailiffs didn't know what to do. Nobody did. Some of the spectators were transfixed in their seats, not daring to look at and identify a man who could deliver a sound that welled deep from within himself. The bailiffs were upset because Franklin was obviously making a disturbance, but he was just as obviously not demonstrating, clearly not agitating and demonstrably doing nothing but crying. They stood there, as words were coming out of the clerk dealing with the charge of kidnap.

Ben Davis was sitting directly in front of Franklin. He was holding his mother's hand so tightly that all the black was squeezed out of their knuckles. "Not guilty."

More tears. Franklin was still sobbing, his cadence the same as when he began. But now there were others, along with sharply intaken breaths, crying at the verdict. Then, silence, for conspiracy is what the trial was all about, and Art Vanick was again reading the preliminaries. There it is, "not guilty," and joyous but restrained pandemonium ripped through the crowd. Angela and Kendra sitting at the defense table had been crying throughout. They moved toward each other and hugged. Branton stood and began applauding, as though the last two not guilties were encores that he wanted repeated again and again. "Right On's" came from the audience, but the total effect was not yet one of jubilation. It was a collective gasp. Branton actually brought them together. He was a lawyer, he was in charge, and he was obviously aware of proper court decorum. Branton applauded, the crowd followed his lead.

It was a verdict in which everybody could find a reason to express pleasure, a verdict that everyone, particularly those who would not have felt disappointment if Angela had been convicted, had to comment on. Ronald Reagan said the acquittal underscored his belief in the American judiciary. He said he wasn't surprised at the verdict. "I've always said that the establishing of a connection would be extremely difficult." He went on to say that her supporters, "ought to think about whether the demonstrations they've staged are worth the civil disruptions." But, there hadn't been any civil disruptions surrounding this trial, and very few demonstrations.

Marin County District Attorney Bruce Bales said, "I'm shocked beyond belief by the not guilty verdicts. Apparently the jury fell for the purely emotional pitch offered by the defense. Despite what happened I'm still firmly convinced Angela Davis is as responsible for the killing of Judge Harold J. Haley and the crippling of my assistant, Gary Thomas, as Jonathan Jackson and undoubtedly more so because of her age and intelligence." [3]

Governor Reagan subsequently elevated Gary Thomas to the Marin County Municipal Court, the only judgeship the Governor has awarded to a registered Democrat.

Judge Arnason also hailed the decision in his own way, but he came on righteously angry at the applauding crowd, which he could have controlled by simply asking for order. "I will not tolerate misconduct in my court," he shouted, saying something to the effect that if you can't behave, get out. The crowd quieted down, but their mood was now light, carefree and tinged with a "go on and kick us out, we didn't want to be here in the first place." The mood could only get so light, as stretched out across the entire width of the courtroom was Captain Johnson and his eight deputies, scowling, waiting for trouble.

[3] Reported in *San Francisco Chronicle,* 5 June, 1972.

Some of the audience had been in San Francisco on March 27, when the Soledad Brothers had been found not guilty. They left the courtroom moving into the Tac Squad dominated ante-chamber that was formed by handcuffing one set of doors closed, partitioning a hall, and leaving a narrow, well guarded passageway, through which only one person at a time could pass. The audience walked out into the smell of mace, and the certain knowledge that it would take more than repeated verdicts of not guilty to end the police domination of much of their lives. There they were, surrounded by policemen who found the very source of their joy a reason for affront, an incipient demonstration, a political excrescence.

Judge Arnason, on the bench, readjusted his stance, resumed his fatherly air, and settled back to a courtroom that had been instantly controlled.

Art Vanick was protesting. This was the part that the clerk gets to do all by himself. For six months Art Vanick had been marking exhibits, keeping track of documents, putting things up and down on an easel, coping with newspeople, and generally keeping the courtroom operating in an efficient fashion. It was his job to read the verdict and to read it in its entirety, and by damn he was going to do it. The recognition that Vanick wanted to real all of his lines sort of mellowed the audience. Right on, read it all into the record. We want nothing to go wrong now.

Through it all Albert Harris and Cliff Thompson sat numb. They probably expected the verdict, and their position was analogous to a pedestrian who knows a car is going to hit him, and can not get out of the way.

In the back of the courtroom, Franklin had just wound down his sobbing. Two deputies had him on his feet and seemed to be telling him to regain his composure outside. But Arnason, in command again, began to congratulate the jury. The deputies stepped back so that they were not creating a disturbance, and Franklin sat down again.

"Our civilization has decided, and very justly decided, that determining the guilt or innocence of men is a thing too important to be trusted to trained men.

"If it wishes for light upon that awful matter, it asks men

who know no more law than I know, but who can feel the things I felt in a jury box.

"When it wants a library catalogued, or the solar system discovered, or any trifle of that kind, it uses up its specialists. But when it wishes anything done that is really serious, it collects 12 of the ordinary men standing about. The same thing was done, if I remember right, by the founder of Christianity."

Arnason was quoting G. K. Chesterton, whose lines were inspired by his serving on a jury. Arnason said that he had selected the passage, so as to be certain that he made appropriate remarks at the close of the trial. He congratulated the attorneys, reminding them that he had once said he would make barristers of them all, but that they, in fact, were barristers. "If nothing else, I just have a feeling each of you can walk the streets of our society with your heads a little higher. You've conducted yourselves admirably, forcefully. You've conducted yourselves as advocates."

Branton jumped up again, he was not going to be denied. He congratulated the judge, calling him "a credit to the judiciary of the state and the country."

"The law declares us to be equal, but it took a selected man to make us equal."

Leo Branton, Jr. has never been above making the grand gesture, but his tribute was for real. Branton had insisted throughout the trial that Arnason was the best thing that had happened to it. Branton and Arnason admired each other's ability, both as lawyers and as performers in the courtroom. They were both men of talent, legal knowledge and strength, and they each respected the other for it.

Arnason had particular reason to like Branton. The judge said that prior to Branton coming into the case in January, that it was impossible to get the defense and prosecution together in a relatively relaxed situation. "I knew it would be a long trial, and it was essential that the lawyers get to know each other and understand each other's positions, so that we could take care of the business that all sides in a lawsuit have to take care of if the trial is to run smoothly.

"In Marin County, there was a coffee machine in my chambers. I would invite both sides in for a cup of coffee during a recess. I'd always end up alone. Albert Harris would walk in one direction and Howard Moore in the other. Those two would never speak to each other until Branton came into the case. He's a total professional, an excellent counselor. It's my belief that if Leo Branton had to prosecute, that he could handle the job with the same effectiveness that he does as defense counsel." [4]

It's doubtful that Leo Branton, Jr. can see himself as a prosecutor, he has represented the defense too long, and has lived all of his life with the recognition that state power, misapplied state power, is often handled by prosecutors.

Howard Moore, Jr. jumped up after Judge Arnason discharged Angela Davis from the custody of the court and had ordered the $102,500 bail exonerated, and raised both fists, his arms bent at the elbows, shouting, "power to the people, all power to the jury." That broke up the set. This was the last adjournment.

Angela came out of the well of the court first, to walk, unimpeded, through well wishers who were now on their feet, to her mother, Sallye, who was standing in the aisle crying. Members of the audience were hugging each other, even the newshawks were happy—something about good news. The courtroom emptied.

After the verdict, about 40 of the National Guardsmen who were hanging around the Civic Center moved in close to the courtroom. They had heard that the verdict was in Angela's favor. One of them said gleefully, "that's great, now we can go home." Private Ramiro Perez said that, "we just came over from our meeting across the street to see what was really happening." The guardsmen apparently had been called out for security reasons, but were to be activated in force only if the defense lost its case. One of the guardsmen, Specialist 5th Class Tom Costa, who would have been one of the security force deployed to control the anticipated riot, said to a newsman, "Yea, I'll tell you how I feel and you can quote me.

"It's a shame this trial happened at all. It wasted two years of Angela's life and a million bucks. The prosecution case was a sham, based entirely on speculation. We all knew what the verdict was going to be." It's a good thing he knew, for despite his personal

---

[4] Judge Richard E. Arnason, post trial interview with the author.

opinions, Mr. Costa had been sent there to control the people. If orders were given to do so, he probably would have done his duty.

An impromptu press conference was formed outside, with Angela surrounded by her attorneys, lots of cameras and hundreds of well wishers. She stood on a ledge outside the court building, while Franklin Alexander had to admit that for the first time in his experience he was at a loss for words. He asked the attorneys to say a few words.

Leo Branton, Jr. replied, "I have been speaking for ten weeks along with the other lawyers. I had my final say when I concluded my final arguments to the jury. This day belongs to Angela Davis and to the people, and so rather than my saying something else, I'd like for Angela to say something."

"I guess I'm like everybody else today, I'm just speechless," Angela began, and then there was applause. It was not for her, but for the jury. The twelve were filing into the cyclone fenced security area, which was still being manned by deputies, and moving through the crowd as the applause rang out. Angela joined in, and one of the jurors, Ralph Delange, threw a fist in the air to accompanying cheers.

"This is not only the happiest day of my life," Angela continued, "but I'm sure that all the people, all across this country, all across the world, who struggled so hard for my freedom, see this as an example of all of the victories that are to come. Because, starting from this day, we're going to work to free every political prisoner and every oppressed person in this country and in the court buildings.

That was it. A statement had been made to her supporters, who now filled the entire space between the superior and municipal courts buildings.

Next was the press conference inside, where all the jury were lined up with mainly Mrs. Timothy doing the talking.

No comment on the prior defense statements that Angela could not get a fair trial in Santa Clara County.

Yes, the idea of women's liberation probably affected the choice of a woman as foreperson.

No comment on whether the jury thought it was a political trial.

No comment on why they wanted to hear the indictment again, "it was really a matter of organization rather than anything else."

They reached a verdict at 10:30.

Yes, the experience of being jurors at that trial had changed their lives, but they had not had enough time to think of the ways.

No, there were not any sharp disagreements among the jurors.

No, they did not want to discuss the way in which they came to a decision.

The jury became a bit more responsive later, after the battery of cameras had folded up, the congratulatory messages passed backward and forward, and the first of a number of victory parties was well on its way.

Eight of the jurors showed up at a party in San Jose that was swinging away less than two hours after the verdict had been returned. Collectively, they agreed, that the prosecution had failed to prove its case. One factor which could not be weighed was the elimination of Janie Hemphill from the jury.

The elimination of the only black on the panel, a person whom several of the jurors had come to know and respect might have left them with a feeling that somehow they had been complicit in a racist act. They remembered Mrs. Hemphill's, "there's been a lot of things I've had to put out of my mind," knowing that she probably would never forget the experience of having been eliminated from a jury solely because of race.

The combination of pre-trial publicity describing Angela as a black militant communist gun provider, coupled with the security around the trial, predisposed the jury to be apprehensive of Angela Davis. The jury had a collective sense of unease, one which was helped along by the prosecution's constant reminder of the fate of three women hostages on August 7. As the trial proceeded much of this feeling of dread was abated as the panel had an opportunity to see Angela Davis in action. Many of them were present when Angela conducted the voir dire of one prospective juror which resulted in his disqualification for being prejudiced against Angela for being a communist. They were impressed by her opening statement, but more important, they observed her day after day, taking notes, conferring with her attorneys, and acting like any defendant concerned with the problem of confronting a number of serious charges.

Apprehension flared up again during the closing days of the trial when the jury discovered that Fleeta Drumgo and John Cluchette were to be witnesses. The jury couldn't help themselves. The baliffs were tense, the search formalities were fully observed, and when they came into the courtroom the jury quickly discovered that Fleeta Drumgo was seated chained in the witness chair.

Only one juror thought that Angela was guilty, but she could not maintain that position, primarily because she felt that the state had not proven its case. The others, in addition to feeling that the prosecution had not established Angela's guilt beyond a reasonable doubt, were satisfied that she had proven her innocence. Part of the jury's reasoning was based on a rejection of Harris' theory that the purpose of August 7 was the freeing of the Soledad Brothers. They felt that if Angela and Jonathan had been so motivated, that they would have waited for the Soledad Brothers to go on trial and then attempted their rescue operation.

The conspiracy charge had been decided first on Saturday afternoon, with the murder and kidnapping charges voted on Sunday. Only two jurors, both of them women, kept the verdict from being returned even sooner than it had been. Stephanie Ryon was not one of them. She appeared at the victory party greatly surprised that the entire press corps, as well as the defense, counted her as the number one prosecution juror. On the other hand, one of the women who balked at a not guilty verdict at first was Michelle Savage, who at 20 was the youngest member ever to serve on a jury. The defense was happy to get her on the jury, assuming that a combination of youth, and being a woman, would move her toward the defense.

The jurors were not particularly interested in newspaper interviews, although in the days following the trial some of them succumbed. One of them, Ralph Delange, seemed a little embarrassed by the fact that he had saluted with his fist. At first he tried to avoid the subject, and then noted, "I did it because I wanted to show I felt an identity with the oppressed people in the crowd.

"All throughout the trial they thought we were just a white

middle class jury. I wanted to express my sympathy with their struggle." [5]

The jurors, as a group, said that they were not bothered by the security arrangements. A couple of them found the repeated searches, "annoying but necessary." One male member of the panel ridiculed the security arrangements. "I could have walked into that courtroom with pounds of explosive under my shirt, and nobody could have done anything about it," he said, preparatory to a 15 minute dissertation on the various methods that could have been used by a member of the jury panel to explosively disrupt the trial. His remarks indicated that there was a wider cross section of political opinion represented on the jury than anyone had suspected.

After the house party, which had been restricted to people who had been fairly close to the defense, there was a public victory party at the Safari Club in San Jose. The Safari Club, located in an area of San Jose that was fruit orchard just ten years ago, is part of a shopping and entertainment complex. The owner, Dan Magowan, provided reduced rates for drinks, and eliminated the usual door charge, so that upwards of 1,000 people could crowd into the club, sing, dance, drink the free champagne that was circulating, and generally celebrate Angela's acquittal. It was at the Safari Club, in the midst of celebrating, that the reality of the politics surrounding the trial came to light.

Angela, her attorneys and legal defense committee retinue appeared at approximately 10:30, to retire to a raised and enclosed set of tables in a back section of the club. The entire defense team, including Kendra Alexander, who was on crutches because of a fall taken just the day before, went in and out of the secured section where Angela was sitting, to dance, to mingle with other celebrants, or sometimes just to change scenery. But Angela, who credited her victory to the power of the people, was separated from those people by security considerations. There were, in fact, too many people and some sort of clear zone had to be established around her. During the trial she had been descended upon by newsmen. Every day, at the beginning and close of the trial session,

[5] *San Francisco Examiner,* 5 June, 1972.

she would make a 100 yard walk from her car to the court, and have that trip covered by television and news cameras. Howard Moore, Jr. and Leo Branton, Jr. had advised her not to spend too much time at the vigil awaiting the verdict because of the overwhelming press of media coverage.

Reporters weren't a problem at the victory party, but the number of people who wanted to personally congratulate Angela were. As it was, she spent most of her time speaking to one or another well wisher.

There was security outside the party at the Safari Club, provided by the San Jose police, who had units parked at intervals no greater than 100 yards apart, on all the streets in the vicinity of the club. At about 12:30, two blacks, Sidney Moore and William Coman, began to scuffle with each other in the parking lot. Witnesses said that the two were involved in a mock fight. Suddenly, up rolled six squad cars, some with dogs. One of the dogs, off his leash, almost bit a reporter for the Associated Press, who was headed for her car, parked in the lot. The two men stopped their struggle and attempted to return inside the club, only to be arrested. Both of them were wrestled to the ground by policemen applying head holds, and one of them was attacked by another of the unleashed dogs.

Charlene Mitchell came out and asked the crowd to recognize that the police presence was an attempt to provoke a riot. She was right, because if that was not their direct intent, riot was clearly an implication of their forceful entry into the parking lot.

There is not a great deal to be said for a contingent of police and dogs charging into a parking lot to keep the peace that is barely being broken by two men who immediately respond to the police presence by quietly attempting to go somewhere else. To ring the party with police officers was provocative in the extreme. Fortunately, there was just one minor incident, provided one can ignore the fact that the manager of the club was stopped by police when he was driving home. Coincidence? No. Police politics which determines where trouble is likely to break out, and prepares for it by provoking the action they are ostensibly there to prevent.

Most of the people who came to the victory party were Angela Davis supporters. It was a predominantly black crowd, many of them not political in the sense of belonging to some political organization.

Angela Davis and George Jackson had a basic political disagreement. Where Jackson insisted that the United States was a fascist country, Angela was only willing to assert that pre-conditions for fascism were present. Essentially, they were both talking about police power, the political use of the coercive divisions of government to assure political orthodoxy, and agreeing that it was oppressively prevalent. George Jackson didn't manage to live long enough to enjoy an acquittal, he wasn't far from the courts, just too close to prison guards. If their guns had been controlled he might have been freed. Angela received her acquittal, and immediately after, those guns were deployed around the people who came out to celebrate that acquittal. Perhaps the disagreement between George Jackson and Angela Davis was one of degree.

Both the condition and the pre-condition of a police state is the instant readiness to circle selected portions of a citizenry with armed threat. What was being patrolled that night in San Jose was a portion of that collective political expression which has come to be called "the movement."

The movement cannot be precisely defined. It embraces a number of elements, some of which, at times, seem to contradict others. There is an important essence. The movement is dedicated to liberation, and therefore generates the idea that laws were meant for men and not the other way around.

The movement is a mass of people who have come to understand that the laws which govern their lives do not work for them, and who, in seeking to get those laws to operate in their behalf, are moving toward revolution. The movement is essentially nonviolent, but it is not pacifistic.

"People have said that I am obsessed with my brother's case and the movement in general," Jonathan Jackson once remarked. "A person that was close to me once said that my life was too wrapped up in my brother's case and that I wasn't cheerful enough for her," he continued. "It's true, I don't laugh very much any more. I have but one question to ask all of you people and people that think like you. What would you do if it was your brother?" [6]

[6] *San Francisco Examiner,* 14 August, 1972.

What Jonathan did is history. Albert Harris theorized that Jonathan was involved in an elaborate plot to exchange hostages for the Soledad Brothers. Those who took Jonathan at face believe that he went into a courtroom to free three prisoners. A prosecutor's understanding is limited by his role as the advocate of the people. He cannot recognize the existence of a mass movement separate from, and opposed to, the abstraction which defines the people and the state as two interchangeable terms.

A lot of movement people, including those who did not agree with Jonathan's acts, understood his reasons. He was a part of the movement. He was also a revolutionary.

Angela Davis, his friend, comrade and fellow revolutionary said that, "Jonathan Jackson was a unique part of his group, for he brought with him the angry frustrations and concerns of a young man who has no memories of his older brother except those which have been obscured by prison bars. Jonathan was a child of 7 when his brother was first taken to prison, and for 10 long years he accompanied various members of his family to various prisons throughout the State of California to visit with his brother. These visits must have left an indelible impression on him about what a prisoner's life was like. I know, though he was only 17 years old, he must have been extremely and intimately sensitive to the plight, the frustrations, the feelings of depression and futility that men like James McClain and Ruchell Magee and William Christmas must have felt, and I might say that now, in retrospect, I understand the frustration, the very deep frustrations and the very deep desperation that Jonathan must have been experiencing." [7]

The meaning and the practicability of his move on the Civic Center provoked tremendous debate. Most of those arguing began with the premise that Jonathan had a purpose in mind which was linked to the aims of the movement. There were regrets that lives had been lost, but an unwillingness to accept the idea that the death of Judge Haley was somehow a greater loss than the deaths of Jonathan Jackson, William Christmas and James McClain.

The coalition which formed in support of Angela Davis included a number of people and organizations who thought they knew what Jonathan Jackson was about, and who respected his memory. Some

[7] Angela Davis, opening statement, 28 March, 1972.

were drawn from the ranks of those active in the prison movement, and others were people who knew from their own experience, or that of close relatives, the yearning for freedom and humaneness developed by prisoners. They guaranteed that the Free Angela Movement would not coincidentally become a Condemn Jonathan Organization.

Henry Winston published a pamphlet [8] in August 1971, harshly condemnatory of Jonathan Jackson. He saw a contradiction which was irreconcilable, between isolated terrorist acts and mass struggle. To him, Jonathan's was a courageous act but an unnecessary self-sacrifice. Winston, while considering Jonathan a sad loss to to the movement did not think he relied on the mass movement nor did he hope to relate his act to it.

This position was opposed within the Party by Angela Davis and those around her on the defense committee. They stood by the statement released by the Soledad Brothers Defense Committee saying: "We want it to be understood that we feel the action which led to his death was not an isolated incident but rather an even clearer expression of the growing feeling of hopelessness in regards to obtaining justice from the courts of this nation when it pertains to Black and Brown people." [9]

The fact is that a revolutionary act, if it is to be successful, must commit others to revolution, while raising the recognition on the part of those who have not considered armed struggle that the movement must operate on a higher plane. Don Cox, once Field Marshall of the Black Panther Party, published an adaptation of Carlos Marighella's *Mini-Manual of the Urban Guerrilla,* for an Afro-American readership.

In his pamphlet [10], Cox argued that tactically, armed struggle could be firmly established as a tool that the masses would accept and use only if actions were placed within a context they, the masses, could relate to and perceive as serving their needs. He maintained

---

[8] Henry Winston, *The Meaning of San Raphael,* New Outlook Publishers, New York.

[9] Soledad Brothers Defense Committee press release, August, 1970.

[10] Field Marshall D.Cox, *On Organizing Urban Guerrilla Units* (pamphlet), October 8, 1970.

furthermore, that time was not to be wasted on polemics and that those who disagreed could disagree for, only action, not rhetoric, could prove one man correct and another man wrong where there was a difference of opinion.

Even as the argument about the correctness of August 7 was being debated in the movement, there was an increase in activity, both legal and extra legal, in the prison movement. New or heightened activities ranging from providing prisoners with reading material to vigorous advocacy of radical prison reform, came in the months following August 7. This is not to imply that the prison movement, as a whole, approved of Jonathan's act any more than the civil rights movement, as a whole, approved of the nonviolent demonstrations and civil disobedience exercises engaged in by many movement members in the late 50's.

At that time there was a role for those who disapproved of specific tactics, while understanding that the punishment, or threat of punishment issuing from officialdom, was more a blow towards the movement, than a reasonable exercise of retributive governmental power. These people provided bail, held protest meetings, formed defense committees, signed petitions, visited legislators, wrote letters, and otherwise committed themselves further to the objectives of the movement. Sometimes they developed different methods of pursuing these objectives, tactics more in accordance with their own ideas of seemliness. They did the best they could to push the movement forward.

Reactions to Jonathan Jackson were similar. For instance, in May, 1972, a *Communication on Human Rights* was presented to the United Nations by a portion of the movement represented by Mrs. Georgia Jackson, the National Conference of Black Lawyers, the United Church of Christ Commission for Racial Justice, the National Youth Congress, the Congress of African People, and the Coalition of Prisoners Representatives. These groups had decided, as Jonathan Jackson apparently had, that they had no remedy at law available under the United States Constitution. They maintained that the Constitution did not recognize human rights as a matter of law and was solely concerned with that subdivision of human rights called civil rights.

"The government of the United States of America has violated the fundamental freedoms and human rights of all prisoners held in the United States, especially those of black prisoners, and is therefore in violation of international law and fundamental principles of human rights," the declaration averred.

Both Jonathan Jackson and the sponsors of the *Communication on Human Rights* were seeking methods by which their position could be made clear outside of the accepted structure of law in this country. Jonathan's act had grown out of prior movement activity. The *Communication on Human Rights* was conceived after the deaths of Jonathan and George Jackson, the slaughter at Attica, and the rising homicide rate affecting prison guards. Both were political statements premised in the belief that established procedures were inadequate to remedy their complaints.

Because of its open opposition to many established procedures, and its periodic efforts to mobilize people around particular demands, the entire movement has been treated as a threat to law and order. Anyone gaining any degree of prominence as a political activist is subject to surveillance. Police jurisdictions regularly send photographers and observers to public demonstrations, in order to identify those who participate regularly. The label "militant" or "radical" is quickly appended to those people who speak regularly at these demonstrations, or whose names appear as members of a defense committee, an anti-war organization, or a mass mobilization effort. They are also classified as potential criminals, and are prime suspects as conspirators if someone with whom they can be associated politically is charged with a crime.

Prosecutor Harris repeatedly denied, throughout the entire trial, that there had been any political motivation in bringing charges against Angela Davis. In his closing statement the prosecutor went one step further. "If there was a frameup of Angela Davis, if facts have been distorted in order to present some sort of charge against her, I think what you are going to have to conclude is that it was not the prosecution who did that . . .

"Jonathan was present on July 25 when Nancy Conrad sold Angela Davis a carbine . . ." He pointed out that Jonathan was also at the Eagle Loan Office on August 5th, when Angela bought the shotgun.

"You know that Jonathan Jackson, at least, had to put the

books that were found in the briefcase into the briefcase, two of them with Angela Davis' signature on them, some of them in the French language, not likely to be attributed to Jonathan Jackson.

"So it seems to me that what you come down to is this: That either Angela Davis knew what Jonathan Jackson was going to do with her guns, with the shotgun, with her books, with that yellow van, or that Jonathan Jackson, for reasons that are beyond—I think beyond the comprehension of anyone, beyond human comprehension—somehow attempted to connect her and implicate her in this crime because he knew these things.

"He knew he was going into a venture with a very high probability of failure, that he might be killed, as indeed so many were killed.

"Why her books? It seems to me that unless you believe that Angela Davis knew about this venture so that when she bought the shotgun on August the 5th, she knew the purpose for which it was going to be used, you have to believe that Jonathan Jackson was trying to implicate the one person in this world who probably shared his own devotion to his brother."

There are other alternatives. One of the books Jonathan brought with him to the Civic Center was Carlos Marighella's *Mini-Manual of the Urban Guerrilla,*[11] which Harris referred to in his opening statement. Marighella speaks of firing groups, with a maximum of five men, who plan and execute actions. Each group sees it as an obligation to act without sitting idle, waiting for orders from above; and any individual urban guerrilla who so desires, can set up a firing group and begin action whenever it suits him.

That is what Jonathan seems to have done. He had an opportunity to act, knowledge of where arms could be found, and a plan of action. He acted, and some of the objects he used could be identified with Angela Davis. If he came out of it alive, he could do his own explaining.

Harris said that Jonathan "was abandoning his brother, and he was betraying perhaps his closest friend, was letting her hold the bag." Not hardly. Jonathan was engaged in armed revolution. He had every reason to expect that the movement, which included

[11] Carlos Marighella, *Mini-Manual of the Urban Guerrilla,* Tricontinental, 1969.

friends, relatives and comrades, would understand his imperatives, absorb the backlash and utilize what they learned from his actions to further advance the struggle.

As a result, Angela Davis became a fugitive for two months, was in jail for almost a year and a half, and was acquitted after a trial which spanned 20 months. All of the resources of the State of California were used in an attempt to convict her. Security costs alone must have exceeded one million dollars.

It was an unequal contest, and her acquittal did not vindicate the courts. The defense, and the movement which supported it, contributed time, money and energy to counter charges based on an abundance of tenuous evidence. Angela is once again politically active, but her place in court will be occupied by others, whose guilt will amount to nothing more substantial than evidence that they were active and vocal in the struggle for meaningful change.

The Angela Davis trial was a passion play, an exercise in courtsmanship, which ended with Angela repeating the same lines she had used in the beginning, "A fair trial would have been no trial at all."

2/6/56	Ruchell Magee convicted of attempted aggravated rape, sentenced to 12 years at Angola State Penitentiary, Louisiana
10/9/62	Ruchell Magee paroled to Los Angeles after serving 6 years, 8 months at Angola State Penitentiary
3/23/63	Ruchell Magee arrested in Los Angeles charged with kidnap and $10 robbery
6/25/63	Ruchell Magee found guilty and sentenced to life imprisonment
12/18/64	California State Court of Appeals reverses Ruchell Magee's 1963 convictions
7/28/65	Ruchell Magee found guilty in retrial of 1963 charges and sent to San Quentin to serve life sentence
9/19/69	University ôf California Board of Regents vote to fire Angela Davis because of membership in the Communist Party
10/20/69	California Superior Court Judge Jerry Pacht rules that University of California Board of Regents cannot fire Angela Davis because of Communist Party membership
1/13/70	Three black inmates of Soledad prison, W. L. Nolan, Cleveland Edwards and Alvin Miller are killed by Soledad prison guard
1/16/70	John V. Mills, Soledad prison guard, found dead
2/16/70	Soledad Brothers, John Cluchette, Fleeta Drumgo and George Jackson indicted for murder of guard John Mills
2/25/70	San Quentin inmate Fred Billingslea killed by San Quentin prison guard

3/2/70	San Quentin inmate James McClain accused of assaulting San Quentin prison guard
5/8/70	Angela Davis attends Soledad Brothers hearing for first time
6/4/70	James McClain trial ends in hung jury, declared mistrial
6/19/70	University of California Board of Regents vote to dismiss Angela Davis because of inflammatory off campus statements
7/30/70	Jonathan Jackson and Angela Davis are stopped at border returning from Mexico
8/3/70	Second trial of James McClain begins
8/5/70	Huey P. Newton released from prison
8/7/70	Jonathan Jackson, William Christmas, Judge Harold Haley and James McClain killed at Marin County Civic Center. Ruchell Magee, Maria Graham and Gary Thomas wounded
8/14/70	Soledad House raided without warrant, Fania Davis Jordan taken to police headquarters for questioning
8/14/70	Federal fugitive warrant issued for arrest of Angela Davis
8/15/70	Angela Davis leaves Los Angeles for Chicago
8/15/70	Funeral of Jonathan Jackson at St. Augustine Church, Oakland, California
8/18/70	Angela Davis placed on FBI Ten Most Wanted List
9/4/70	Marin County Grand Jury indicts Rutchell Magee for murder
10/13/70	Angela Davis arrested in New York
11/10/70	Grand Jury drops indictment against Ruchell Magee and indicts Angela Davis and Ruchell Magee as co-defendants on charges of murder, kidnapping and conspiracy
12/22/70	Angela Davis extradited from New York to California
12/23/70	Angela Davis makes first court appearance in Marin County, California. Judge E. Warren McGuire issues gag rule
1/5/71	Ruchell Magee and Angela Davis appear in court as co-defendants for first time

1/9/71	Gary Thomas named Marin County Peace Officer of the Year
3/12/71	First conference between Angela Davis and Ruchell Magee
3/15/71	California Superior Court Judge John P. McMurray makes first appearance in case
3/17/71	Judge John P. McMurray disqualifies self on Magee's challenge
4/1/71	California Superior Court Judge Alan P. Lindsay makes first appearance in case
4/12/71	David Poindexter found not guilty of knowingly harboring a federal fugitive (Angela Davis)
5/10/71	Ruchell Magee uses preemptory challenge to unseat Judge Lindsay
5/13/71	California Superior Court Judge Richard E. Arnason assigned to case
5/25/71	Presbyterian Church donates $10,000 to Angela Davis defense fund
6/16/71	Bail for Angela Davis denied by Judge Arnason
6/28/71	Angela Davis motion to dismiss indictment is denied
7/8/71	Angela Davis meets George Jackson at conference in Marin County Civic Center
7/19/71	Angela Davis and Ruchell Magee cases severed on Davis motion
7/27/71	Angela Davis enters plea of innocent
8/21/71	George Jackson killed at San Quentin during alleged escape attempt. Three guards and two other inmates, all white, also died
8/21/71	Guard Leo Davis killed by stabbing and black inmates Larry Gibson and Earl Justice charged with murder and assault
8/23/71	Fast by inmates of Cell Block D at Attica Prison, NY, in memory of George Jackson
8/28/71	George Jackson memorial service at St. Augustine Church, Oakland, California
9/13/71	Attica massacre, 32 inmates and 9 hostages die
10/5/71	San Quentin 6, four blacks, Fleeta Drumgo, David Johnson, John Larry Spain and Willie Tate, and two

Chicanos, Hugo Pinell and Louis Talamantes, are charged with five counts of murder and assault, one count of conspiracy to commit murder. Spain is also charged with one count of attempted escape. All charges in connection with August 21 alleged escape attempt of George Jackson

11/2/71	Change of venue of Angela Davis trial to Santa Clara County
12/2/71	Angela Davis moved to jail in Palo Alto, California
1/10/72	Attorney Leo Branton, Jr. enters case for the defense
2/18/72	Death penalty ruled unconstitutional by California State Supreme Court
2/23/72	Angela Davis released on $102,500 bail
2/28/72	Jury selection begins in Angela Davis trial
3/17/72	Angela Davis jury selection completed
3/27/72	Opening statement of prosecution in Angela Davis trial
3/27/72	Remaining two Soledad Brothers acquitted
3/28/72	Jailbreak attempt from Santa Clara County jail, adjacent to Angela Davis trial site
3/29/72	Opening statement of Angela Davis defense
5/15/72	Prosecution completes case
5/23/72	John Cluchette released from prison
5/24/72	Defense rests
6/2/72	Jury begins deliberations
6/4/72	Angela Davis acquitted on all three counts
8/4/72	Gary Thomas appointed Marin County Judge by Governor Ronald Reagan, the only Democrat the Governor has appointed
11/27/72	Ruchell Magee trial begins